Getting To Outcomes with Developmental Assets

▼

TEN STEPS TO MEASURING SUCCESS
IN YOUTH PROGRAMS AND COMMUNITIES

Deborah Fisher

Pamela Imm, Ph.D.

Matthew Chinman, Ph.D.

Abraham Wandersman, Ph.D.

Getting To Outcomes with Developmental Assets: Ten Steps to Measuring Success in Youth Programs and Communities

Deborah Fisher, Pamela Imm, Matthew Chinman, and Abraham Wandersman

At the time of this book's publication, all facts and figures cited are the most current available; all Web site URLs are accurate and active; all publications, organizations, Web sites, and other resources exist as described in this book; and all efforts have been made to verify them. The authors and Search Institute make no warranty or guarantee concerning the information and materials given out by organizations or content found in Web sites, and we are not responsible for any changes that occur after this book's publication. If you find an error or believe that a resource listed here is not as described, please contact Client Services at Search Institute. Parents, teachers, and other adults: We strongly urge you to monitor children's use of the Internet.

10 9 8 7 6 5 4 3
Printed on acid-free paper in the United States of America.

Search Institute
615 First Avenue Northeast, Suite 125
Minneapolis, MN 55413
www.search-institute.org
612-376-8955 • 800-888-7828

Credits
Editor: Kathryn L. Hong
Production Coordinator: Mary Ellen Buscher
Book Design and Composition: Wendy Holdman
Cover Design: JoAnn Holzemer

ISBN-13: 978-1-57482-872-6
ISBN-10: 1-57482-872-X

Library of Congress Cataloging-in-Publication Data

Getting to outcomes with developmental assets : ten steps to measuring success in youth programs and communities / by Deborah Fisher . . . [et al.].
p. cm.
Includes index.
ISBN 1-57482-872-X (pbk. : alk. paper)
1. Youth—Services for—United States—Evaluation. 2. Social work with youth—United States—Evaluation. 3. Youth development—United States. I. Fisher, Deborah, 1951– II. Search Institute (Minneapolis, Minn.)

HV1431.G485 2006
362.7072—dc22

2006005778

About Search Institute

Search Institute is an independent, nonprofit, nonsectarian organization whose mission is to provide leadership, knowledge, and resources to promote healthy children, youth, and communities. The institute collaborates with others to promote long-term organizational and cultural change that supports its mission. For a free information packet, call 800-888-7828.

Licensing and Copyright

The worksheets in *Getting To Outcomes with Developmental Assets: Ten Steps to Measuring Success in Youth Programs and Communities* may be copied as needed. For each copy, please respect the following guidelines:

- Do not remove, alter, or obscure the Search Institute credit and copyright information on any worksheet.
- Clearly differentiate any material you add for local distribution from material prepared by Search Institute.
- Do not alter the Search Institute material in content or meaning.
- Do not resell the activity sheets for profit.
- Include the following attribution when you use the information from the activity sheets in other formats for promotional or educational purposes: **Reprinted with permission from *Getting To Outcomes with Developmental Assets: Ten Steps to Measuring Success in Youth Programs and Communities* (specify the title of the worksheet you are quoting). Copyright © 2006 by Search Institute, Minneapolis, Minnesota, 800-888-7828, www.search-institute.org. All rights reserved.**

Contents

Worksheets and Tipsheets

WORKSHEETS

Question #1. NEEDS/RESOURCES

Question #2. GOALS

Question #3. EFFECTIVENESS

Question #4. FIT

Question #5. CAPACITIES

Note: All these worksheets plus a variety of supplemental resources can be found on the CD-ROM that accompanies this book. The worksheets can be customized for your particular needs.

TIPSHEETS

Foreword

A New Way to Work on Behalf of Children, Youth, and Communities

Community mobilization to improve outcomes for children and youth and the use of evaluation to refine interventions are not new ideas. Unfortunately, many community efforts have been limited by poor design, faulty execution, or disagreement among coalition members. Although evaluation techniques could help prevent these problems, this has rarely happened since evaluation is usually viewed as a hardship that is imposed by some external authority. This book represents a significant advance regarding how communities think about evaluation and how they target their efforts.

Both Developmental Assets® and Getting To Outcomes (GTO) ask community members to think differently about fundamental issues and then to act differently because of their new conceptualizations. In the case of Developmental Assets, it's thinking about what's right with children and youth and building from there—not viewing young people as problems to be fixed. In the case of GTO, the main ideas involve empowering people, both to plan and conduct evaluation themselves as well as to use it to improve collaboration and outcomes—not waiting until the end and hiring outside folks who've not been part of the process.

The linking of Developmental Assets and GTO is important because there is no one "silver bullet" that will help all children and youth to survive life's challenges and to flourish. Research suggests that a combination of three approaches is necessary to build resilience and ensure high life outcomes for all our children and youth:

1. Positive youth development;
2. Risk reduction through universal and early intervention; and
3. Effective treatment and support for children at greater levels of need.

Barry (2001) suggests that for these approaches to work, they must be child- and family-driven, strength-based, empowering, culturally and linguistically competent, ecological, and able to address the variety of individual and geographic needs. Also, the accumulation of practice knowledge demonstrates that to be effective, these approaches must be strategic, coordinated, collaborative, data-driven, results-oriented, accountable, and attentive to capacity building. Doing all of this is challenging. It requires mobilizing the community or schools, using collaborative planning and monitoring to sustain coalitions, selecting the right interventions, and implementing (including adapting) these interventions effectively. It also requires avoiding symbolic or ad hoc solutions as well as weak, ineffective, or even harmful interventions. The combination of Search Institute's approach to asset-driven community mobilization and Getting To Outcomes' data-driven approach to planning, continuous quality improvement (CQI), and evaluation provides communities with powerful, transformative tools to address these challenges.

Positive Youth Development

An increasing body of correlational and experimental research suggests that positive youth development can enhance short- and long-term outcomes for many youth (Catalano, Berglund, Ryan, Lonczak, & Hawkins, 2002; Durlak & Weissberg, 2005). Positive youth development focuses on developing or enhancing individual and environmental assets.

Such an approach is necessary for at least four reasons. We cannot predict what environmental or individual risk factors individuals will encounter during the course of their development. Additionally, some risk factors are not amenable to change, and others (e.g., poverty) will not change in the short run (U.S. Public Health Service, 2000). Further, our knowledge about the impact of individual risk factors is sometimes imprecise and, even when it is correct, only can predict outcomes for groups, not individuals. Because of this, assets such as social competency and connections with adults may provide individual children and youth with the resources necessary to overcome a multitude of risk factors. Finally, as Karen Pittman, Peter Benson, Kristin Moore, and others suggest, we want our children and youth to thrive and flourish, not just avoid problems (e.g., Moore & Lippman, 2005). Search Institute's community mobilization strategy provides communities with an opportunity to coalesce around the goals and principles of positive youth development.

Risk Reduction

However, positive youth development cannot accomplish everything. As Scales and Leffert (1999, p. 217) stated in their book on Developmental Assets, "Building Developmental Assets is only part of what communities need to do to ensure healthy development for all adolescents." Risk re-education is still necessary for some children and youth because the accumulation of risk factors can override protective factors (Pollard, Hawkins, & Arthur, 1999). Although experienced individually, risk is socially structured, making it likely that some children and youth are more likely to be exposed to risk factors than others (Kendziora & Osher, 2004; Osher, 1998). Although, as resilience research suggests, many individuals can survive risk factors (e.g., Rutter, 1989), some will not. A community approach that ignores risk will leave some individuals behind. Hence, it is important to address risk factors as well as create settings that support resilience (Osher, Kendziora, VanDenBerg, & Dennis, 1999a, 1999b).

Communities can address risk through universal interventions (sometimes called primary prevention) that reduce or eliminate factors that place individuals at risk, such as punitive disciplinary practices at home and school (Osher et al., 2004; Reid & Eddy, 1997). When adult behavior itself is the risk factor, eliminating the problematic behavior makes it easier to create positive connections with children and youth. This, in turn, helps young people build Developmental Assets (McNeely, Nonnemaker, & Blum, 2002).

In addition, communities can enhance primary prevention by targeting specific mechanisms that prevent or buffer the impact of specific risk factors. While there is much overlap between protective factors, which have been identified with prevention research, and Development Assets, there are also conceptual and philosophical differences. These differences (in the words of the seminal 1994 Institute of Medicine Report) affect "how people talk about these endeavors, why they participate in them, what they expect to gain, and the manner and extent to which they are willing to support them" (Mrazek & Haggerty, 1994, p. 334). GTO, which was first developed within a prevention context, provides communities with tools that can bridge these conceptual and philosophical differences by focusing on needs, results, and evidence-based practices.

Support for Children in Greater Need

Since some children and youth will be at greater levels of risk, early interventions will be necessary for them. Some young people will be at an indicated level of risk (e.g., children whose behavior is getting them into trouble) and some may have experienced or are about to experience events and processes that research suggests may place them at a high level of risk (e.g., children who have experienced a major loss). Both types of individuals benefit from Developmental

Assets. However, they may also require targeted support to help them address their individual needs (e.g., grief counseling).

Still other children and youth have even more intense needs that require targeted treatment and supports, which can enable them to overcome these problems or manage them effectively. These children and youth also benefit from asset building. However, they may also need different interventions or more support to realize these benefits (Dwyer & Osher, 2005; Osher, Dwyer, & Jimerson, in press). For example, some children with depression or anxiety may benefit from cognitive behavioral approaches, which can help them implement cognitive strategies to deal with their thoughts. Similarly, although mentoring may remain an effective tool for some of these children and youth, its dosage may need to be higher and it may have to be combined with other interventions (e.g., Kendziora, Bruns, Osher, Pacchiano, & Mejia, 2001). Here, too, GTO's focus on needs, the mechanisms of change, and the monitoring of results provides a tool for communities to align interventions efficiently.

To be effective, all three approaches must address the challenges of engagement and attrition, which are related to the poor penetration and outcomes realized by many interventions. Doing this requires moving away from a professional- and provider-driven, deficit-oriented paradigm that ignores individual needs and differences and, instead, elaborating upon empowerment-oriented family- and youth-driven approaches that have gained momentum during the past decade. These approaches attend to relationships, actively involve consumers in planning and evaluation, identify and build strengths, and are ecological (Kendziora et al., 2001; Osher & Osher, 2002). The Developmental Assets model has the potential to do this by mobilizing natural resources, building individual assets, and addressing environmental supports. GTO can support the process when families and youth are engaged in planning, monitoring, and evaluating.

Intervention strategies must also address the fact that interventions may vary in how effective they are with different individuals and in different contexts (Osher, Dwyer, & Jackson, 2004). In fact, prevention research suggests that in some cases, efficacious universal interventions may even have a negative impact on some subpopulations (Gillham, Reivich, & Shatté, 2002). In addition, although assets, risk, and protective factors appear to be consistent across culture groups (Osher, Cartledge, Oswald, Artiles, & Coutinho, 2004; Sesma & Roehlkepartain, 2003), culture mediates and moderates outcomes (U.S. Public Health Service, 2001). GTO provides collaborations with the ability to select the right interventions, monitor impacts across different groups, and identify new interventions, when necessary.

Efficiency and effectiveness depend upon using resources wisely. This requires doing a needs assessment that includes mapping assets, setting realistic goals and objectives, developing a plan that identifies the mechanisms of change necessary to create the changes in individuals and institutions to accomplish the specified goals and objectives, and identifying projects and programs that are consistent with the logic model—interventions that are sufficiently powerful to bring about the planned change and that can be implemented with fidelity, given the human and material resources available. Effectiveness requires assessing implementation to ensure fidelity, identify what is and is not working, and use this information for CQI to enhance outcomes. Assets-GTO provides a planning process that addresses all these matters.

Children and youth experience risk and require support across multiple domains (Catalano et al., 2002). Most schools and communities have multiple interventions and services, which are usually fragmented by funding streams, orientation (i.e., promotion, prevention, or treatment), discipline, and agency turf. This underalignment creates duplications, which waste money and undercut the ability of different initiatives and agencies to support each other (Adelman & Taylor, 2005; Osher, 2002). School and community efforts should be coordinated and integrated in a collaborative manner, which may include pooling resources and/or braiding funding (Osher, Dwyer, et al., 2004).

Effective coordination and collaboration, however, depend upon addressing the barriers to meaningful collaboration, which include professional socialization and agency mandates (e.g., Rappaport et al., 2002). Sustaining collaboration requires that every stakeholder's indicators—not just those of the lead agency—are part of the planning, CQI, and evaluation. The Developmental Assets model has demonstrated an impressive ability to engage the initial interests of potential collaborators. GTO provides the tools for them to use data collaboratively to improve outcomes and deepen their collaboration.

Finally, empowerment is important to both the GTO and asset frameworks—both models ask community members not only to change how they have traditionally viewed youth development and evaluation, but also to then use the new tools to act on their changed understanding. If communities do so and use them to connect with and build powerful supports for *all* their children and youth, many more children and youth will thrive, flourish, and become the types of parents and citizens that we need (Osher et al., 1999a, 1999b).

—David Osher
Managing Research Scientist
American Institutes for Research
Washington, D.C.

References

Adelman, H. S., & Taylor, L. (2005). *The implementation guide to student learning supports in the classroom and schoolwide: New directions for addressing barriers to learning.* Thousand Oaks, CA: Corwin Press.

Barry, M. M. (2001). Promoting positive mental health: Theoretical frameworks for practice. *International Journal of Mental Health Promotion, 3*(1), 25–34.

Catalano, R. F., Berglund, M. L., Ryan, J. A. M., Lonczak, H. S., & Hawkins, J. D. (2002). Positive youth development in the United States: Research findings on evaluations of positive youth development programs. *Prevention & Treatment,* 5, http://journals.apa.org/prevention/volume5/pre0050015a.html

Durlak, J. A., & Weissberg, R. P. (2005, August). *A major meta-analysis of positive youth development programs: Its important implications.* Paper presented at the annual meeting of the American Psychological Association, Washington, DC.

Dwyer, K., & Osher, D. (2005). *Safeguarding our children: An action guide revised and expanded.* Longmont, CO: Sopris West.

Gillham, J. E., Reivich, K., & Shatté, A. (2002). Positive youth development, prevention, and positive psychology: Commentary on "Positive Youth Development in the United States." *Prevention & Treatment,* 5, http://www.journals.apa.org/prevention/volume5/pre0050018c.html

Kendziora, K. T., Bruns, E., Osher, D., Pacchiano, D., & Mejia, B. (2001). *Wraparound: Stories from the field.* Washington, DC: Center for Effective Collaboration and Practice, American Institutes for Research.

Kendziora, K., & Osher, D. (2004). Fostering resilience among youth in the juvenile justice system. In C. C. Clauss-Ehlers & M. Weist (Eds.), *Community planning to foster resiliency in children* (177–196). New York: Kluwer.

McNeely, C. A., Nonnemaker, J. M., &. Blum, R. W. (2002). Promoting school connectedness: Evidence from the National Longitudinal Study of Adolescent Health. *Journal of School Health, 72*(4), 140–146

Mrazek, P. J., & Haggerty, R. J. (Eds.). (1994). *Reducing risks for mental disorders: Frontiers for prevention intervention research.* Washington, DC: National Academy Press.

Moore, K. A., & Lippman, L. H. (Eds.). (2005). *What do children need to flourish? Conceptualizing and measuring indicators of positive development.* New York: Springer.

Osher, D. (1998). The social construction of being at risk. Introduction to R. Kronick (Ed.), *At-risk youth: Theory, practice, reform* (iv–xii). New York: Garland Press.

Osher, D. (2002). Creating comprehensive and collaborative systems. *Journal of Child and Family Studies, 11*(1), 91–101.

Osher, D., Cartledge, G., Oswald, D., Artiles, A. J., & Coutinho, M. (2004). Issues of cultural and linguistic competency and disproportionate representation. In R. Rutherford, M. Quinn, & S. Mather (Eds.), *Handbook of research in emotional and behavioral disorders* (54–77). New York: Guilford Publications.

Osher, D., Dwyer, K., & Jackson, S. (2004). *Safe, supportive, and successful schools step by step.* Longmont, CO: Sopris West.

Osher, D., Dwyer, K., and Jimerson, S. (in press). Foundations of school violence and safety. In S. Jimerson and M. Furlong (Eds.), *Handbook of school violence and school safety: From research to practice.* Mahwah, NJ: Lawrence Erlbaum Associates.

Osher, D., Kendziora, K. T., VanDenBerg, J., & Dennis, K. (1999a). Beyond individual resilience. *Reaching Today's Youth, 3*(4), 2–4.

Osher, D., Kendziora, K. T., VanDenBerg, J., & Dennis, K. (1999b). Growing resilience: Creating opportunities for resilience to thrive. *Reaching Today's Youth, 3*(4), 38–45.

Osher, T. W., & Osher, D. (2002). The paradigm shift to true collaboration with families. *Journal of Child and Family Studies, 11*(1), 47–60.

Pollard, J. A., Hawkins, J. D., & Arthur, M. W. (1999). Risk and protection: Are both necessary to understand diverse behavioral outcomes in adolescence? *Social Work Research, 23*(8), 145–158

Rappaport, N., Osher, D., Dwyer, K., Garrison, E., Hare, I., Ladd, J., Anderson-Ketchmark, C. (2002). Enhancing collaborations within and across disciplines to advance mental health programs in schools. In M. D. Weist, S. Evans, & N. Tashman (Eds.), *School mental health handbook* (107–118). New York: Kluwer.

Reid, J. B., & Eddy, J. M. (1997). The prevention of antisocial behavior: Some considerations in the search for effective interventions. In D.M. Stoff, J. Breiling, & J. D. Maser (Eds.), *The handbook of antisocial behavior* (343–356). New York: John Wiley & Sons.

Rutter, M. (1989). Pathways from childhood to adult life. *Journal of Child Psychology and Psychiatry, 30*, 23–54.

Sesma, A. Jr., & Roehlkepartain, E. C. (2003). Unique strengths, shared strengths: Developmental Assets among youth of color. *Search Institute Insights & Evidence, 1*(2), 1–13

Scales, P. C., & Leffert, N. (1999). *Developmental Assets: A synthesis of the scientific research on adolescent development.* Minneapolis: Search Institute.

U.S. Public Health Service. (2000). *Youth violence: A report of the Surgeon General.* Washington, DC: Author.

U.S. Public Health Service. (2001). *Mental health: Culture, race, ethnicity: A supplement to the Surgeon General's Report on Mental Health.* Washington, DC: Author.

Preface

Picture these scenes:

- Staff and teachers in a suburban Minnesota high school concerned about growing problems among incoming 9th graders design an asset-building program to increase academic support *and* reduce risk behaviors.
- A Colorado nonprofit organization using outdoor activities to build leadership skills in young participants looks for ways to better transfer the lessons of planning, decision making, and personal responsibility into young people's everyday lives.
- A rural community coalition providing educational and recreational activities for its children and youth plans to sustain its work by transitioning from supporting itself through a patchwork of federal, state (or provincial), and local money to embedding its successful programs into other organizations.
- Several statewide initiatives find creative ways to use federal funding to reduce drug and alcohol use among youth while also reorienting deficit-focused prevention programs into strength-based ones, creating new organizational partnerships, streamlining health delivery infrastructures, and building the community's capacity for supporting its young people.

All of these programs, organizations, and initiatives have worthy goals and plans. But each must also cope with expectations and mandates for evaluating the outcomes of its work. For a variety of reasons, all of them need to know if they are achieving their goals and outcomes, not just to fulfill their vision for supporting youth, but to demonstrate to their stakeholders (including funders) and communities that time, money, and other resources are being well spent. Sometimes these programs, organizations, and initiatives grapple with trying to implement long-term, strength-based strategies while responding to outcome-oriented grantors and accountability requirements. While funders typically require grantees to measure the outcomes that result from their interventions, both funders and grantees often struggle to determine what those outcomes should be, how long it should take to reach them, and how to tie them directly to the work being implemented. Evaluation is time-consuming and can be expensive, and many programs, organizations, and initiatives simply lack the capacity and resources to plan, monitor, and measure results as fully as they'd like.

This book has been written specifically to address that situation. *Getting To Outcomes with Developmental Assets* offers a clear, ten-step process to help programs, organizations, and initiatives tailor their own evaluation plans to specific needs and particular focus, no matter the size or budget of the project. The book is structured with the Getting To Outcomes (GTO) process, which weaves together several evaluation and accountability models that include critical elements of program planning, implementation, and outcome measurement. As integrated with the Developmental Assets framework, this book and CD provide a full range of resources for planning your work, ensuring its quality, and measuring and reporting performance.

The blended asset and accountability process, called the Assets-GTO process, has been created for programs, organizations, and initiatives that want to:

- Explore and define their own measures of progress;
- Demonstrate that their strength-based strategies are producing positive, concrete results, but still retain the flexibility to grow and change that they've come to enjoy within an asset-building environment;
- Add rigor and structure to their efforts on behalf of children's and young people's well-being;
- Conduct evaluation that fits within their budget;
- Satisfy funders while achieving stated goals for young people that can also be demonstrated to the community; and
- Use the best practices of both prevention and strength-based youth strategies.

The ten questions that make up the core of this book can be used to examine your efforts at the broad, initiative level or on the ground at the program level. The questions will guide you to plan, design, implement, and measure the results of programs or any structured, intentional project you're using to carry out your goals. Assets-GTO can also assist you in designing new strength-based efforts or infusing Developmental Assets into existing ones. Whether you want to measure your success to receive funding or you want to have a clearer idea of exactly how your long-term change plan is having an impact, this book offers a planning tool that can help any asset-building communities, youth organizations, and programs build sustainability and continuous improvement into their efforts.

The Assets-GTO process is flexible and customizable; it does not dictate a rigid set of outcomes, nor does it require the use of specific programs. It can help you build a valid structure for your work that puts you in a good position to meet widely accepted accountability criteria. Assets-GTO can be used if you are employing asset building as your primary strategy or if you are combining asset building with different approaches, such as Communities That Care, America's Promise, or other youth development activities. By combining the strengths of both the Developmental Assets framework and the Getting To Outcomes process, Assets-GTO can help you achieve your goals in an organized, effective way.

Developmental Assets: The Power to Protect, Promote, and Prevent

For more than 45 years, Search Institute has studied adolescent development and its connection to community change. The framework of 40 Developmental Assets (see page xx) was first published in 1997. Rooted in the study of child and adolescent development, with additional focus on the applied literature of prevention, thriving, protective factors, and resiliency, the framework establishes a set of opportunities, experiences, and supports crucial for positive child and adolescent development. The model was crafted from the beginning to apply to all kids. Search Institute emphasized identifying a set of developmental factors that would be particularly robust in predicting healthy outcomes across gender, race/ethnicity, and family income differences.

Half of the 40 assets are *external assets,* which focus on the support young people get from the people in their lives, including a sense of feeling valued, clearly defined boundaries, high expectations, and opportunities to participate in structured activities. The other half are *internal assets,* which focus on young people's commitment to learning, their sense of self-worth, their positive values, and the skills they possess to make good life choices.

In creating the Developmental Assets, the researchers at Search Institute wanted to name the "building blocks" of development that not only have scientific credibility but would also resonate across gender, race/ethnicity, and

40 DEVELOPMENTAL ASSETS FOR ADOLESCENTS

(Ages 12–18)

Search Institute has identified the following building blocks of healthy development that help young people grow up healthy, caring, and responsible.

EXTERNAL ASSETS

Support

1. **Family support**—Family life provides high levels of love and support.
2. **Positive family communication**—Young person and her or his parent(s) communicate positively, and young person is willing to seek advice and counsel from parents.
3. **Other adult relationships**—Young person receives support from three or more nonparent adults.
4. **Caring neighborhood**—Young person experiences caring neighbors.
5. **Caring school climate**—School provides a caring, encouraging environment.
6. **Parent involvement in schooling**—Parent(s) are actively involved in helping young person succeed in school.

Empowerment

7. **Community values youth**—Young person perceives that adults in the community value youth.
8. **Youth as resources**—Young people are given useful roles in the community.
9. **Service to others**—Young person serves in the community one hour or more per week.
10. **Safety**—Young person feels safe at home, at school, and in the neighborhood.

Boundaries and Expectations

11. **Family boundaries**—Family has clear rules and consequences and monitors the young person's whereabouts.
12. **School boundaries**—School provides clear rules and consequences.
13. **Neighborhood boundaries**—Neighbors take responsibility for monitoring young people's behavior.
14. **Adult role models**—Parent(s) and other adults model positive, responsible behavior.
15. **Positive peer influence**—Young person's best friends model responsible behavior.
16. **High expectations**—Both parent(s) and teachers encourage the young person to do well.

Constructive Use of Time

17. **Creative activities**—Young person spends three or more hours per week in lessons or practice in music, theater, or other arts.
18. **Youth programs**—Young person spends three or more hours per week in sports, clubs, or organizations at school and/or in the community.
19. **Religious community**—Young person spends one or more hours per week in activities in a religious institution.
20. **Time at home**—Young person is out with friends "with nothing special to do" two or fewer nights per week.

INTERNAL ASSETS

Commitment to Learning

21. **Achievement motivation**—Young person is motivated to do well in school.
22. **School engagement**—Young person is actively engaged in learning.
23. **Homework**—Young person reports doing at least one hour of homework every school day.
24. **Bonding to school**—Young person cares about her or his school.
25. **Reading for pleasure**—Young person reads for pleasure three or more hours per week.

Positive Values

26. **Caring**—Young person places high value on helping other people.
27. **Equality and social justice**—Young person places high value on promoting equality and reducing hunger and poverty.
28. **Integrity**—Young person acts on convictions and stands up for her or his beliefs.
29. **Honesty**—Young person "tells the truth even when it is not easy."
30. **Responsibility**—Young person accepts and takes personal responsibility.
31. **Restraint**—Young person believes it is important not to be sexually active or to use alcohol or other drugs.

Social Competencies

32. **Planning and decision making**—Young person knows how to plan ahead and make choices.
33. **Interpersonal competence**—Young person has empathy, sensitivity, and friendship skills.
34. **Cultural competence**—Young person has knowledge of and comfort with people of different cultural/racial/ethnic backgrounds.
35. **Resistance skills**—Young person can resist negative peer pressure and dangerous situations.
36. **Peaceful conflict resolution**—Young person seeks to resolve conflict nonviolently.

Positive Identity

37. **Personal power**—Young person feels he or she has control over "things that happen to me."
38. **Self-esteem**—Young person reports having a high self-esteem.
39. **Sense of purpose**—Young person reports that "my life has a purpose."
40. **Positive view of personal future**—Young person is optimistic about her or his personal future.

political and religious affiliations. In field-testing the framework, Search Institute looked for language that unified communities, creating a sense of common good around which people could rally. The framework goes beyond naming what all children need to grow up happy and healthy in that it also describes a set of factors likely to unite, energize, and mobilize communities around preventing risky behaviors as well as promoting positive ones.

The primary tool for measuring levels of Developmental Assets in a community's youth is the 156-item *Search Institute Profiles of Student Life: Attitudes and Behaviors* survey, typically administered anonymously in a classroom setting. With more than two million young people having completed the survey, Search Institute has found that, on average, the young people report having only about 19 of the 40 assets. This is unfortunate, since research links high levels of Developmental Assets to young people's academic achievement, leadership, involvement in the community, and healthier, safer lifestyles. In a nutshell, the most important research findings from years of surveying young people about their levels of assets is that the more Developmental Assets young people have in their lives, the more likely they are to succeed in school, show leadership, take care of their health, and value diversity, and the less likely they are to be involved in violence, in using alcohol, tobacco, and other drugs, and in early sexual activity.

For example, 53% of young people who report 0–10 assets used alcohol three or more times in the past month or got drunk at least once in the last two weeks. However, only 3% of students with 31–40 assets report such alcohol use. Students with 11–20 assets are ten times more likely to have problems with alcohol use than students with more than 20 assets. These same patterns exist for other behaviors, including drug use, tobacco use, sexual intercourse, depression and/or attempted suicide, antisocial behavior, violence, school problems, driving and alcohol, and gambling. These patterns also apply across differences in students' race, ethnicity, age, socioeconomic status, and gender.

Search Institute has also found that the survey results inform community members about the strengths and needs of their community through their own young people's eyes; the resulting data often give a jump-start to programs, initiatives, and community collaborations working on behalf of young people. Communities large and small have discovered that the Developmental Assets framework gives them a common language that allows them to validate the work they are already doing to support the healthy development of children and youth while finding common ground for connecting with other programs, strategies, organizations, and coalitions doing the same work. The framework offers inspiration, motivation, and a simple tool for looking at what your community and its young people already have going for them, as well as for finding areas that need increased attention.

Search Institute and many of its partner initiatives have been able to document the impact of this asset-oriented community mobilization movement. Between 1997 and 2002, The Colorado Trust funded a statewide initiative dedicated to promoting the use of the 40 Developmental Assets. The Trust contracted with the Denver-based social science research firm OMNI Research and Training, Inc., to assess the initiative's impact on youth using key informant interviews, youth focus groups, site visits, document reviews, and surveys. OMNI found that by promoting new collaborations among diverse community sectors, more than 600 entities reported using, or supporting the use of, the Developmental Assets framework within the first five years. Youth reported gains in their sense of belonging, relationships with adults, self-confidence and positive view of the future, empathy for others, valuing of community service, and sense of self-efficacy.

These findings support community use of the asset surveys and other techniques to elicit the input of young people to define the changes that need to be made; the collective youth voice contributes inspiration and momentum to community change. This voice often pulls community members together, helping them transform a general wish for improvement into focused action.

The implications for preventing risk behaviors are especially compelling. Without adding costly new programs, a community can strengthen prevention efforts by infusing existing prevention programs with the positive approach of the Developmental Assets framework and by engaging all adults to connect with young people in positive ways.

LEARN MORE: For more information on the research, application, and evidence base for Developmental Assets, please see *Appendix B.* Research on and Evidence for the Developmental Assets Model in the Appendix to this book starting on page 273. For more on the Developmental Assets for children younger than 12, visit www.search-institute.org.

Getting To Outcomes: The Power to Build and Sustain Measurable Success

While researchers have developed many successful programs and policies to address positive youth development, local communities, schools, and youth-serving organizations can face significant challenges in trying to achieve positive outcomes. Often the significant amount of knowledge and skills required, the amount of resources needed, and the policies that need to be in place present barriers to success. Hoping to bridge this apparent gap between what works in the lab and the capacities in real life, Drs. Matt Chinman, Pam Imm, and

Abraham Wandersman wrote their manual, *Getting To Outcomes 2004: Promoting Accountability Through Methods and Tools for Planning, Implementation, and Evaluation* (www.rand.org/publications/TR/TR101).The manual was initially tailored to substance abuse prevention, but numerous practitioners have found the Getting To Outcomes (GTO) steps applicable for a wider range of strategies that aim to prevent any type of behavioral health problem and promote positive development.

GTO weaves together several overlapping theoretical strands of evaluation and accountability into a system that includes all of the critical elements of program planning, implementation, and evaluation needed in order to achieve results. Alone, each strand of evaluation is incomplete in providing the guidance needed for prevention practitioners to achieve positive results; by weaving the strands together, GTO provides a more complete model for planning and outcome measurement.

The GTO approach is based first on *traditional program evaluation,* which is usually conducted by external (neutral and objective) evaluators to assess the effects of programs created and implemented by practitioners. While this traditional approach is the foundation of evaluation, in recent years additional approaches to evaluation have been proposed that support more collaborative relationships between evaluators and practitioners.

One such approach, *empowerment evaluation,* is the second theoretical strand of GTO. While still retaining the basic tenets of traditional evaluation, it calls for evaluators to provide program implementers with both the tools and the opportunities to plan, implement with quality, evaluate outcomes, and develop a continuous quality improvement system themselves, thereby increasing the probability of achieving results. (For more on this strand, see D. Fetterman & A. Wandersman [2005], *Empowerment Evaluation Principles in Practice.* New York: Guilford Press.)

The third theoretical strand of GTO is *results-based accountability* (RBA). Based in part on Osborne and Graebler and on the Government Performance and Results Act of 1993, RBA moves practitioners away from collecting only outcome or output information—such as counting the number served—toward answering bottom-line questions about program effectiveness.

The fourth strand is *continuous quality improvement,* a technique in Total Quality Management (TQM). Developed for industry and successfully used in health-care settings, TQM suggests using an ongoing process to improve quality, reduce errors and costs, and increase customer satisfaction.

The GTO model interweaves these strands to enhance the capacity of practitioners and initiative members by empowering them to address all the key tasks involved in planning, implementing, tailoring, evaluating, and sustaining their own programs and policies.

The original GTO model synthesizes the leading prevention research into ten easy-to-follow questions that address these tasks:

1. Needs/conditions/resources
2. Goals
3. Evidence
4. Fit
5. Capacities
6. Planning
7. Process
8. Outcomes
9. Continuous quality improvement
10. Sustainability

The GTO model has already demonstrated its value and impact. An earlier version of the GTO manual was used with an elementary school in rural South Carolina to build character, increase social and academic competence, and improve classroom behavior. In that effort, Dr. Wandersman and colleagues collaborated with members of a community-based prevention coalition—using GTO—to plan, implement, and evaluate their programs in the local elementary school. Compared to a school without the program or GTO, children in the experimental school exhibited significantly lower levels of acting-out behavior, higher levels of on-task behavior, improved spelling and reading grades, and increased levels of self-esteem. Later, in 2001, the GTO manual won an award for the best self-help manual from the American Evaluation Association. Beyond its use at the local level, the GTO model has been used to organize the prevention systems of entire states.

Recent tests of the revised GTO manual in two substance abuse prevention coalitions in California and South Carolina suggest the GTO process has improved program staff's capacity across the various areas of prevention known to be associated with outcomes. For example, survey data of coalition members who used the GTO model show that participation was associated with more positive prevention attitudes (e.g., evaluation data can be used to improve programs) and more frequent evaluation practice (e.g., how often one engages in evaluation) across almost all of the important prevention domains specified by the ten questions. Qualitative data from both coalitions' staff showed that GTO provided them with "a new language" about how to make their programs more accountable. Also, it helped them be more "proactive," "focused," and "orderly" so that key details about the programs were not accidentally neglected. In particular, staff noted that GTO helped them with various aspects of planning such as communicating with grant writers, understanding the limits of their own capacity, structuring priorities, developing realistic goals and objectives, and assessing whether new potential programs were evidence-based.

While the original GTO model was grounded in drug and alcohol prevention research, it is now being used more widely in other content areas, such as HIV/AIDs prevention, teen pregnancy prevention, intimate partner violence and sexual violence prevention, juvenile justice, media literacy, and school readiness. Besides GTO's usefulness across many types of initiative activities, the ten steps of the GTO process are applicable at both the broad community level and the specific program level.

LEARN MORE: For more information on the research and evidence base for Getting To Outcomes, please see the article titled "Getting To Outcomes" in Appendix C of this book starting on page 299.

Combining Developmental Assets and Getting To Outcomes

The Assets-GTO process provides practitioners, program directors, and initiative leaders with the full range of perspectives and activities needed to improve the quality of prevention and positive youth development services, as well as to measure and report on performance. The two approaches are highly complementary, bringing together compatible language, perspectives, content, tools, and resources. Each system offers expert guidance in certain areas of high-quality prevention and community mobilization on which the other system has not concentrated and is therefore less well developed.

For example, GTO, as a generic process that can be used to plan, implement, and evaluate any prevention strategy, has less information about community mobilization and coalition building. The Developmental Assets model, with its community empowerment approach, has extensive materials in these areas. Search Institute's community-based approach emphasizes the integration of the assets model into community and program activities, while GTO offers concrete guidance in the form of text and tools to plan the details of such a process, implement it with high quality, and then evaluate its effectiveness. While GTO includes data collection tools for design, implementation, and evaluation, Search Institute has a strong positive youth development framework and well-developed and validated community assessment processes and measures, which can be used for conducting the needs, strengths, and resources assessment for either programs or community initiatives.

Succinctly, the Assets-GTO process is described in the following sequence of ten questions:

1. What are the needs, risks, resources, and conditions to address? (NEEDS/RESOURCES)
2. What are your goals and desired outcomes? (GOALS)
3. How will you achieve your goals effectively? (EFFECTIVENESS)

4. How does your work fit with existing programs and community-wide initiatives? (FIT)
5. What capacities will you need to implement your program or asset-building initiative? (CAPACITIES)
6. What is your plan? (PLAN)
7. How will you assess the quality of implementation? (PROCESS)
8. How will you determine if the program or asset-building initiative is working? (OUTCOMES)
9. What continuous quality improvement efforts do you need to improve your initiative or program over time? (CQI)
10. If the program or asset-building initiative is successful, how will it be sustained? (SUSTAINABILITY)

How This Book Is Organized

Using ten questions, this book describes the basics of how to structure either a program or an initiative so that it can be planned, implemented, and evaluated. Starting with Question #1 about conducting initial assessments of assets, thriving indicators, risks, conditions, and resources, each question builds upon the preceding ones as you develop the priorities, goals, and outcomes that you will eventually measure, document, and report. You will build and refine the most important aspects of your process over the course of answering the ten questions. For example, you will develop the first draft of your outcomes in Question #2, but you will have a chance to learn more and refine those outcomes in Questions #3, #6, and #8.

Assets-GTO is a dynamic process. It works best if people work together in groups to answer the questions, complete the worksheets, and develop plans. For initiatives or programs with limited resources, the book offers suggestions about how to modify or select worksheets that will yield the basic information you need to complete this process. For those of you who might want more detailed materials, the CD-ROM that is included with this book contains additional worksheets and resources. Special notes throughout the book titled *CD FEATURE* will point out what's available.

You don't have to be just starting out on the work of your initiative or program to use this book. You may, for example, have already completed needs and resource assessments or even have developed goals, outcomes, and a logic model. You could begin the Assets-GTO process with Question #3 or even later, depending on where you are in your work. Once you've had a chance to glance through the structure of this book, you can decide where it is most appropriate for you and your working group to start. You may also find that, at some point, you wish to cycle back and rework an earlier step, then move forward again. Assets-GTO has been designed to work flexibly for you, depending on your needs.

The ten Assets-GTO questions are organized into three sections.

PART ONE: Starting Points, Conditions, and Goals

Introduction. Getting Started describes some of the key information you need to get started on this process, including an overview of Search Institute's model for asset-based community capacity building, which is built into the infrastructure of this process; the importance of developing a coherent vision to unifying your evaluative work; and the critical elements to employ that will begin to build the sustainability of your work from the beginning, such as the deep engagement of youth and diverse communities in your work.

Question #1. What are the needs, risks, resources, and conditions to address? (NEEDS/RESOURCES)—The first question takes you through the steps of determining what kinds of needs and resource assessments you want and how to conduct them. There are useful summaries about which Search Institute surveys you can use to get the information you need, as well as other places from which to gather data. When you finish this chapter you will have developed a basic set of priorities from your assessments.

Question #2. What are your goals and desired outcomes? (GOALS)—The second question helps you build on your basic set of priorities from Question #1, leading you through the process of specifying the goals and the outcomes you hope to measure.

PART TWO: Projects and Programs, Fit, and Implementation

Building upon the work you do in the first two questions, this next set of questions guides you through researching the best activities to use to reach your goals, how to make sure your goals will fit with your community, and determining whether your initiative or program has the capacity needed to implement your plans.

Question #3. How will you achieve your goals effectively? (EFFECTIVENESS)—This question offers more background on the evidence-based Developmental Assets and prevention principles you can integrate into your initiative or program. You will learn how to select effective programs and principles to use in your work. You will also design your logic model, which will form the basis of the work you do in subsequent questions.

Question #4. How does your work fit with existing programs and community-wide initiatives? (FIT)—This question guides you through assessing the congruence between what you are planning and what your community needs. This question also helps you determine if you need to modify or adapt selected programs and offers tips on how to do so.

Question #5. What capacities will you need to implement your program or asset-building initiative? (CAPACITIES)—This question helps you assess your initiative's, organization's, or program's capacity for carrying out the plan you have begun to develop, including whether you have the operational infrastructure needed to sustain your work.

PART THREE: Launch, Monitor, and Evaluate

This set of questions guides you through launching, monitoring, and evaluating the plans you developed in Questions #1–#5. Each of these three chapters has a "planning" phase and a "doing" phase. By this point, you will have a clear idea of what you can successfully measure when you're done. Some of the worksheets in this section will bridge across chapters.

Question #6. What is your plan? (PLAN)—This question helps you bring all the information you've developed so far into a coherent, detailed plan for how you will carry out your project(s) and program(s).

Question #7. How will you assess the quality of implementation? (PROCESS)—This question guides you through evaluating how your overall process is working.

Question #8. How will you determine if the program or asset-building initiative is working? (OUTCOMES)—This question guides you through evaluating the outcomes of your work. In addition to the planning and doing sections of this question, there is also a section on "reporting" that helps you organize your results into meaningful ways of communicating your successes to the community.

PART FOUR: Improve and Sustain

Once you have successfully completed your work, the questions in this section show you how to use all you've learned to continuously improve and sustain what you're doing.

Question #9. What continuous quality improvement efforts do you need to improve your initiative or program over time? (CQI)—This question takes you through a simple self-assessment of your work so far with tips on how to make improvements the next time you conduct your program.

Question #10. If the program or asset-building initiative is successful, how will it be sustained? (SUSTAIN)—The final Assets-GTO question brings the sustainability tips embedded in each of the previous questions into an overall plan you can use to make sure your work continues.

There are several useful features in each chapter of this book, including:

- A *rundown* of what each question will help you do;
- A *quick list* of what you'll need to get started;
- A *snapshot* of what each step looks like in action, featuring the work of existing asset-building initiatives and programs from around the country;
- *Tipsheets* that will extend your knowledge and supplement your work;
- *Worksheets* that will guide you through each of the critical steps you need to take to complete each question;
- *Sidebars* that contain useful, additional shots of information;
- *"Learn More"* tips that suggest additional resources you may want to consult to extend your knowledge;
- *CD Features* will tell you about other resources, reports, or more detailed worksheets that can be found on the CD-ROM included with this book; and
- *Sustainability tips* at the end of each question that will get you thinking about how to develop and strengthen your work as you go.

As with other books written to guide you in your asset-building journey, this one must conform to a linear form to be useful, even though the process of developing initiatives, programs, and evaluation plans doesn't always happen in a straight line. The material has been sequenced into a series of easy-to-follow steps to help organize your work, but you should adapt the information and suggestions to the needs of your unique, creative process.

PART ONE

Starting Points, Conditions, and Goals

Before you begin your Assets-GTO journey, you need to have some idea where you're starting from. Just as if you were embarking upon a car trip, the starting point is your home base. You have your end point or destination in mind, but before you leave, you determine what you'll need to take with you to make the trip comfortable and successful. You check out weather and road conditions along the way, which helps you prepare for changes you might need to make in your itinerary, depending on what you encounter. You assess the resources you have to make sure you can pay for your trip.

The chapters in this first section will help you get off to a good start. They include:

An **Introduction** that lays out the key concepts that form the foundation of this book. (For detail on the research background of Developmental Assets and Getting To Outcomes, see Appendix B and Appendix C.) The Introduction discusses important ways to ensure a successful journey, such as developing an overarching vision and engaging youth and diverse communities in your efforts. By taking time to incorporate these preliminary steps, you can also begin to build sustainability into your work. *The Introduction begins on page 3.*

Question #1. What are the needs, risks, resources, and conditions to address? (NEEDS/RESOURCES)—This question helps you discover what risks and deficits exist in your community that you wish to address, as well as which assets and resources exist that will help you combat those risks and deficits. *Question #1 begins on page 19.*

Question #2. What are your goals and desired outcomes? (GOALS)—This question shows you how to take what you've learned from your needs and resources assessments and shape them into goals and outcomes that will form the basis of the work to come. *Question #2 begins on page 49.*

INTRODUCTION

Getting Started

You may be either entirely new to or already deeply involved in the process of building Developmental Assets; in charge of managing a program, organization, or community coalition, or involved in running a prevention program. *Getting To Outcomes with Developmental Assets* is designed to assist you at any level of professional or organizational experience and to apply across a wide variety of programs and issues. Your work with the Assets-GTO process will guide you from the big picture of your vision all the way to the details of your implementation and evaluation. But let's start first with the larger context.

When people get started with asset building, they usually begin with a vision of transforming their community, even the larger society, into one in which all young people are valued and thrive, and they use the framework of Developmental Assets to guide them in creating projects and programs that lead toward bringing that vision into reality. They use Search Institute's Five Action Strategies—Engage Adults, Mobilize Young People, Activate Sectors, Invigorate Programs, and Influence Civic Decisions—to provide a structural look at the five main areas in which action needs to take place to accomplish societal change.

Ultimately, an initiative needs to be working in all Five Action Strategy areas with multiple projects and programs, but you may choose to focus on just one or two strategies in the beginning. Programs focus on the Invigorate Programs strategy, but can usefully look at the four other action strategies for the potential of enhanced impact. For example, a youth-oriented prevention program might think about the Engage Adults and Activate Sectors strategies, and then may consider how to involve adults such as parents and neighbors in the program and how they might hook up with nearby schools to broaden the program's reach.

To give you a view of how your initiative or program fits in the framework of asset-based community building, Tipsheet A on page 5 shows you the Five Action Strategies and how they fit within the overall context of building the community's capacity for asset building.

LEARN MORE: If you've not yet begun organizing your initiative and/or are unfamiliar with the asset approach, we recommend that you take some time to review the excerpts from the following resources on the CD-ROM before beginning the Assets-GTO process:

- *Assets in Action: A Handbook for Making Communities Better Places to Grow Up.* This book takes you through the how-to of each of the Five Action Strategies and provides stories, tips, and ideas for each.
- *Putting Assets in Action: Making Your Community a Better Place for Young People . . . and for You.* This brochure is based on the book and offers a cogent overview for getting started.
- *The Asset Activist's Toolkit: Handouts and Practical Resources for Putting Assets into Action.* This is a collection of materials complementary to the above resources, designed to help you effectively communicate the asset message.

CD FEATURE: Excerpts from the resources listed above can be found on the CD-ROM included with this book.

TRAINING AVAILABLE: If you wish to have assistance in using the Assets-GTO process, contact Vision Training Associates at 800-294-4322 or go to www.search-institute.org/training.

Here's a description of the key components of this asset-based community capacity-building framework.

Cultivate Community Readiness, Energy, and Commitment. Cultivating an asset-building community is conceived as a mobilization of public will, power, capacity, and commitment to create a culture in which all residents are expected to contribute to young people's healthy development. Thus, a strong focus is on stimulating community passion, commitment, and capacity not only for strengthening programs but also for uniting the entire community in supporting

Tipsheet A

A FRAMEWORK FOR ASSET-BASED COMMUNITY BUILDING

The asset approach can be used to increase community capacity to support children and youth by bringing energized youth and adults together with the resources and experience of community organizations and existing networks. You can see that the Five Action Strategies are at the heart of this framework.

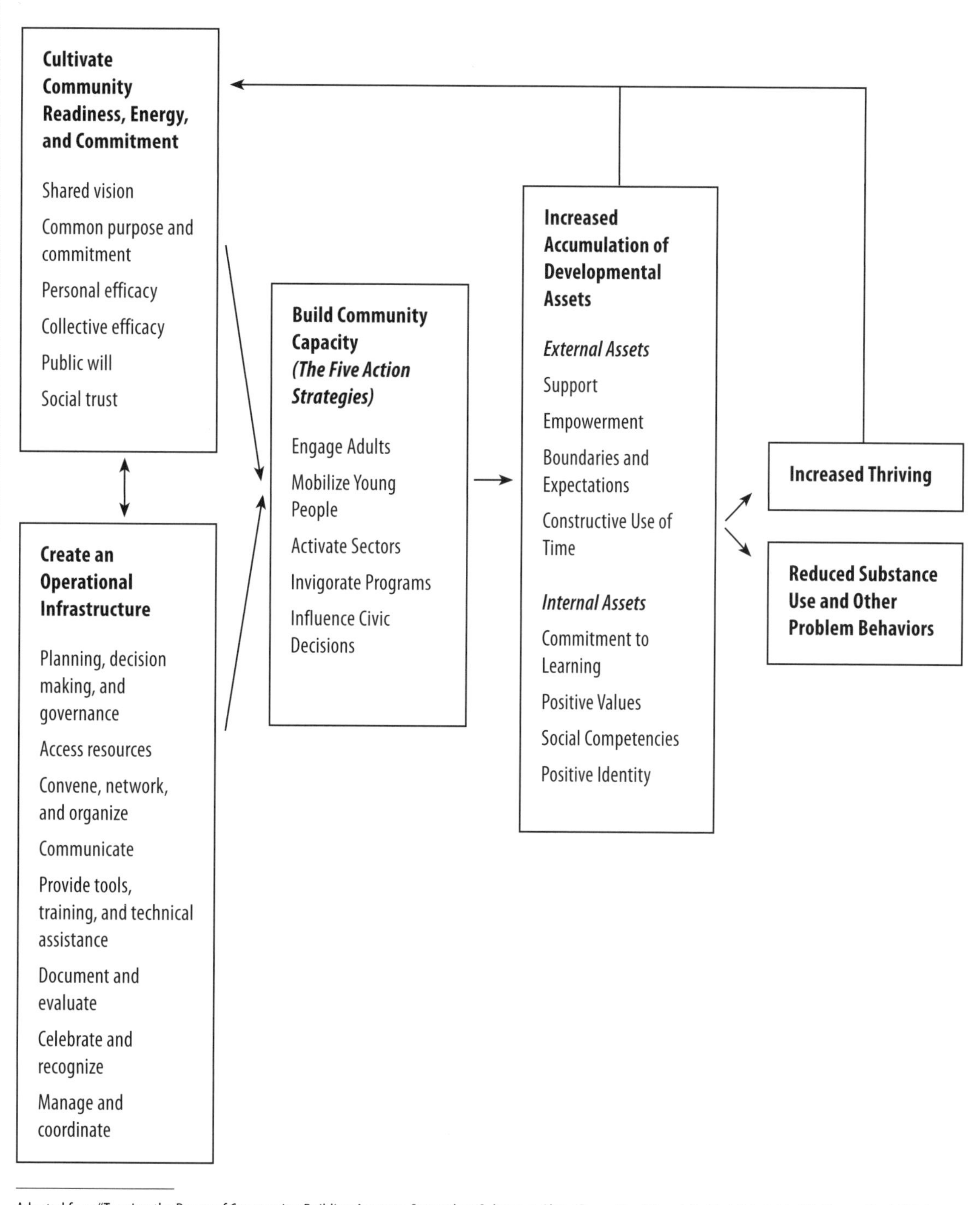

Adapted from "Tapping the Power of Community: Building Assets to Strengthen Substance Abuse Prevention," Search Institute's *Insights & Evidence,* March 2004.

and contributing to all young people's healthy development. Components of creating this culture of sustained commitment include:

- *A shared vision* that unites multiple community sectors, systems, policies, and leaders across political, ideological, religious, economic, and/or racial/ethnic differences;
- *Common purpose and commitment* that allow for collaboration and synergy across different initiatives and agendas in the community;
- *Personal efficacy* in which young people, residents, parents, and nonparents recognize their own capacity and power to contribute to young people's healthy development and community life;
- *Collective efficacy* in which people, organizations, and formal networks recognize and act upon their shared strengths and capacities to work together for common goals;
- *Public will* for investing individually and collectively in young people's lives and in the policies, programs, and practices that support their healthy development; and
- *Social trust* that comes from being in relationship with others and recognizing commonalities and mutual respect, even in the midst of ideological, cultural, or economic differences.

Create an Operational Infrastructure. The formal asset-building infrastructure in a community (i.e., the initiative, coalition, or organization) plays the vital role of linking, promoting, and supporting asset-building efforts in the community. It typically includes the following core functions:

- *Planning, decision making, and governance* to guide both the maintenance issues of the infrastructure and the mission priorities of building community capacity;
- *Accessing resources* (e.g., financial, personnel, skills) needed to support the core functions and capacity-building efforts;
- *Convening, networking, and organizing* committed "champions" who have the passion to spread the word and help make the vision a reality;
- *Communicating* broadly to the community to inspire and support engagement by distributing information, making presentations, and tapping the media to raise awareness about asset building and local efforts;
- *Providing tools, training, and technical assistance* that increase the capacity of individuals, programs, and organizations to engage in, deepen, and sustain their asset-building efforts;

- *Using formal documentation, assessment, and evaluation* to examine community life through the asset lens and to identify how well a community ensures youth access to multiple opportunities across the age span;
- *Celebrating* asset-building efforts and progress in the community; and
- *Managing and coordinating* schedules, budgets, and other administrative tasks, as needed.

Build Community Capacity. Search Institute has identified Five Action Strategies that highlight the areas within a community that need to be tapped in order to create asset-rich communities. These strategies are:

- *Engage adults* from all walks of life to develop sustained, strength-building relationships with children and adolescents, both within families and in neighborhoods.
- *Mobilize young people* to use their power as asset builders and change agents, tapping the power of peer influence in substance abuse and other risky behaviors as well as in healthy development.
- *Activate all sectors* of the community—such as schools, congregations, youth organizations, businesses, human services, and health-care organizations—to create an asset-building culture and to contribute fully to young people's healthy development.
- *Invigorate, expand, and enhance programs* to become more asset rich and to be available to and accessed by all children and youth. The asset framework offers a tool for reflecting on current practices to determine how they can be strengthened.
- *Influence decision makers and opinion leaders* to leverage financial, media, and policy resources in support of the positive transformation of communities and society. This strategy involves providing a lens for decision making in the media, foundations, and public policy.

LEARN MORE: Numerous examples illustrating the Five Action Strategies can be found in *Assets in Action: A Handbook for Making Communities Better Places to Grow Up.*

OUR MISSION

Quakertown Area Healthy Communities • Healthy Youth Coalition mission:

To build a community of youth and adults working and dreaming together to build an environment where every individual's unique gifts, talents and strengths are discovered, nurtured, and employed.

The Georgetown Project mission:

IMAGINE—a community where no child is hungry, hurt, alone or rejected . . . and where all children and youth believe they are loved, respected and treated with dignity . . .
. . . **Imagine Georgetown!**

It All Starts with Vision

Experienced leaders and participants in programs, organizations, and initiatives know it's important to develop a shared vision. A shared vision not only guides your work, it also engages new participants and fosters connection. "It's more than just having a discussion around a vision statement," says Lee Rush, coordinator for the HC • HY (Healthy Communities • Healthy Youth) of Upper Bucks initiative in Pennsylvania. "It's about providing an experience where everyone gets input so they develop more ownership. Vision helps sustain people's involvement in the work on a higher level."

Vision is also central to the success of the Assets-GTO process. A unified vision logically knits your work on the ten steps of the GTO process together in a coherent manner and gives you a touchstone against which to measure your progress. "As we evolved through our first years in the planning stages, I thought sometimes we'd never get 'there,'" says Georgetown, Texas, Project Director Barbara Pearce. "But we'd go back to this vision that was driving us and then move forward again. We created our activities to contribute to that vision."

The longer term efforts to sustain your initiative or program will start with your vision, too. The buy-in of participants, combined with conceptual clarity about what you want to accomplish in your community, will help you plan for the future.

If you don't already have a shared vision, consider creating a vision team to work together to adopt or create one. An emphasis on making sure young people are always part of the vision team helps keep an initiative dynamic and creative and contributes to the efficacy of a program's responsiveness to its messages. You may want to start by considering the vision Search Institute has developed for its Healthy Communities • Healthy Youth (HC • HY) initiative:

> All children and youth need to be surrounded with networks of individuals and institutions that provide them with support, opportunities, boundaries, and structure, and that nurture in them the commitments, values, competencies, and positive identity they need to grow up healthy and competent.

LEARN MORE: You can find out more about Search Institute's national Healthy Communities • Healthy Youth initiative at www.search-institute.org.

Your vision can be used as a touchstone throughout your entire process. The interconnectedness of vision to the ten steps of the Assets-GTO process is depicted in the graphic on page 10. More information on how to develop a vision can be found in *Assets in Action: A Handbook for Making Communities Better Places to Grow Up.*

Use Assets-GTO at Both the Program and Initiative Levels

Assets-GTO is written so that you can apply it at the initiative or community level or on the ground at the program level. The chart on pages 11–12 shows you a quick view of how each of the ten Assets-GTO questions may play out at both the program and community level. The points summarized in the chart will be more fully explained in the chapter corresponding to each question.

Both the circular graphic found on page 10 and the chart on pages 11–12 may be useful to copy and distribute to staff, volunteers, participants, partners, funders, and other interested constituents as you work your way through the Assets-GTO process.

Critical Elements for Integrating Assets-GTO

To better ensure the success of your work, Assets-GTO needs to be fully integrated into everything you're doing, whether at the community initiative or at the program level. Your work will be much more effective if you make Assets-GTO the process for how you do business rather than just an "add-on" to what you're already doing. For example, using many of the worksheets you'll find in this book as tools for developing and communicating your plans will help everyone involved with your work learn and speak the language of Assets-GTO. These same worksheets can also be used as the foundation for progress reports to stakeholders.

Given the busyness of most people's lives, you may have a concern about the depth of this process and the numerous worksheets and steps it involves. It will be important for you and those working with you to arrange to spend some good-quality time on the process. As we lead you through it, we'll show you how to use the exercises and worksheets to your advantage. Integrating the Assets-GTO steps

The Relation of the 10 Questions to the Healthy Communities • Healthy Youth Vision

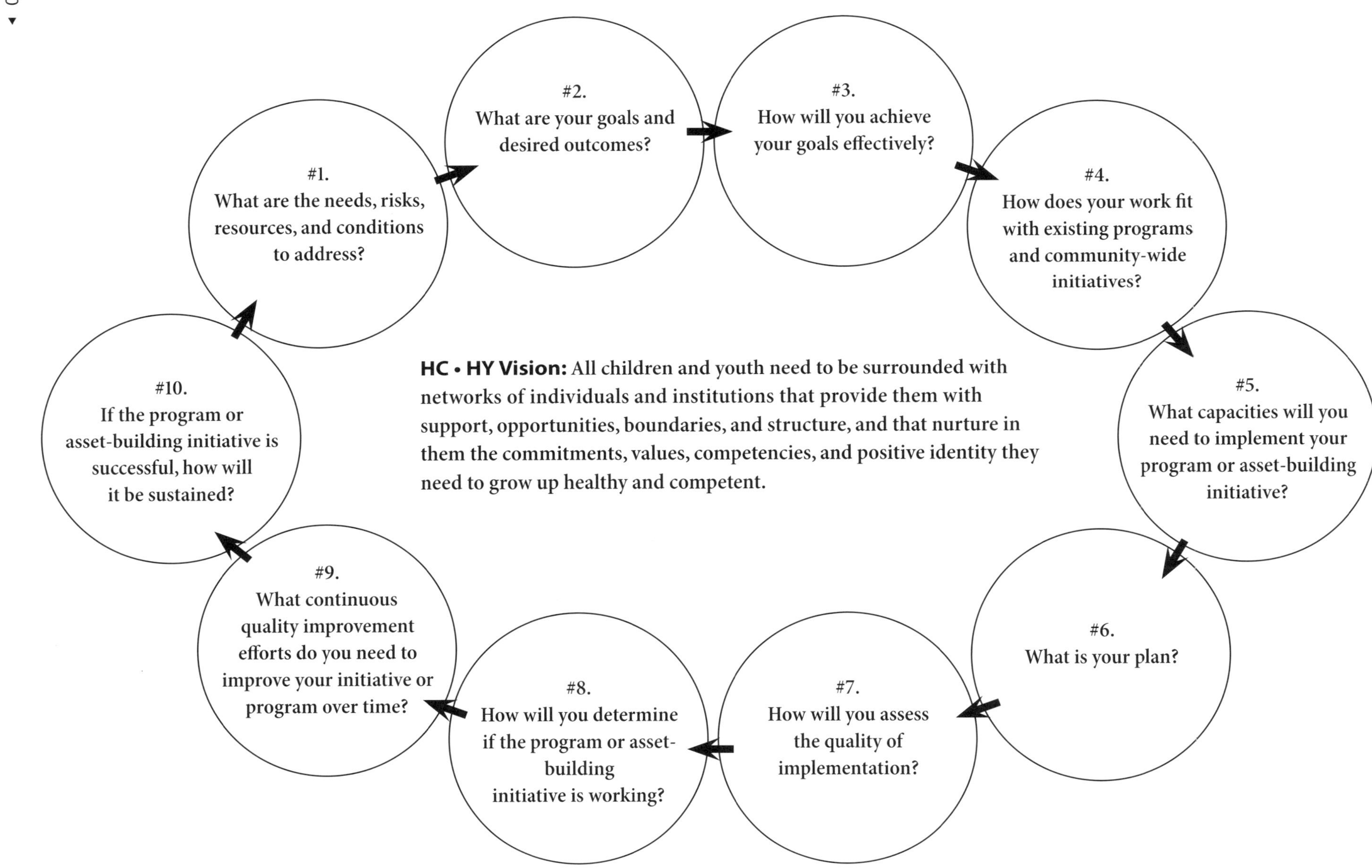

The Ten Assets-GTO Questions

Accountability Questions	What this looks like at the program level	What this looks like at the community initiative level
1. *What are the needs, risks, resources, and conditions to address?*	The program (within an organization or initiative) assesses its interests, then gathers asset, thriving indicator, risk, and deficit information to help select priorities for attention. Existing resources are also identified.	A community initiative conducts a broad asset, thriving indicator, risk, and deficit assessment to help select asset priorities for attention. Existing resources are also identified.
2. *What are your goals and desired outcomes?*	The program shapes its priorities into specific, attainable asset-oriented goals and outcomes.	The community initiative shapes its priorities into specific, attainable goals and outcomes tied to the Five Action Strategies.
3. *How will you achieve your goals effectively?*	The program reviews evidence-based strategies to see if any address their chosen goals and outcomes, infuses assets as necessary, and/or creates the appropriate strategies using proven Developmental Assets and prevention principles. A logic model is developed.	The community initiative reviews and selects relevant existing models, infuses assets if necessary, or creates the appropriate projects and programs. The initiative also prioritizes its actions with regard to which of the Five Action Strategies it will use in order to build the overall initiative capacity. A logic model is developed
4. *How does your work fit with existing programs and community-wide initiatives?*	The program determines how well it fits into the organizational setting and larger context in which it will be implemented.	The community initiative determines how ready the broader community is for its proposed work and what resources already exist that address goals and outcomes.
5. *What capacities will you need to implement your program or asset-building initiative?*	The program determines which capacities it has and what it needs to build the chosen Developmental Assets.	The community initiative determines if it has the capacity needed to conduct its plans and then develops what it needs.
6. *What is your plan?*	The program specifies the details of its implementation plan and anticipates its process and outcome evaluation.	The community initiative specifies the details of its implementation plan and anticipates its process and outcome evaluation.

The Ten Assets-GTO Questions, continued

Accountability Questions	What this looks like at the program level	What this looks like at the community initiative level
7. How will you assess the quality of implementation?	The program is implemented and its process evaluated.	The community initiative implements its strategies and programs, and evaluates its process.
8. How will you determine if the program or asset-building initiative is working?	The program measures its impact.	The community initiative measures its impact across the Five Action Strategies.
9. What continuous quality improvement efforts do you need to improve your initiative or program over time?	The program reviews what happened in steps 1–8 and then makes improvements before the program is repeated.	The community initiative reviews what happened in steps 1–8 and makes important changes as it moves forward.
10. If the program or asset-building initiative is successful, how will it be sustained?	The program continuously looks for ways to sustain its work both structurally and financially, using its data to support its success.	The community initiative continuously looks for ways to sustain its infrastructure and its work both structurally and financially, using its data to support its success.

and materials will lead you to a more efficient and coherent planning process that will enhance your work and ultimately save you time by increasing the efficiency of your efforts.

For the Assets-GTO process to be fully successful, it is very important that you not skip any of the questions! All ten questions are designed to build upon each other, so skipping questions will lead to less-than-satisfactory results. Some of the questions will require more work than others, but it should not take an unreasonable amount of time to follow them. In fact, you may find, as you work through this book, that you're doing some of the steps already. This process will help you better organize and document your efforts. The more closely and systematically you follow the questions, the more likely you'll be able to demonstrate accountability in a variety of ways. This will be useful in communicating with a variety of funders and constituents.

A summary of the critical elements for integrating Assets-GTO is shown in Tipsheet B on page 13. Whenever you see this symbol ◆ in other sections of this

Tipsheet B

CRITICAL ELEMENTS FOR INTEGRATING ASSETS-GTO INTO YOUR WORK

These tips can help programs, organizations, and initiatives more fully integrate the Assets-GTO concepts into your work:

1. ***Get buy-in.*** Work on getting all levels of the initiative, organization, or program to endorse and use Assets-GTO. Buy-in starts on the inside with staff, management, volunteers, board members, peer educators, and anyone else connected with everyday activities. Buy-in also means regularly encouraging leaders and decision makers to promote and model the Assets-GTO concepts, as well as asking support staff and participants to do the same.

2. ***Always orient new personnel and participants to Assets-GTO.*** Build training for new staff, employees, volunteers, and participants into your work. Orient them to the view that the process is an integral part of the operational framework. Trainings should ground all participants in the basic concepts. By providing copies of all the materials along with assistance in learning how to use Assets- GTO, you will help newcomers more easily adopt the model as part of their work.

3. ***Structure all reporting around Assets-GTO.*** Reports structured around the ten questions can facilitate regular communication among participants and staff about operations and results. Such communication helps keep information fresh and can be used to integrate new participants into the process. High-quality reporting will also play an important role in continually improving and sustaining your process.

4. ***Provide regular access to Assets-GTO information.*** As forms and reports are updated and completed, materials can be collected and made available to all relevant staff and participants. Many of the worksheets provided in this book can easily be turned into useful reports. To make the best use of completed Assets-GTO reports, gather groups of staff, volunteers, participants, stakeholders, and youth together for regular meetings based on the Assets-GTO questions. Regular meetings can be used to update responses to each question as work continues. The Assets-GTO materials can be especially effective as communication tools for initiatives with a wide range of participants.

5. ***Use Assets-GTO to complement strategic planning.*** You can maximize your results by making the Assets-GTO process (especially Questions #1–6) part of your larger strategic planning efforts. Assets-GTO can be used very effectively at both the individual program level and at the organization and initiative levels.

6. ***Employ what you're learning to build capacity.*** The Assets-GTO process can be integrated into varying levels of your work to build capacity in a variety of ways. For example, if an initiative or organization gives out grants or mini-grants, the application process can mirror the Assets-GTO model so that the questions that need to be addressed in the application are based on the same ten accountability questions. Reports can be similar and the granting organization can provide Assets-GTO training for its grantees. Alternatively, the ten questions plus a budget, the articles on the evidence base of Developmental Assets and GTO, and a list of staff qualifications together can make up a strong grant application. Future reports to funders can consist of your answers to the ten questions.

book, you'll find specific tips and examples on how to more fully integrate Assets-GTO into your work.

Striving for Equality and Diversity

One of the important ways in which asset building is distinguished from many other efforts is the depth and degree to which *youth are equal partners*—you strive to work *with* and *for* youth. They are equal partners in all activities and should be invited to work as equal partners in the Assets-GTO evaluation process, too. Youth can play many roles in your efforts, including bringing a fresh perspective to the kinds of information you gather, as well as defining and legitimizing the strategies you develop as a result of following the Assets-GTO process. Many initiatives and programs are finding that youth are eager to participate in evaluation efforts and can sometimes elicit different results than adults can. Chanteal and Rhonda Garcia, a daughter-and-mother team, canvassed their neighborhood in Montebello, California, asking residents to identify individual and community treasures as part of a project called Neighborhood Matters! sponsored by Safeco Insurance and the YMCA. "Going door-to-door with Mom was really good because people won't always listen to someone my age," says Chanteal. "It was really good because I had someone older with me." "Younger kids see any adult as an authority figure," says Rhonda, "but they'll look up to a teen more. The kids we invited to help with our plans listened to her."

Researchers Barry Checkoway and Katie Richards-Schuster conclude in their article "Youth Participation in Community Evaluation Research," from the *American Journal of Evaluation,** that youth are equal to the task of fully participating in evaluation alongside adults. They not only benefit from the support they receive from the adults, they also develop and share knowledge that better prepares them to participate in the community. Young people exposed to such a dynamic exchange are more likely to engage in positive social action, and the community benefits because young people have important views and information to contribute, especially in evaluating programs directed at them.

If you are in the early stages of your work and do not yet have significant youth involvement in your efforts, you can refer to a number of resources Search Institute has developed that can help you. *Assets in Action* has an entire chapter on mobilizing youth as one of the Five Action Strategies. *Working Shoulder to Shoulder: Stories and Strategies of Youth-Adult Partnerships That Succeed* is another book that can take you through all the steps of building an effective and rewarding collaboration.

**24*(1), 21–33.

CD FEATURE: For more information on how to involve youth and work in intergenerational groups, see the tips found on the CD-ROM included with this book.

Intergenerational diversity is just one of the many important aspects asset-building initiatives, organizations, and programs integrate into their efforts. For Assets-GTO to be fully effective, attention must also be paid to incorporating ethnic and racial diversity into your efforts, as well as geographic, religious, economic, organizational, tribal, and sector diversity.

For a community-wide initiative to enhance the developmental experience of *all* children and adolescents, *cultural competence* must become just as deeply embedded in asset-building work as a focus on helping young people build Developmental Assets. Writing in *The Spirit of Culture: Applying Cultural Competency to Strength-based Youth Development,* former executive director of Assets for Colorado Youth (ACY) María Guajardo Lucero distinguishes cultural competence from the related concepts of diversity and inclusiveness in the following ways:

- *Diversity* refers to the people asset builders are trying to reach—the young people we build assets for and with *and* the community members of all ages we invite to become asset builders with us. Diversity includes race and ethnicity, but is broader in its definition to include political, religious, gender, age, sexual orientation, ability, and economic groups as well. The goal is to build bridges of unity and cooperation across the many diverse groups within a community.
- *Inclusiveness* is the process of how initiatives engage audiences. It means paying deliberate attention to involving, reaching, and empowering all members and segments of a community. The lens of inclusivity can be used to examine how decisions are made, who is asked to lead, where dialogues are held, and how resources are distributed. For example, groups with members from a variety of different cultures often find that using consensus models for decision making, which take time and patience, is more successful overall than using democratic models, in which voting processes can lead to "winners and losers" and thus alienate some members from further participation.
- *Cultural competence* refers here to the overall change process that occurs personally and professionally as people are exposed to various cultural strengths and traditions and learn to do things differently and enhance efforts as a result. For the asset message to be most effective, it needs to be culturally inclusive, relevant across ethnicities, and respectful of the diverse approaches to nurturing a child.

Central to the process of developing cultural competence, says Guajardo Lucero, is the building of relationships—the sharing and offering of oneself while embracing the richness of another. The asset framework works for individuals of many cultures and can itself be considered an "inclusivity" tool because it invites *everyone* to come together around these common words and concepts for a common goal: to improve life for all children.

Guajardo Lucero continues in her book: "Just as asset builders learn to reach out and connect with youth, culturally competent individuals learn to engage and connect with people of different ethnic and cultural backgrounds. The process is similar and the results are equally as profound. Asset builders who make a conscious effort to give their support to a young person are engaging in behavior similar to a culturally competent individual who asks a person to share the story of her or his cultural background. It goes beyond celebrating culture, which is often short-term and time limited, to promoting a new way of thinking that fully embraces diversity. Embracing means getting to know someone, developing a relationship with them, and engaging in a process of sharing with them."

Embracing culture and diversity changes people individually and, consequently, changes the trajectory of initiative work in the community. This is especially important for all of the young people asset builders seek to develop relationships with. Assets for Colorado Youth offers these three guiding principles for engaging ethnically diverse youth:

1. *Culture influences behavior; culture does not determine behavior.* While there are shared qualities and experiences within ethnic groups, it is important to remember that there is diversity within ethnic groups.
2. *Relationships are key.* Programs don't change people, people do. Relationships based on strengths will provide a platform for skill development, behavioral change, and informed decision making.
3. *Culture influences one's worldview, as both a provider and a recipient of services.* Youth and adults may not be able to articulate the influence of culture, but this does not mean it should be ignored. Naming and sharing cultural experiences will allow for worldviews to be more meaningfully understood.

Building relationships—especially with youth and diverse segments of your community—will also be essential to building sustainability into your work, at both the initiative and the program levels. "Relationships are important," says Lee Rush of Pennsylvania's HC • HY Upper Bucks initiative, "but it also has to be fun for people to keep doing it. It has to be more than just part of their jobs. It has to be personally satisfying."

Planning Ahead for Sustainability

Get started right now on thinking ahead to how you will sustain your efforts. As we've suggested with the evaluation process itself, sustainability shouldn't be something you do *after* you've finished implementing your program. Your plan for sustainability starts at the beginning of your work at the same time your program and evaluation planning begins. Planning for sustainability now—and at each step of the way as you work through the ten Assets-GTO questions—will improve your chances of being able to successfully repeat and continue the good works you accomplish.

Soon after launching a federally funded project to reduce underage drinking, the Wisconsin Positive Youth Development Initiative, for example, also instituted its own system analysis along with a set of prevention system change indicators of success. This ongoing process guides the coalition partners through a regular self-review of fourteen different aspects of the project from vision to sustainability. "Building your system *is* an act of sustainability," says Sue Allen, the initiative's coordinator. "By creating a lasting collaborative system that builds expectations including sharing data into the way agencies, institutions, organizations, municipalities and counties 'do business,' then we have a chance at a long-term sustainable process. Prevention *plus* building assets means we're all thriving."

CD FEATURE: You can review a copy of the Wisconsin Coalition's Prevention System Analysis grid and a summary of the initiative's success indicators on the CD-ROM included with this book.

To begin the journey of sustainability from your initiative's or program's inception, remember to ground all of your work in these three important ways:

1. *Develop a shared vision:* Vision provides conceptual clarity and allows for future-oriented planning. One example—a Kansas Health Foundation effort that asked the citizens of McPherson County, Kansas to participate in Vision 2010, a grassroots method of identifying the county's five most significant issues and designing solutions to address them.
2. *Build strength-based relationships:*Emphasize building relationships as the basis of all your work. They will provide a platform for skill development, behavioral change and informed decision-making. "We found during one of our regular reviews," says Renie Kehres,

coordinator of Prevention Partners for Youth Development (PPYD), "that the networking benefit was significant during supervisors training. We made sure subsequent trainings included a networking period where individuals could have structured time to network and share information."

3. *Cultivate diversity:* Embracing culture and diversity changes people individually and consequently changes the trajectory of your program or initiative's work in the community. Continually cultivate diverse youth and community engagement and active participation in all levels of your work.

Remember to also emphasize building relationships among your diverse participants—focus on forming trusted relationships with members of different community groups and working with those folks first to be sure that members of each group feel safe, welcomed, and accepted in a meeting or at an event. This will help keep your work relevant as well as strengthen and sustain your members.

Initiative organizers in both Alaska and Colorado, for example, have conducted formal processes to help shape culturally relevant translations of the asset framework. Adult and youth members of diverse communities have contributed stories, language, and cultural traditions to both illuminate and expand the asset framework beyond a simple, literal translation. Both the process and the result have helped build trust and relationships among participants.

LEARN MORE: *Helping Kids Succeed—Alaskan Style* is available from Search Institute (www.search-institute.org) or from the Alaska Initiative for Community Engagement (www.alaskaice.org). Different translations of the asset framework, including Spanish translations that include *dichos* or traditional proverbs, are available from Assets for Colorado Youth in their publication, *The Spirit of Culture: Applying Cultural Competency to Strength-based Youth Development* at 1-888-543-7871.

Now you're ready to move onto the first Assets-GTO question.

QUESTION #1

What are the needs, risks, resources, and conditions to address?

(NEEDS/RESOURCES)

Before you take action, you need to know what's going on in your community. Your current asset-building initiative or community program was started for a reason—there was a specific issue in the community people wanted to address, or perhaps a core group of people (e.g., youth organization leaders, community activists, teachers) was inspired by hearing about Developmental Assets and wanted to do something with the framework. Answering this first question by examining your community's needs, issues, and available resources will help you learn more about what's going on in your community. Perhaps there are concerns about rising rates of substance abuse or violence among local youth. You might be looking for fresh ways to tackle an ongoing issue, such as creating deeper connections with diverse communities. Or you might have a fired-up group of teens interested in developing community service projects. Whatever your reasons and issues, the activities in this chapter will help you gather the information you need to begin bringing more focus to your actions and to help get people on board with you.

Conducting meaningful needs and resource assessments will not only help you gain a clear understanding of issues or problems you want to address, but also determine exactly who will benefit from your interventions and what existing strengths and resources you can leverage as part of the solution. This chapter leads you through a process to assess the existing assets and resources that will help solve problems, improve conditions, or even keep problems from emerging in the first place—whether you are developing a program or a structured set of intentional activities in an initiative. Gathering specific data and information in this first step will also help you design more meaningful, measurable outcomes later on.

The activities in this chapter will guide you to:

- Establish a work group that includes youth and other key stakeholders—anyone who has a vested interest in your eventual outcomes—who will help you manage your assessment.
- Identify the data and information you want to gather to create an accurate picture of your community of interest, including asset surveys, resource mapping, and risk behaviors analysis. You'll want to examine the existing data as well as determine the sorts of data you will need to complete your analysis.
- Create and implement a plan for data gathering.
- Analyze, interpret, and report your data and information.
- Select the priorities you wish to address and which groups will benefit from your proposed interventions.

The priorities you develop in this chapter will form the basis for developing your goals and outcomes in Question #2, as well as selecting the projects and programs you will use to achieve your goals, which will be discussed in Question #3.

Here's what you'll need to get started:

- *A small group of people interested in helping* begin your assessment. This group should include what we broadly call "stakeholders": anyone with an interest in what you're doing, including youth, internal program staff, members of local boards, and diverse community members who may help shape or benefit from your programs. Stakeholders can also include organizations that might be involved in eventually delivering services, funders who may support your work, or local policy and decision makers who could later help sustain your efforts.
- *Some preliminary data or information* to present to your group to get them started. These materials could easily be drawn from existing resources such as a series of newspaper articles that have sparked concerns or health survey data gathered by your school district. You could also use existing Search Institute survey data drawn either from its most recent aggregate data set or from your own local results.
- *A simple structure for getting started,* including a central, comfortable location for people to meet, someone who's agreed to facilitate, and a set number of initial meetings (people may find it easier to commit if they know they're only being asked to participate in four work

sessions). To make youth involvement easier, consider having after-school meetings at schools they attend. To more easily engage diverse communities, consider identifying and attending existing meetings and asking for input about the issues you're examining in addition to helping them with their mission.

- *Copies of worksheets* from this chapter.
- *A recorder* willing to fill in the worksheets and make copies of the completed forms for the whole group.

A SNAPSHOT OF THIS STEP IN ACTION

The St. Louis Park High School 9th Grade Program

Children First, Search Institute's first Healthy Communities • Healthy Youth (HC • HY) initiative in St. Louis Park, Minnesota, is an example of a mature initiative that has had a deep impact on an entire community's understanding of asset building on behalf of its youth. While the initiative itself does not run programs, the visibility and success of Children First have created a strength-based, community-wide context in which successful asset-building programs have begun to flourish.

One prominent example is the St. Louis Park High School 9th Grade Program, initiated by school counselor Angela Jerabek. In 1998, state health survey data showed an increasing percentage of students using marijuana and alcohol. High school staff were also reporting among incoming 9th-grade classes a growing constellation of problems commonly associated with drug and alcohol use, including increasing truancy, and discipline and failure rates. Further, the school's student assistance staff team data showed that 50% of the students discussed at weekly meetings were 9th graders. The staff feared that the atmosphere of 9th grade was becoming a culture of failure.

Using data to bolster the case, Jerabek worked with staff to create an asset-building program for incoming 9th graders that concentrated on the asset categories that would help reduce risk behaviors as well as promote thriving ones, such as more relationships with positive adults, increased connections to school, and greater involvement in extracurricular activities. While the program was funded by a 2000–2003 State Incentive Grant from the Center for Substance Abuse Prevention, it is notable for its proactive orientation toward incoming students' strengths, needs, and challenges, rather than an intervention model that is triggered only by the occurrence of problem behavior.

The program's success in reducing academic failure rates, truancy, and drug and alcohol use has led to increased support for the program by the school district, fueled, in part, by the development of clear, measurable outcomes as well as enthusiastic buy-in and participation by staff and parents. In this and subsequent chapters, you'll learn more about exactly how participants in the 9th Grade Program used their assessment data to select their priorities, develop goals and outcomes, and design their activities. Eventually the process they followed allowed them to clearly evaluate their effectiveness.

How to Conduct a Meaningful Needs and Resource Assessment

Chances are you've participated in a project that involved some sort of a "needs assessment." Too often these assessments focus only on deficits, and while they can be momentarily useful, they quickly end up dated and on a shelf somewhere. We want to guide you through the doable tasks of conducting a meaningful needs and resource assessment that examines assets and thriving indicators as well as risks and deficits. This assessment will give you a well-rounded, working picture of your community that will form the basis of the work you do with the rest of the questions in this book.

Once you've established a work group to help you sift through information, you'll want to discover what information you can access that already exists and what information you'll need to generate to answer the questions you have. We're going to offer you ideas about how to find what's already out there and then decide what else you need to know, all organized into an easy-to-follow plan. But remember: This first step, like all the steps presented here, is dynamic. You should plan to update your information regularly to freshen your data and to make sure your assumptions, goals, outcomes, and plans remain relevant.

Start by Establishing a Work Group to Help You Manage Your Assessment

You've probably already noticed people working in your initiative or program who like to crunch data and information. Ask some of them if they are willing to take on the task of managing your assessment process. Determine up front if they're willing to do a short series of planning meetings or if they're interested in longer-term participation. Be sensitive to people's time constraints, and help them determine what will fit with their current work priorities or volunteer commitments.

You're looking not only for the best people to handle the task of gathering and reviewing data, but also for those who are interested in doing so. Your participants don't have to be professional data crunchers, but you might want to try to recruit a few people who have some technical experience. Ask members of your community initiative or program to suggest people they might know, or look for potential recruits among those who work in academic or research fields. You could also consider recruiting an eager graduate student from a nearby college or university who needs some course credit or experience in data analysis.

Here are two examples of different kinds of work groups:

Short-term work group. The genesis of the Together We Care initiative in Ohio County, Kentucky, was a community concern about high rates of youth drug and alcohol use, teen pregnancy, and violence. The Ohio County School Board agreed to convene a series of meetings to find out more about youth assets, thriving indictors, risks, and deficits. Forty adults and youth were asked if they would commit to four meetings. At one such meeting, Bill Scott from the Kentucky School Board Association presented participants with a Profile of Ohio County culled from existing studies. The initial findings revealed that a shocking 42% of the county's children were living in poverty and 48% of the area's adults over 25 had not received a high school diploma or GED. The administration of the *Search Institute Profiles of Student Life: Attitudes and Behaviors* survey also revealed key strengths of Ohio County's children—including that 75% of 6th- to 12th-grade students reported attending church regularly. These findings figured prominently in the formation of the initiative and the development of its priorities. Many of the original group of 40 participants readily committed to becoming involved in the initiative, too.

Longer-term work group. An HC • HY initiative in Iowa—the Mason City Youth Task Force—organized its assessment group out of a larger pool of initiative participants. The group calls itself the Data Divas and Dudes, or 3D Group, and is composed of about 20 adults and youth in the Task Force who come from local social services agencies, community coalitions, United Way, YMCA, education, and health organizations. Some are planners, some supervisors, some coordinators or directors, and many are grant writers. Their primary job is to gather and analyze data when a specific project is proposed, then construct summaries and recommendations for the Youth Task Force. Depending on what's needed, the 3D Group draws on a wide variety of relevant, locally produced data, such as regional health indicators, community assessments, and *Search Institute Profiles of Student Life: Attitudes and Behaviors* reports.

The group also lends its data-crunching expertise to other community groups participating in the initiative, such as helping the Girl Scouts develop a pre-/post-test survey process for all of their programs to demonstrate positive development for their youth participants. Whenever summary information is presented, at least one or two members of the group attend to provide background and answer questions. Young people from several communities in and around Mason City have also been trained by the 3D Group to be Community Research Assistants to help with resource inventories and other data-gathering projects.

Tipsheet C

IDEAS FOR DEVELOPING A STRONG ASSESSMENT WORK GROUP

Keep these ideas in mind as you recruit and develop your own data and resource assessment work group:

- ***Identify roles for each work group member.*** Participants usually feel more comfortable getting involved if they know what's expected of them. Different roles can include gathering data, developing survey questions, doing library research, running focus groups, analyzing data, or facilitating priority-setting sessions. For example, the members of the 3D Group share responsibility for helping the Youth Task Force conduct its own assessments, evaluations, and outcome measurements. Some concentrate exclusively on the Youth Task Force; others participate in additional committees. Several members also participate in multi-county planning groups.

- ***Engage key stakeholders in the assessment process.*** Stakeholders include anyone (adult or youth) who has a vested interest in your eventual outcomes. The more you engage interested people in your process, the more you increase the likelihood that your findings will be useful and used. Many members of the 3D Group are invested in the asset-building and drug reduction goals of the larger Youth Task Force by virtue of their jobs and their interest in young people. Some work for agencies specific to the immediate Mason City community; others work for larger entities such as the state health department. The broad representation of this data-gathering group ensures that there is useful information flow among all those working on positive youth development. Some initiatives, such as the GivEm 40 Coalition in Traverse City, Michigan, have identified local evaluators as stakeholders and invited them to join efforts early on to help develop and shape outcomes. Be sure to include youth and members of diverse groups.

- ***Find creative ways to involve diverse groups.*** Your data gathering will benefit from the involvement of diverse groups in your community. The following two examples describe creative ways two different groups have received input that could be considered part of their assessment efforts:
    - Essex CHIPS (Community Helping to Inspire Young People to Succeed) in rural Vermont recruits young people in grades 6–8 to serve on work groups and the teen center's governance board. Not only does the initiative gain youth voice and involvement, but young people often stick with CHIPS all the way through high school, providing continuity to the initiative and mentoring to the next crop of students.
    - In response to the need to increase access to local resources in Bellevue, Washington, nearly 100 members of Chinese, Vietnamese, Russian, Hispanic, and Korean communities participated in writing a multilingual guide called "Helpful Connections." The Eastside Refugee and Immigration Council helped identify and recruit community members from each of the immigrant groups to write and translate the material, then worked with the Eastside Human Services Forum to get the guide published in English and in the language of each ethnic community. The guide goes beyond just listing phone numbers; sections specific to each culture were designed to help immigrants, refugees, and other newcomers understand and find local resources, activities, and social services.

On page 24, we've gathered together some tips on how to recruit and develop a strong assessment work group. There are two very important things to keep in mind at this early stage of your Assets-GTO work:

INTEGRATE ASSETS-GTO by *getting buy-in* right now. Invite participants who might be able to share what they know with you and who will find it useful to have you share what you learn with them. You can further enhance the integration of Assets-GTO by *using the filled-in worksheets* from this chapter as the format for your reports back to the community and your participants.

Begin sustainability by developing relationships. By involving stakeholders early, you'll learn right away what their priorities might be and can build alignment among plans, concerns, and needs—both yours and theirs. Refer to the capacity-building model on page 5 in the Introduction and you'll see that starting here and now, you're also developing a common purpose and commitment integral to your efforts. The willingness to share what you learn with participants and stakeholders will help you begin to establish the relationships you'll need not only to get the job done, but also to keep your efforts going well later on.

On page 27, you'll find a simple worksheet you can use to help develop the composition of your assessment work group. This worksheet can help you see where you need to recruit people to make sure you have the breadth of representation and skills to complete the task in a high-quality, timely manner. You can also copy and distribute this list among your work group members to help them get to know each other's areas of expertise—and help build relationships!

Instructions for Using the Developing Your Assessment Work Group Worksheet

The process for completing Worksheet 1.1 is as follows:

1. Make one copy of the worksheet.
2. Brainstorm a list of potential participants, paying attention to the perspectives they bring to the table and whether they have any previous assessment or evaluation skills and experience.
3. Write down the names of individuals you know or, if you don't know any of the specific people, write down the groups, organizations, or perspectives that you'd like to have represented.
4. Review your list to see what other skills and expertise are needed.

5. Use a blank copy of this worksheet as a sign-up sheet at meetings to keep gathering contact information, or if you modify it slightly, you can use it as an attendance sheet to document participation for grant-reporting purposes.
6. Eventually you may want to distribute a complete list of contacts among participants so they can share information.

Seek representation from the organizations and groups that are most interested in the results of your assessments and, perhaps, your later evaluations. We also recommend that you identify at least one work group member who has some experience in doing assessments and/or evaluations. If you can, also involve funders, or at least review your assessment plans with them so that any differences will surface and be resolved early in the process.

Identify the Data and Information You Want to Gather

On the basis of your vision for your community and your community's young people, the next logical step is to decide what you need to know. Do you think building Developmental Assets among your community's youth is the direction you want to take? Then you'll need to first determine the present number of assets youth have where you live. Has the community been shaken by a recent rash of teen suicides? Then you'll need to find out more about what factors in your community might contribute to teen suicide, as well as what resources are in place that target those factors. Do you want to increase children's access to the arts and the outdoors? Then you'll want to find out what organizations in your community already provide arts and outdoors education, if any, to see how you can best fill the gaps and use the resources you have to offer. Do you want to prevent tobacco use by teenagers? Then you'll want to discover, among other things, the most current research findings about the factors that lead young people to try smoking and which local organizations are already working to limit teen access to tobacco.

Developmental Assets Surveys

Let's assume you'll be starting your data and information gathering by looking at levels of Developmental Assets. Many communities find it effective to spark local action by conducting their own asset surveys, although this is not a requirement for starting an HC • HY initiative or asset-building program. In fact, communities working under Alaska's statewide initiative have often chosen to lay the asset-building groundwork *before* conducting the surveys. You can decide within your community which strategy will work best for you.

WORKSHEET 1.1

Developing Your Assessment Work Group

Name and contact information	**Perspectives member brings and/or organizations member represents** *(youth, youth-serving experience or organizations, adults, funders, business, congregations, schools, etc.)*	**Previous evaluation skills or experience?** *(circle one)*
		Y / N
		Y / N
		Y / N
		Y / N
		Y / N
		Y / N
		Y / N
		Y / N
		Y / N

If you do decide to begin your work by assessing levels of assets in young people's lives, here is a quick guide to help you determine which Search Institute survey instrument would best fit your needs:

- ***Search Institute Profiles of Student Life: Attitudes and Behaviors.*** This survey provides baseline aggregate data from which to develop asset-building strategies and is particularly useful for community mobilization. It gives you a portrait of the Developmental Assets, thriving indicators, deficits, and risk behaviors of youth in grades 6–12 in your community. The survey cannot be used as an assessment of an individual student's level of assets, nor is it designed as a pre-post program evaluation tool.
- ***Me and My World.*** This survey, like the *Profiles of Student Life: Attitudes and Behaviors* survey above, provides baseline aggregate data on which to develop asset-building strategies. It gives you a portrait of the Developmental Assets, thriving indicators, deficits, and risk behavior patterns for young people in grades 4–6. The survey cannot be used as an assessment of an individual student's level of assets, nor is it designed as a pre-post program evaluation tool.
- ***Developmental Assets Profile (DAP).*** This survey provides an assessment of an individual adolescent's Developmental Assets within the context of the four external asset categories (Support, Empowerment, Boundaries and Expectations, Constructive Use of Time), the four internal asset categories (Commitment to Learning, Positive Values, Social Competencies, Positive Identity), as well as within five social contexts (Personal Assets, Social Assets, Family Assets, School Assets, and Community Assets).

  The 58-item DAP is available for use with children and youth ages 11–18, and you can aggregate the individual scores for a group of young people. This tool can be used for planning individual interventions and/or for pre-post program evaluation. It is available to those professionals who are appropriately trained to administer, score, and interpret psychological tests. Increases in these asset categories and related contexts can serve as the outcomes in an evaluation, which will be discussed in upcoming chapters. The DAP was not designed to yield information about the presence or absence of each of the 40 Developmental Assets.

Using any of these surveys can help spark interest among people who may be interested in joining your initiative or supporting your program because often local data are more meaningful to local community members. The surveys also provide a more balanced picture of both the assets and risks faced by youth and the results can help communities shape a more concrete vision and goals.

LEARN MORE: For more information on these and other Search Institute tools, please go to www.search-institute.org/surveys or phone Survey Services at 800-888-7828.

Existing Community Data

The next area to examine is what existing data and information are already available in your community. This type of historical and archival data, regularly collected by a variety of groups and agencies, is generally easily accessible, and using it will save you time and money. What you want to collect for review will depend on the breadth and scope of what you are trying to examine. In the case of St. Louis Park High School, for example, staff gleaned specific data for program planning on its incoming 9th graders from asset surveys as well as state and local school district health surveys. A larger community coalition or interagency partnership might want to know about the needs and resources of a neighborhood, a community, several counties, or an entire state.

For example, the Healthy Communities Coalition of Lyon and Storey Counties in northern Nevada produced a report called "The Millennium Report for Change," which started its assessment by profiling challenges, priorities, and goals in its six diverse partner communities. Communities were identified and prioritized through a combination of mapping both resources and risk factors. In some cases, this was done simply, as in the town of Yerington in Lyon County, where youth and adult members of the Asset-Building Task Force conducted interviews with, among others, the mayor, a public health nurse, and a substance abuse counselor to help shape their focus and goals.

The larger coalition in northern Nevada also utilizes multiple sources of data popular with funding agents, such as the Office of Juvenile Justice and Delinquency Prevention and the Centers for Disease Control and Prevention (CDC), including:

- The *Youth Risk Behavior Survey* is used to assess youth alcohol and tobacco use in combination with *tracking tax revenue* from liquor license sales and taxes on alcohol and cigarettes.
- *Education databases* provide information about school dropout and teen pregnancy rates, standardized test scores, and attendance records.

- *Voting turnout statistics and numbers of building permits* are used to provide a sense of the level of community connectedness.

Aim for a balance of data that focus on deficits/risks and strengths. Whatever you decide to gather, be realistic about the resources you have available as you go about developing your data collection plans. Ideally, your data collection efforts should match the size of the area in which you are interested and be affordable both in terms of money you have to spend and the amount of time your work group can devote to your efforts. If you are interested in learning about a single high school, for example, national data will provide some context, but you will likely be better off concentrating your efforts on collecting existing regional and local data more immediately relevant to your community.

CD FEATURE: If you would like to learn more about how to match your assessment efforts to your available resources, please look at "How to Determine Assessment Levels Based on Resources" on the CD-ROM included with this book.

Tipsheet D on pages 31–33 shows you a variety of existing data that may be available for you to use and how to find such data.

Existing Strengths and Resources

The next area of available information to gather within your community is what resources already exist. By resources, we mean existing programs, funding sources, cultural institutions, communities of faith, local government supports, hospitals, parent organizations, educational institutions, service groups, recreational activities, and volunteer groups. This resource assessment will help you understand what's already being done in your communities of interest, how effective these resources are, and perhaps show you any gaps that exist. You can then target your efforts, save time, and increase the likelihood of positive impact. A thorough understanding of existing resources will also help you leverage existing and new resources and avoid duplicating efforts as you design your projects and programs later on.

The Northeast Community Challenge Coalition (NECC) is a large HC • HY initiative in Cincinnati, Ohio, that conducted a thorough resource assessment of all of the important organizations and institutions that support youth in their community. Dozens of organizations belonging to the coalition helped gather the information that went into the assessment, which documented the work of faith-based organizations, government, law enforcement and safety departments,

Tipsheet D

TYPES OF INFORMATION AND WHERE TO GET IT

Programs, projects, and organizations, as well as city, county, state/province, and federal entities, all collect a variety of data that may be useful to you. Schools and academic institutions are good sources of information, too. You can use aggregate results on Developmental Assets or national data on youth risk behaviors as starting points for figuring out what local data you want to gather. These days, a lot of information is available online. You may be able to access existing materials, or in some cases, such as with surveys, conduct your own data gathering. The following list of options to explore is not exhaustive, but may be helpful in getting you started. Forming a relationship with a reference librarian at your local library is one way to streamline your efforts to access these kinds of data.

Archival Data

- ***Health indicators.*** Various social services and public health departments maintain information on a variety of health conditions, including teenage pregnancy, HIV/AIDS diagnoses, substance abuse admissions, families receiving welfare benefits, unemployment levels, and percentage of households below the poverty line. In Canada, one such site is the Canadian Institute for Health Information at http://secure.cihi.ca/cihiweb/splash.html.
- ***Census records.*** Census data provide demographic information for the United States (www.census.gov/index.html) and Canada (http://www12.statcan.ca). Census record data may also be available for the population and demographic distribution of your specific community. Many states have similar information on their own Web sites.
- ***Annie E. Casey Foundation.*** The foundation's annual KIDS COUNT report tracks the status of children at both the national and state level. www.aecf.org/kidscount/
- ***Police and court data.*** Police arrest and court tracking figures provide information about crime in various areas of the community, including the types of crimes being committed and the ages of offenders.
- ***School data.*** School districts and individual schools track their own data or glean it from state surveys regarding college attendance, graduation and truancy rates, test scores, and students receiving free or reduced-cost lunches. They also document diversity among students.
- ***Local government records.*** Many cities and counties track such information as income levels, numbers of children in school, and home ownership.
- ***Federal data.*** Many communities are specifically working on reducing drug and alcohol use. You might find this federal Web site useful for information on national drug policy, data, and programs: www.whitehousedrugpolicy.gov/index.html.
- ***Centers for Disease Control and Prevention (CDC).*** The Youth Risk Behavior Surveillance System (YRBSS) was developed in 1990 to monitor priority health risk behaviors that contribute markedly to the leading causes of death, disability, and social problems among youth and adults in the United States. Data can be viewed online at the city and state levels at http://www.cdc.gov/HealthyYouth/yrbs/index.htm.
- ***Asset-Based Community Development Institute (ABCD).*** The institute provides a wealth of resources on community asset mapping, organizing, and capacity building that were developed by John L. McKnight and John Kretzmann. www.northwestern.edu/ipr/abcd.html

Tipsheet D continues on next page ▶

Qualitative Data

- ***Key informant surveys.*** These surveys are conducted with those individuals who are important or natural leaders in their communities, such as elected officials or community elders. They know the community and are likely to be aware of the extent of its needs and resources.
- ***Community meetings/forums.*** Many municipalities and organizations regularly invite various community individuals to provide input and information in a series of meetings about community issues. Although key leaders are often present, the meetings are held to obtain information from the general public.
- ***Focus groups.*** In a focus group format, 6–12 individuals (adults and/or youth) convene and answer a predetermined set of open-ended questions from a facilitator. Focus groups may be particularly useful in getting information quickly and gathering opinions from an established group. Focus groups are a useful format for getting at the underlying attitudes, feelings, beliefs, and behaviors of a group through discussions.

CD FEATURE: There is more information about how to conduct focus groups found on the CD-ROM included with this book.

- ***Appreciative Inquiry***. This is a highly effective, organized way of facilitating discussion among groups about positive or peak experiences in the community. It is designed to elicit thoughts and ideas about what works to help shape positive solutions. It is also a useful interviewing process for youth to use with adult stakeholders, one that engages youth and helps the key stakeholders reconnect with their positive vision for the youth of the community. http://appreciativeinquiry.cwru.edu.
- ***Legislative records.*** Records or transcripts from legislative meetings and hearings on pertinent topics.

Surveys (Quantitative Data)

- ***Service provider surveys.*** Service providers, such as local child care providers or business coalitions, possess knowledge about the nature of problems in a community, what programs and resources are available, and who is and is not being served.
- ***Client or participant surveys.*** Clients and program participants are excellent sources of information on what needs are being met and what more should be done. They can also offer information on useful resources that exist.
- ***Targeted population problem behavior surveys.*** Self-report surveys and comprehensive assessments on a specific community of interest or targeted population can provide useful information on the extent and nature of their problem behaviors and other issues.
- ***Youth participant surveys.*** Many programs, youth-serving organizations, cities, and initiatives regularly gather information about who uses their offerings as well as asking young people about program effectiveness and satisfaction.

Tipsheet D continues on next page

Community Resources

- ***Resource mapping.*** Mapping available community resources includes noting existing programs and services that address identified issues and providing evidence on where problems are already being addressed, as well as where there are gaps in service.
- ***City and county surveys.*** Many communities conduct residence surveys that provide demographic and cultural data and document trends such as home ownership versus transient housing. Youth councils also gather information from young people about service use and priorities.
- ***Evaluation data on other programs and projects.*** Evaluation data on existing programs and projects may be publicly available.
- ***Community Youth Mapping.*** Instituted by the AED (Academy for Educational Development) Center for Youth Development and Policy Research, Community Youth Mapping (CYM) is a process that mobilizes youth and adults as they canvass their neighborhoods to identify resources and opportunities in their community that may not be found in traditional directories. www.communityyouthmapping.org/Youth

Environmental Climate

- ***Environmental scan.*** The scan is a method for assessing local environments to determine the presence or absence of environmental risk factors consistent with problem behaviors, such as inadequate lighting, signage/billboards, tolerance for loitering, or density of alcohol outlets near schools.

health organizations, parent groups, schools, businesses, senior services, social and service organizations, recreational activities, youth-serving organizations, and volunteer groups and helplines. In addition to using the information to learn about all the resources available in the community, NECC partnered with the Community Press to publish the information in a 32-page booklet distributed to the public that also includes background on the initiative and its asset-building goals. This resource-assessment-turned-guide serves to inform the community about asset building as well as identifying which organizations and programs build which assets.

You can use Resource Assessment Worksheet 1.2, provided on page 36, to help you gather information on existing resources in your community. In general, you will be looking for the following types of information:

- The name of the activity, program, or resource;
- Where it's located;
- Hours of operation;
- The ages of the people who use the program or resource;
- How often the program operates;
- Who uses it—youth? adults? seniors?
- What assets the resource builds;
- What risks the resource reduces; and
- Evidence of its effectiveness.

Instructions for Using the Resource Assessment Worksheet

First, decide what slice of information about existing resources you want to gather. Are you going to assemble information about all types of organizations and programs in the your community that serve youth or only those that provide health services? If you already have an idea about a specific group that will receive your attention (15- to 17-year-olds, for example), you may want to focus your information gathering on resources that address the same group. Narrowing your focus will help you target your efforts.

Also consider how you want to do the work itself. If you live in a smaller community, it may be possible for a small group to sit down and, over the course of an afternoon, fill in most of the information in the resource assessment together. If you have a lot of information to gather or are trying to cover a large geographic area, you may want to identify a key leader or group with general knowledge about the resources in your community who can help complete the assessment. For example, when legislatively mandated community Public Health and Safety Networks in Washington State first organized to deal with juvenile crime and adolescent health risks, many of the networks began with a series of meetings at which different groups were invited to educate the boards of directors. Over a period of several months, the community members of these boards received a series of educational presentations from police officers, public health officials, educators, sexual assault victim advocates, and others about issues and resources related to youth in each topic area.

Finally, consider how you'll check the accuracy of the information you gather. Do you have access to independent reviews of the effectiveness of local programs, for example, or do you need to correlate data from different sources? If you have a lot of information to gather, you may want to develop a timeline for completing your task that's reasonable but allows you to bring this task to conclusion. The assessment can be challenging to complete, but give it your best shot. Consider, in practical terms, the scope of what you need and what you can do with the staff and/or volunteer resources you have available. One or two people working in a very focused way, using readily available materials from the library or online, may be able to gather the basics of what you need in a full day or two. Be clear about what you want to know, how much information you'll need, and how long you want to take to pull the information together.

The process for completing Worksheet 1.2 is as follows:

1. Make as many copies of the worksheet as you and your work group need to do your work. You may want to do the work on worksheet drafts and then use clean copies of the worksheet to pull together all the final information.
2. Remember to ask young people themselves about existing programs and initiatives for children and youth in your community!
3. In column 1, write down the description or, if you know it, the name of the program or resource.
4. In column 2, indicate where the program or resource is delivered. List the geographical setting and list the address if you know it to provide the most specific information.
5. In column 3, indicate the ages of the participants the program or resource serves.
6. In column 4, write down the hours of operation for the program or resource and note how often it operates. This information will help you determine the "dosage" of the program, that is, the frequency and intensity of services. It will help to be as specific as possible. You may notice important gaps in the availability of after-school activities, for example.

WORKSHEET 1.2

Resource Assessment

Name of resource	Location	Ages served	How often it operates	Who uses it?	Assets addressed	Risks addressed	What's working?

7. In column 5, specify who uses the program or resource. This information will help you understand more about the demographic characteristics the program or resource primarily serves. In general, try to report which groups or primary neighborhoods are typically served by the program or resource.
8. In columns 6 and 7, fill in both the assets and risks/deficits the program or resource addresses.
9. In column 8, fill in any information you have about the effectiveness of the program or resource. Is there research or evidence that shows the program works well? In some cases, the program may be a replication of an existing evidence-based program; if so, note this on your worksheet. If this is a "home-grown" program, indicate what evidence is available (if any) to show its effectiveness. This might include sustained funding by United Way or another local funder. *Note:* You'll use the information in this column in Question #3.
10. If you don't yet have all the information to fill in all the columns, leave them blank for now. Just fill in what you have. Doing so will show you some of the gaps you need to fill in order to get the information you need.

Consider customizing this worksheet to adapt it to your needs. If you are conducting a community-wide effort, you can retitle, expand, or revise the columns to reflect the kind of information you want to gather. You can also use this worksheet as the basis for creating your own database of information.

Many youth-serving organizations, congregations, schools and programs are already providing many great services for and with youth in your community. Many are already doing asset building even if they don't call it that. Knowing what all these resources are and which ones are already working will keep you from reinventing the wheel and give you a good foundation on which to develop partnerships or leverage your efforts. You can also use what you learn to recognize, publicize, and affirm these efforts and the volunteers and professionals who work on behalf of positive youth development, and to reinforce their commitment and inspire others to take similar action.

Create and Implement a Data Collection Plan

By now, you probably have collected the most relevant and easily accessible data having to do with your issues or communities of interest. *After examining the available data, it becomes clearer which data still need to be collected.* Your group can brainstorm about data sources or you can seek collaborators in the broader community to help you come up with ideas. Look for ways to obtain reports of similar efforts that have been conducted in the recent past. The kind of data you need to collect will depend on the overarching goals of your community initiative or program. It may also be dictated by the particular grant under which you're operating. For example, if you have a federal Safe and Drug Free Communities grant, Search Institute Developmental Assets surveys can provide some of the key information you need, such as self-reported rates of substance abuse in the past 30 days, but you will have to use other sources to get other required data, such as the perception of harm from drug or alcohol use.

As you compile this information and begin thinking about a data collection plan, these common assessment questions, which are used in prevention initiatives, may guide you:

1. What are the major issues and problems in your community of interest?
2. How important are these issues and problems to different sectors of the community, such as parents, youth, service providers, schools, the faith community, and policy makers?
3. How widespread are these issues and problems among your community of interest?
4. What community, individual, peer, family, and school risk factors in your area underlie or contribute to these problems?
5. What resources in your community, families, or individuals help to protect people from these problems and issues?

Once you've determined what data still need to be collected, you can begin to identify ways to collect those data. Having a clear data collection plan will help you ensure that the collection process stays on track.

You may find that getting some of the information you want takes a bit of negotiation with the agencies, organizations, or individuals who have the data you want. If that's the case, it's best to explain your purpose clearly in order to get people's interest and investment. You may find that someone already participating in your initiative or program is particularly suited to make the request through more informal, rather than formal, channels. Or you can invite a person from a new organization who may be resourceful in obtaining data to join your group, or even invite someone to join from the group you are trying to get information from. If necessary, get clout on your team by recruiting some "asset champions" (messengers who intentionally promote assets, successfully engage others in asset building, and advocate for youth—especially in forums where youth voices might rarely be heard). People in influential roles can often get access to information that otherwise may be difficult to obtain.

One tactic the Mason City Youth Task Force uses to encourage the free flow of information is to make sure that everyone who shares data gets copies of the reports that are later generated. Not only is the information useful, but all the participating agencies have a better idea of what everyone else in the community is doing, lending more congruence to everyone's work.

The Data Collection Plan Worksheet 1.3 on page 41 will help you get organized. The tips found in the sidebar on page 40 will also help the overall plan move smoothly.

Instructions for Using the Data Collection Plan Worksheet

The process for completing Worksheet 1.3 is as follows:

1. You may find it helpful to work on this plan as a group. It may take more than one meeting to fully develop this plan.
2. Make as many copies of the worksheet as you need to do your work.
3. In column 1, describe in general terms what needs to be assessed. For example, one area of assessment that the Nevada HC • HY initiative tracks is how Developmental Assets are operationalized in the participating counties.
4. In column 2, describe the specific indicators you need to measure. This could include assets and thriving indicators, as well as risks and deficit indicators (thriving and deficit indicators are measured along with levels of Developmental Assets in the Search Institute Developmental Assets surveys). The Nevada HC • HY initiative measures the impact of service-learning projects, a central vehicle for operationalizing Developmental Assets.
5. In column 3, describe the method for collecting the information you need. The Nevada HC • HY initiative uses what's called a Civic Responsibility Survey to assess the impact of service-learning.
6. In column 4, briefly describe where you'll get the information.
7. In column 5, indicate who will be responsible for getting the information and by when.
8. Feel free to fill in any part of the tool you readily have information for, even if you don't yet have *all* the information. This will show you some of the gaps you need to fill in order to get the information you need.

Continue to integrate Assets-GTO into your work by using copies of this filled-in worksheet as a quick way to keep reporting back to your participants and information providers.

CD FEATURE: If you want more information on the relationship between Developmental Assets and other youth development frameworks to help you fill in the resources and factors you are examining, please look at the chart on the CD-ROM included with this book.

Analyzing, Interpreting, and Reporting the Data

Communities face a wide variety of situations and circumstances that can make this step difficult. The complexity (or simplicity) of this task will depend on how well you have identified which data will be relevant and how much data you have to analyze and present. Think of this task as beginning to tell your story. At this point, the interpretation of your data may only be for internal use among your assessment work group and initiative or program leaders. Or you may have a wider variety of audiences interested in what you have to say that could influence what you say and how you present it. No matter who you're sharing results with, you want to make sure your audiences can readily understand your findings and reports. Try to present information to your stakeholders in the ways they find most accessible. For example, youth may want to hear stories and hold

TIPS TO HELP IMPLEMENT YOUR DATA COLLECTION PLAN

1. *Identify key leaders to help in this process who are organized, responsible, and good planners.* It may be necessary to check in with them to see how their tasks are progressing and whether they need some additional assistance.
2. *Try to stay true to your data collection plan.* If you must modify it, have a logical reason for doing so. Staying true to the timeline may be the biggest challenge.
3. *Be a good partner.* If you promised a nonprofit agency or a community group that you would share data or partner with them in some way, follow through with that promise. Be mindful, though, of any promises of confidentiality that were made in the course of data collection.
4. *Remember to collect the data you will use and use the data you collect.* Gathering information that is not useful is a waste of valuable time.

WORKSHEET 1.3

Data Collection Plan

What needs to be assessed?	What indicators will be measured?	What is the method for data collection?	Where is this data located?	Who will be responsible for data collection / by when?

discussions, while an immigrant audience may respond well to a trusted community leader who can make a presentation in the group's first language.

Here are a few guidelines to keep in mind as you analyze and interpret your data:

- *Use the most recent information.* Archival data have a long time lag, so they may not be as current as you would like. Therefore, don't place too much emphasis on this type of data unless they are confirmed by other sources.
- *Emphasize data with personal perspectives.* When confronted by conflicting information between archival data and more subjective data (e.g., what people tell you in focus groups or on surveys), lean toward placing greater emphasis on what local people say. After all, they may have more recent information in the form of personal observations and reports from others, and they may know the targeted area best. For example, a key informant living on one block may accurately reveal that there are methamphetamine labs in his neighborhood, but the state or local data show no indication of the availability of methamphetamine or its increased popularity and use because of the time lag in gathering this type of objective data.
- *Get a complete picture.* Using a combination of data sources is necessary in order to get a complete picture of the problem or issue. One single data source is difficult to interpret in isolation. However, multiple sources of both subjective and objective data add greater clarity to the discussion and increase accuracy in defining a problem or the resources available to address it, while instilling confidence and creating common understanding among program stakeholders. Where data sources do not suggest similar patterns (e.g., adults report being very involved with youth, but the youth perception of how the community values them is low), it's important to examine the issue from both perspectives. Some responding adults may be volunteering in a mentor program, and so report themselves as being very involved with young people, but if few youth have access to the mentoring, their view may be quite different. The juxtaposition of these findings may help you craft suitable goals. Asking a focus group of youth why they don't feel valued by their community and what would help them feel valued could also help identify specific strategies you might employ.
- *Look for patterns.* Remember that interpretation of data can be tricky. When your data say more teens are getting ticketed for drunk driving, are DUI arrests rising because there is more drinking and driving or is the enforcement better? Interpreting data can be difficult and is

> not always an exact science. In going through this process of interpretation, spend a lot of time asking "why?" and "how do you know?" questions, trying to determine why the data suggest certain patterns. Now is the time to convene with your partners and key stakeholders (adults and youth) to help make sense of the data.

Keep in mind that at this stage, you are looking at the big picture. In subsequent chapters, especially Question #4, you'll use these data and resource assessments again to go more in depth into the effectiveness of local supports and determine how well your proposed projects and programs will fit with existing ones.

CD FEATURE: Some community groups prefer (and can afford) to hire an outside expert to assist in data analysis and interpretation. Tips on how to hire an evaluator can be found in the Question #2 folder on the CD-ROM included with this book.

Select the Priorities You Want to Address

Your assessment work group has gathered and sifted through the most salient data and information related to the issues and communities you're interested in. You've taken some time to analyze, interpret, and perhaps even report on the patterns and findings revealed by your data gathering. You've identified the resources in your community that address the issues you're interested in. Now you're ready to take on the final task in this chapter: selecting the priorities on which you want to focus. This important task will lay the groundwork for developing your specific goals and outcomes in the next chapter.

Keep in mind that you won't be able to do everything at once and you shouldn't try to. The more specific you can be, the better. For example, when the Asset Building Task Force in Yerington, Nevada, finished its interviews and data analysis, the group prioritized these risks, assets, and goals:

> **Risks:** (1) availability of drugs/substance abuse; (2) economic deprivation; and (3) family management problems, including peer and domestic violence.
>
> **Developmental Assets:** Constructive-Use-of-Time category, Sense of Purpose, Integrity.
>
> **Goals:** Raise/secure funds to ensure success; get more youth involved in asset building; organize a communication campaign that links to the

public and other youth-focused groups; and focus on what is doable and get it done on time.

Among the interviews conducted, conversations with the mayor, a public health nurse, and a substance abuse counselor led the local task force to believe that focusing on three key Developmental Assets to begin with would help the group focus its time and energy. Some of the goals were developed to help jump-start this new effort and to build some support as they figured out the best way to tackle the identified risks.

The Developing Priorities Worksheet 1.4 on page 46 will guide you through organizing your findings.

Instructions for Using the Developing Priorities Worksheet

The process for completing Worksheet 1.4 is as follows:

1. Gather the relevant data into an easily usable form that will help with the flow for the planned discussion about priorities. Using tools such as bar charts and graphs will assist you in effectively communicating the findings.
2. Bring the group that's going to be selecting the priorities together in a comfortable setting so they can think, listen, and talk as a team. Consider designating one person to facilitate this discussion so the participants are free to really dig in and talk things over.
3. Make as many copies of the worksheet as you and your work group need on which to do your work.
4. In column 1, describe the most prevalent assets and risks you've discovered from your data collection and analysis. You are looking for trends about what the community is telling you. What is your group's interpretation of the data, and what are the possible explanations for what you're seeing? What assets are most prevalent on which you can build your projects and programs? What risk factors are major sources of serious or immediate consequences that need attention, such as a pattern of teen suicides?
5. In column 2, describe what you've learned from your resource assessment about which of the supports or programs are already addressing the prevalent assets and risks you've identified.
6. In column 3, describe the issues and priorities you believe you can address, modify, or prevent that fit within your time frame, budget, and resources.

7. In column 4, describe what you can most easily measure. Base this on what you have measures for, what you have experience in measuring, or where you know of existing measures that are already being administered (i.e., a situation in which you can access another group's data).
8. In column 5, describe the factors that you believe you can have an impact on. For example, while it may be true that many youth in your school district live in low-income families, you may not be able to get the state legislature to raise the minimum wage. You can, however, work with community organizations to provide services for those young people in their schools. *Note: Later in the Assets-GTO process, you'll turn these insights into desired outcomes that you can actually measure.*
9. In column 6, describe an identifiable group of assets that can be built, or risks that can be addressed, that could provide a synergistic response to the prevalent issues you've identified. After reviewing Search Institute survey results, many communities and initiatives choose to focus on steps to increase a specific cluster of assets that are less prevalent among their own youth. Many communities are currently tackling youth drug, alcohol, and tobacco use through a combination of building assets and reducing risk factors.
10. Finally, in column 7, describe the people you hope to affect. Who will benefit from the actions you plan to take?

Remember to keep in mind the vision of what you are trying to accomplish (for example, print it at the top of each meeting agenda) and use it as a touchstone for developing your priorities. You may not feel entirely sure at this point whether the priorities you've selected are exactly the right ones. Don't worry; you'll have opportunities to modify or refine these priorities as you continue working through the Assets-GTO questions. We'll show you how to incorporate changes as you go.

Looking Ahead to Sustainability

Believe it or not, you've already learned a great deal about your community and your work that may help you sustain your initiative and program(s) in the long run. We've already suggested that you pay attention to the needs, interests, and priorities of the stakeholders who've already joined you at the table. You want to know what's important to them and look for creative ways to develop congruence

WORKSHEET 1.4

Developing Priorities

Prevalent assets/risks (what our data tell us)	
What's already getting focus and resources? (what our community assessments show)	
What can we address with our resources, time, and budget? (what our internal assessments show	
What can we easily measure? (what's under our control)	
What priorities do we think still need attention? (where's the best place for our resources)	
What actions can we take that will have the greatest potential for success? (our preliminary goals)	
Who will these actions affect? (who benefits)	

between their priorities and yours. By paying attention, you're also beginning to develop relationships, as well as a common purpose and commitment, which are all key to maintaining your work. A study of community done by the Kansas Health Foundation found, for example, that the town of McPherson had many existing community assets that provided not only a solid economic base but a hospitable environment for raising healthy, responsible youth. Such existing qualities, when folded into the results of the Vision 2010 process, were used as the foundation of ongoing work in the community.

Here are some other things you can do now to help set the stage for sustainability:

- *Start to identify places in which to integrate asset building.* Your resource assessment has shown you a full range of programs and supports in the community. Identify which ones you think might be good places to start the conversation about integrating asset building into their work.
- *Offer trainings.* Community leaders and programs might be interested in what you have to offer, but don't have the resources to extend themselves. Providing trainings is a way to build relationships and help create a larger, operational infrastructure (again, look back at that capacity-building model on page 5 in the Introduction for where this fits in the bigger picture).
- *Identify potential homes for your programs.* While no one likes to think about what would happen if they can't continue their program, look ahead to logical organizations or programs to take on your work if your funding ends.
- *Talk about larger policy goals now.* It never hurts to think ahead to how you might want to influence decision makers about your issues, priorities, and goals. If you are discussing now whom you eventually want to influence and what information you know they'll need to hear, you can build some of those ideas into your evaluation. For example, specific goals and objectives aimed at enforcing existing police and community policies or creating new ones are built into the alcohol-use reduction strategies implemented by the Wisconsin Positive Youth Development Initiative.

All of these actions will help make your work more relevant in the community. You'll have a clear understanding of how your initiative or program fits into the larger picture of what's going on in your community and you can take steps to integrate your work into community and organizational efforts.

Before Going on to the Next Chapter

Think of some easy ways to regularly update your formal and informal surveys of community issues and concerns and reassess resources so you know when to make appropriate adjustments in your work. You might note on your worksheets, for example, or on an initiative or program calendar, when certain key surveys are redone each year so you can remind yourself to get the new data.

It's a good idea to set up a three-ring binder into which you'll collect all your filled-in worksheets. Then you can look at how all the information is coming together at one time or more easily refer back to specific material you need. The notebook also can make a good tool for showing funders your planning, process, and results so far. In the next chapter, we will show you how to use the preliminary information you've gathered in the Developing Priorities worksheet to begin developing specific goals and outcomes.

QUESTION #2

What are your goals and desired outcomes?

(GOALS)

This chapter is going to help you look ahead to what *you* want to accomplish with your initiative or programs and describe those accomplishments in concrete, measurable terms through goals and outcomes that will satisfy you, your stakeholders, and your funders. Then you'll take your goals and outcomes forward to help you map out the rest of your steps, so you'll know exactly where you're going by the time you get to actually evaluating your work.

Establishing clear goals puts you in the position to evaluate the progress of your work. Planning your evaluation is as crucial as the evaluation itself. Without a good plan, you could have an initiative or program that's accomplishing a lot, but no clear outcomes to demonstrate your progress. Planning and implementing evaluation require some stretching, though; you're trying to take action and reflect on your actions at the same time. As you continue on in the Assets-GTO steps, you will begin to formulate the questions you need to ask to measure your formal progress. Being able to communicate both informal and formal results will give you the potent mix of stories and data that will help you communicate the success of your work.

You are going to be building on the priorities developed from the assessments of assets, needs, risks, and resources you conducted in Question #1 to begin shaping exactly what you're seeking to do and how you're planning to do it. First, we'll walk you through how to turn your priorities into goals—a set of specific statements that describe the larger picture of what you believe you can achieve through your initiative's or program's actions. Then you'll move to developing a set of desired outcomes—the specific, measurable changes you expect as a result of your actions. This is the first time you'll draft your outcomes;

you'll have a chance to refine your outcomes further in Question #4 and again in Question #8.

The steps in this chapter will guide you to:

- Develop a set of clear, realistic goals; and
- Create a set of measurable, desired outcomes tied to those goals.

The priorities from the previous chapter and the goals and desired outcomes you choose in this chapter will all go into the logic model you'll build in Question #3. Creating the logic model in the next chapter will help ensure that the assets, resources, and needs you identified in Question #1, the goals and desired outcomes you develop in this question, and the projects or program(s) you will be selecting in Question #3 are logically linked and, hence, likely to help you realize the intended outcomes.

Here's what you'll need to get started:

- *A work group ready to continue moving forward.* This could be the assessment group you've already brought together or a new group that comes together at this stage. You could also work with members of your initiative or program to develop these next steps. Remember, it will be important to have youth and members of diverse communities involved in developing your goals and outcomes.
- *Filled-in worksheets* from Question #1.

Developing Goals and Desired Outcomes

The first task we're going to work on now is to look at the priorities you developed in Question #1 and think through what you want to do and why. This will make it easier to develop clearer goals and outcomes. Before beginning, you may find it helpful to read a 16-page report from Search Institute called "Making Evaluation Integral to Your Asset-Building Initiative: Employing a Theory of Action and Change," written by researcher Dr. William Mesaros. Let's highlight just a few key points from this paper. Mesaros writes:

> Since initiatives are generally formed for the purpose of effecting community-wide change, there may be a natural inclination to want to show funders community-wide outcomes. A problem arises when an initiative wants to show such outcomes while conducting activities that target narrow audiences and select organizations. Such a disconnect between global, long-term goals and current targeted, local activities sets the stage for weak linkages among the goals, activities, and outcomes.

A SNAPSHOT OF THIS STEP IN ACTION

Educo, Fort Collins, Colorado

Educo Colorado in Fort Collins is an outdoor experiential leadership nonprofit serving youth and adults. One of Educo's objectives (the name comes from the Latin root word for education and means "to lead or draw forth") is to increase key leadership assets in young participants such as caring, planning, decision making, and personal responsibility through outdoor activities like rock climbing, snowshoeing, and backpacking. Educo's programs are designed to create connections between learning the skills needed to overcome the challenge of intense, outdoor experiences and transferring those practical skills into young people's everyday lives.

Educo serves more than 1,300 participants annually with three and a half full-time staff and numerous community volunteers. Operating in the United States since 1988, Educo assimilated asset building into its activities beginning in 1999, choosing to concentrate on three internal assets from the categories of Positive Identity, Social Competencies, and Commitment to Learning. Educo made these choices because the group's assessment of needs and existing assets revealed that youth in Fort Collins were not demonstrating leadership skills or a sense of purpose.

The program is based on the theory that kids who feel connected to the natural world will feel a greater connection to the human community. This logically connects with the program's long-term outcome: having youth feel a sense of purpose in life. But how do you get from a weekend wilderness experience to a changed worldview? What Educo offers to youth is essential, yet intangible to many people in today's society. Educo works to effectively communicate the greater value of these wilderness programs in part through its evaluation process, which measures outcomes in regard to young people and the program itself.

"Educo is in the fourth full year of the evaluation process" says Educo Executive Director Shane Butterfield, "and we are making revisions based on what we have learned in order to accurately measure the quality of our programs." For example, while early evaluations revealed that each Educo program was extremely successful in accomplishing overall goals, documentation was a challenge. There was a low rate of return on surveys mailed to students who participated in the Cornerstone Co-Op program, for instance. The staff is considering scheduling evaluation time into the daily curriculum to alleviate the problem, as well as giving students some of the responsibility to conduct the surveys to further enhance leadership skills development.

Educo's short-term desired outcomes for the Teen Leadership Programs are to have kids learn some basic planning skills while having fun outside. During after-school and weekend meetings, kids learn the first steps of planning for an outdoor event. Then on a summer expedition, they get to use what they've learned. But in order to move kids from a few simple skills to feeling a larger sense of purpose requires some interim steps, so Educo's intermediate outcomes became the deliberate transfer of knowledge from one step to the next. After the weekend's outing, for example, staff may teach kids how to transfer their newfound planning skills from a camping trip to planning the steps of their next homework assignment. Ultimately, Educo hopes that kids will demonstrate more personal responsibility, interpersonal competence, and understanding of their larger role in life.

But how do you measure that? To gather quantitative data, Educo does pre- and post–tests and surveys. To get qualitative data, they conduct interviews and train staff in observational techniques so they can write short reports after expeditions. All of this information helps the organization examine the accountability, effectiveness, and impact of the programs.

These weak linkages are bound to make the evaluation effort frustrating as the initiative simply lacks in the short term the wherewithal to make its case globally. The inability to make the case globally can then lead to general dissatisfaction among stakeholders.

The solution to these weak linkages is to consider a more realistic scope for your activities and outcomes. Having a sense of how large or small your effort will be will help you develop suitable goals and desired outcomes now, preparing you to select the most logical things to do in Question #3. We'll return to useful material from the Mesaros report in Question #3 when we discuss more about how to choose projects and programs.

CD FEATURES: You can read the entire Mesaros report on the CD-ROM that is included with this book.

How to Develop Goals

Goals indicate your overall direction and reflect the impact you hope to have in the future. They are broad statements that describe the desired longer-term impacts of what you want to accomplish. To plan projects and programs, and eventually describe measurable desired outcomes, an organization or group must first establish specific, attainable goals for moving toward its vision.

Goal statements should *not* just be a description of an activity (e.g., "To implement a mentoring program"). Goals state what is to be accomplished by a combination of many activities. You can develop goals at the larger initiative or organizational level on which your group works together, or you can develop goals that are more at a programmatic level, describing work that one organization is doing or several are focused on collectively. It's best if your goals describe behavioral changes. You're asking questions at this stage: What are we trying to accomplish? Who are we trying to reach? What are the results we expect? How would we like conditions to change?

Here are some examples of goal statements to illustrate a variety of approaches:

National initiative level. Search Institute's Healthy Communities • Healthy Youth (HC • HY) Initiative Goal #5: *Youth empowerment*—To help children and adolescents build assets in their own lives, in the lives of their peers, and in contributing to community-wide initiatives.

Local asset initiative. Virginia City, Nevada's Asset-Building Task Force Goals #2 and #3—To make sure all kids have equal starts/steady starts (food, school supplies, etc.); involve more youth in the community in leadership and asset-building roles to serve as cross-age coaches and mentors.

Organizational level. Seattle, Washington's Art Corps's top goals—To positively impact the lives of young people, model a different approach to education, energize and unite communities, and bring recognition and support to the value of art in life.

Program level: Educo's Teen Leadership Program goal—Youth develop a personal environmental ethic, show an awareness of personal leadership styles and goals, become interpersonally competent, and have a sense of purpose.

Remember to revisit your vision statement and describe your goals in ways that connect to that vision. You want to describe positive accomplishments that naturally flow toward making your vision a reality. Just as developing a shared vision encourages buy-in, common purpose, and commitment, shared goals will also help everyone involved in your efforts work toward the same ends. Clearly articulated goals can facilitate clear communication with stakeholders and the larger community as well.

One final note: As you move ahead, you may decide to implement an evidence-based program (discussed in more depth in Question #3), which may already have identified goals and outcomes that you can use. In these cases, most program developers and funders have already worked out, through their own evaluation studies, which goals are appropriate to expect the program achieve.

On page 55, we have provided a very simple Developing Goals Worksheet 2.1 to help inspire your thinking. You don't need to have goals for all Five Action Strategies, nor do you need to have goals for five years; adapt the format of this worksheet to your needs.

Discussing these questions can help you develop your goals:

- How do your goals connect with your vision?
- Are all of the goals attainable?
- Are you pushing yourselves enough?
- Are you focused on positive outcomes with a reachable audience?
- How will you know when you get there? What will have happened?

CD FEATURE: You can review "Seven Essential Goals for Community-Based Asset Building" on the CD-ROM that is included with this book. This document will give you some ideas about how overarching asset-building goals can be worded.

Instructions for Using the Developing Goals Worksheet

The process for completing Worksheet 2.1 is as follows:

1. Make as many copies of the worksheet as you and your work group need on which to do your work.
2. Also have copies available of the Five Action Strategies information from the introduction to this section found on page 5.
3. Set up your work session in ways that encourage brainstorming and creativity to generate as many ideas as possible for discussion. You might ask youth and adult participants to imagine and describe (in words or in drawings) what the future of their community or program will look like based on your vision. These creative ideas could help form the basis for effective goal statements.

How to Develop Outcomes

Outcomes are the specific changes you expect as a result of your actions, whether you are designing them for an initiative, organization, or specific program.

The first level at which you can describe desired outcomes is related to changes in the individuals participating in programs, such as:

- *Knowledge.* What people learn or know about a topic. One goal for the Storey County, Nevada, Asset-Building Task Force, for example, is to "educate the school board and other formal groups/general public regarding the task force, healthy communities model, and the programs targeting substance abuse prevention among youth."
- *Attitudes.* How people feel about a topic. The foundational goals of the Brother to Brother program at Liberty Hills Baptist Church in Little Rock, Arkansas, include helping young African American males recover their cultural roots and develop a more positive identity, which will instill a greater sense of confidence and lead to increases in areas such as academic success.

WORKSHEET 2.1

Developing Goals

Action Strategy	Year 1 goals	Year 2 goals	Year 3 goals	Year 4 goals	Year 5 goals
Engage adults					
Mobilize young people					
Activate sectors					
Invigorate programs					
Influence civic decisions					

- *Skills.* The development of skills to resist risky behavior and choose healthy behavior. For the Educo Teen Leadership Program, one outcome is "youth feel comfortable demonstrating 3-5 wilderness skills (planning for trip; tying figure eight knots) by the end of the program." Components of this broad goal are designed to lead youth into learning more leadership skills and developing a sense of purpose.
- *Behaviors.* Changes in behavior. One goal for the St. Louis Park High School 9th Grade Program, for example, is for teachers and staff to "improve the consistency of enforcement of school boundary rules." One important such rule is keeping students on campus so they're less likely to engage in risky behavior and, eventually, more likely to be successful in school. In this case, the behavior of both staff and students is targeted for change.

The next way you can describe desired outcomes is at higher, community levels. These outcomes may measure changes in individuals or in larger groups. Sample outcomes for community-wide efforts might include changes in:

- *Community awareness and mobilization.* One outcome for the substance abuse environmental strategies plan in Marquette County, Wisconsin, is to "reduce alcohol use by 12- to 17-year-olds in Marquette County by 5% by December 2005."
- *Policies.* One of the short-term outcomes developed by Maine's Communities for Children and Youth initiative—working under the Governor's Children's Cabinet—is "The Children's Cabinet develops policy about incorporating the asset development approach into the relevant work of all member departments, and works together to share resources for ongoing program development."
- *Local laws or ordinances.* Youth in Essex, Vermont, have a long-term outcome of getting state legislation passed that would allow students under 18 to become voting members of school boards. In the meantime, they've been successful in the shorter term by getting students into advisory positions on local school boards.
- *Increased cooperation and collaboration among community agencies.* One of Maine's high-level goals is to create and support a statewide prevention/health promotion infrastructure. One of the specific outcomes is to "ensure that every community in Maine has the opportunity to participate in a comprehensive needs, resources, and readiness assessment, and develop a cross-disciplinary prevention plan grounded in the [federal] Strategic Prevention Framework steps and principles."

Another way to describe desired outcomes is to use the levels of Developmental Assets experienced by youth. Assets are great outcomes to target because they are all examples of knowledge, attitudes, skills, and behaviors that are related to increasing healthy choices and reducing youth engagement in high-risk behaviors. For example, some assets involve knowledge, such as knowing how to plan ahead and make choices (Asset 32. Planning and Decision Making). Some involve attitudes, such as caring about school (Asset 24. Bonding to School). Some involve skills, such as those needed to resist negative peer pressure and dangerous situations (Asset 35. Resistance Skills). Others involve behaviors, such as doing at least one hour of homework every school day (Asset 23. Homework).

Asset categories can be measured at the individual, peer, school, family, and community levels by using the Developmental Assets Profile, or DAP. The DAP is a self-report survey developed by Search Institute researchers that provides an individual assessment of an adolescent's levels of categories of Developmental Assets for youth ages 11–18.

Outcomes using the DAP can be based on any of the eight asset categories:

- Support
- Empowerment
- Boundaries and Expectations
- Constructive Use of Time
- Commitment to Learning
- Positive Values
- Social Competencies
- Positive Identity

Or outcomes can also be based on the levels of assets experienced in the five important domains of life:

- Personal (individuals)
- Social (peers)
- Family
- School
- Community

LEARN MORE: Find out more about the DAP by visiting www.search-institute.org/surveys/dap.html.

For all of these, you can develop desired outcomes linked to a goal and addressed by a certain set of activities. For example, Educo's overarching mission is to use outdoor expeditions as a way to teach basic planning and leadership skills, which fall into the personal domain as well as the asset categories of Social Competencies and Positive Identity. Their four high-level outcomes are:

1. Short-term outcome: Youth acquire basic skills for expedition behavior.
2. Intermediate outcome: Youth show interpersonal competence.
3. Longer-term outcome: Youth feel a sense of purpose in life.
4. Longer-term outcome: Youth develop a personal leadership style.

An example of the specific targets Educo has established to measure its first outcome looks like this:

- 90% of youth feel comfortable demonstrating 3–5 wilderness skills by the end of the program, such as putting up tents or using camp stoves.
- 75% of youth can list 4–7 ethics statements by the end of the program, such as "leave what you find" or "respect wildlife."
- 75% of youth demonstrate an increase in planning and decision-making skills by one point.

To develop useful outcome statements, remember to describe the specific change(s) you expect to occur as a *direct* result of your initiative, program, or project. As you think about developing your outcomes based on the goals drafted so far, keep these tips in mind:

- *Create realistic outcomes.* Focus on what you can do within the scope of your resources and what's really under your control. You can't really assess youth tobacco use in the whole state if you're implementing a cessation program in only one school district. Think about short-term, intermediate, and long-term outcomes, as well as outcomes on the community level (for initiatives), program level, and individual youth level.
- *Make your outcomes specific.* An outcome should be specific, observable, and measurable. An outcome should specify *what will change* (e.g., certain assets, risk factors, or attitudes); *for whom* (e.g., grade 7 students); *by how much* (e.g., decreased approval of peer smoking by 10%); *by when* (e.g., by the end of your program, at a six-month follow-up). Remember that some of your outcomes may involve behavior change on the part of adults as well (e.g., parents of participants will have expressed their wish that their children not smoke directly to their children).
- *There is likely to be more than one measure for each outcome.* Although you must have at least one measure for each outcome, it's actually better to have two or more measures since not all outcomes can be adequately expressed just one way. Educo, for example, measures the

increasing leadership capacity of its youth participants in five different ways using pre-post surveys, staff observations, and parent surveys.

- *The outcome statements should be logically linked to support the attainment of your goal(s).* For example, the St. Louis Park High School 9th Grade Program strives to decrease alcohol, tobacco, and other drug use by increasing the consistency of enforcement of school boundary rules. To help increase the more consistent enforcement of school rules, the program (a) trained security staff to consistently enforce school rules, (b) reminded teachers of their roles and responsibilities to consistently enforce rules, (c) developed written procedures for security staff and teachers, and (d) instituted individualized contact by the dean with students who violate rules.
- *Use the shortest survey instruments possible.* When you are using surveys, find an established measure with the least number of items. Shorter measures will reduce the time needed to complete the survey and to analyze whether you have attained your outcomes.

We've provided a Developing Outcomes Worksheet 2.2 on page 61 to help get you started on drafting your desired outcome statements. This worksheet will also help you link the goals you drafted in the previous worksheet with the outcomes you hope to achieve. This will be your first opportunity to develop your outcomes. You'll be able to work on them again in Question #4 and have a final look at them before you implement your plans in Question #7.

Instructions for Using the Developing Outcomes Worksheet

The process for completing Worksheet 2.2 is as follows:

1. Gather together the designated work group that will be developing your outcomes. This can be the small group you started out with who helped design your vision or data gathering, or, if you're working on a larger community level, it may be a group of participants specifically interested in this phase of your work.
2. Collect the relevant needs and resources assessments as well as other data and documents you need to inform the development of your outcomes.
3. Have copies of the filled-in Developing Goals Worksheet 2.1 on hand.
4. Make as many copies of worksheet 2.2 as you and your work group need on which to do your work.

5. Starting on the left-hand side of the worksheet, fill in your goals. If relevant, include information from the Developing Goals worksheet about which of the Five Action Strategies each outcome will link to.
6. For each goal, answer each of the four questions listed, keeping these ideas in mind:
   a) *What will change?* When you describe what will change, make a clear statement about the *behaviors, attitudes, knowledge, and/or skills* you expect to change.
   b) *By how much?* How much of a change do you think you can achieve?
   c) *When will the change occur?* What is your time frame for implementation and measurement? This can include the description of *short-term* changes (immediately to six months or one year), *intermediate* changes (from one to two years or longer), and *long-term* changes (anywhere from three to five years or longer). These can become your short, intermediate, and long-term outcomes.
   d) *How will it be measured?* How will you measure changes? Here you'll need to think about what kinds of surveys, tests, focus groups, and other methods you'll need to evaluate your outcomes.
7. On the right-hand side of the worksheet, fill in who you expect will be affected by your work and how many people you hope to serve or involve.

Finally, if you have not already begun a discussion while working in Question #1 about how to match the level of work you plan to the level of resources you have available, now may be a good time to start. Consider what is needed to produce the change you seek, and what you can realistically accomplish and measure with the resources you have.

INTEGRATE ASSETS-GTO by continuing to *get buy-in* while using the development of your goals and outcomes to *complement your strategic planning.* By continuing to invite and involve stakeholders in the development of goals and outcomes, you will continue to connect your collective efforts through a common vision, purpose, and commitment. The clarity and success of your goals and outcomes will also help inform the kinds of longer-term goals typically incorporated into strategic planning.

WORKSHEET 2.2

Developing Outcomes

Goals	What will our outcomes be?		For whom (and how many)?
1.	What will change?		
	By how much?		
	When will the change occur?		
	How will it be measured?		
2.	What will change?		
	By how much?		
	When will the change occur?		
	How will it be measured?		
3.	What will change?		
	By how much?		
	When will the change occur?		
	How will it be measured?		

Looking Ahead to Sustainability

Involving youth, diverse communities, other stakeholders, and the community in the development of your goals and outcomes builds excitement and investment in collective success. Your goals and outcomes become important features of the story you want to tell about your program or initiative and what you hope to achieve. They provide a clear road map for you and the community to follow as you implement, measure, and talk about your accomplishments. Logically linking your community's priorities with the goals and outcomes you develop makes your story easier to tell. You can more easily identify what you want to say and who you want to say it to.

For example, the Moorhead Healthy Community Initiative was originally launched in 1995 in direct response to community concerns about increasing crime among its youth, both as perpetrators and as victims. The initiative was able to report many successes by 2000, when it decided not only to review its progress, but also to gather feedback from the community to help develop a five-year strategic plan. A total of 16 focus groups involving 126 participants were conducted throughout the community. The findings were reported back to the community in a variety of ways, and the key findings became the basis of priority planning for the initiative. Both the process and the plan kept community priorities and progress logically connected.

To help set the stage for sustainability:

- *Develop a simple communications plan now.* Use what you're learning through your planning and evaluation efforts to continually communicate with your participants, community, and stakeholders.
- *Repeat your story.* Redundant messages about your goals, outcomes, and successes are necessary to build your identity so that your work becomes an important part of the fabric of the community.
- *Always discuss policy goals.* Continue to discuss, wherever relevant, what your policy goals are; include communications and engagement with policy makers in your plans.
- *List your desired outcomes for sustainability.* For example, ask yourself: what portions of your work do you wish to sustain?

All of these actions will help create a viable operational infrastructure. If you develop and successfully measure realistic outcomes while making the best use of your available resources, you'll demonstrate efficacy to your stakeholders through your successful planning, decision making, and governance. This helps you build your capacity for continuing your work. Measurable outcomes not only have a positive impact on the young people you're working with, they also increase everyone's confidence so that you can garner the support and resources you'll need to repeat your successful program or build your initiative.

Before Going on to the Next Chapter

Take a little time to rewrite or reorganize final, clean copies of your goals and outcomes worksheets that you can distribute to all those who participated in the groups that worked on them. You may want to bring together an informal group of agency staff, youth leadership, or others who didn't participate in the original development of the goals and outcomes to hear a presentation about your plans so far and get their feedback on the goals and outcomes. Ask: Do they make sense?

Once you have finished developing your goals and desired outcomes, you're ready—in Question #3—to choose what you're going to do to achieve those goals and outcomes. We'll also suggest how to develop your "theory" of how those activities will work together to achieve your desired outcomes, and you will build your logic model. Also in Question #3, you'll learn how to make sure that what you choose to do has been shown to be effective.

PART TWO

Projects and Programs, Fit, and Implementation

Now you've spent some time gathering the information you need to lay the groundwork for the implementation and evaluation of your asset-building initiative or program. You have brought together a core group of like-minded people, including youth and interested members of diverse communities, and they have developed a stake in your plans. This group and others have worked on assessing the community's resources and youth Developmental Assets, thriving indicators, deficits, and risks, which you used to develop a set of priorities for action. You've also gained a clearer understanding of what types of resources are already available in your community, both in general as well as the specific programs addressing some of the priorities you identified. From those initial priorities, you have drafted a set of goals and desired outcomes. Taking these goals and outcomes forward—combined with all that you have learned about your community—you'll now move into the next phase of Assets-GTO.

In this section, we will show you how to pick—or, if necessary, create—effective projects and programs for reaching your goals and outcomes. We will also guide you in developing a clearer understanding of how well your plans fit within or are aligned with initiatives and programs already operating in your community. Better alignment increases your chances of success, as well as making better use of everyone's resources. Finally, we'll help you assess whether your initiative, organization, or program has the capacity to implement your plans.

If you've already got a pretty good idea about the direction you're going to be taking, you may not need to spend a lot of time working on these steps; the three chapters in this section will help you check the accuracy of your choices so far and better prepare you for actually implementing, monitoring, and evaluating your plans. The questions in this section are as follows:

Question #3. How will you achieve your goals effectively? (EFFECTIVENESS)— This question guides you in determining the types of programs and projects you want to use to implement your goals and outcomes. You will learn the important principles of asset building and effective prevention programs, apply those principles to your program and project choices, and then build a logic model to organize your plans so far. *Question #3 begins on page 67.*

Question #4. How does your work fit with existing programs and community-wide initiatives? (FIT)—This question will show you how to determine if your chosen asset-building goals, outcomes, programs, and projects will fit into the fabric of what's already going on in your community. *Question #4 begins on page 103.*

Question #5. What capacities will you need to implement your program or asset-building initiative? (CAPACITIES)—This question will help you further explore the capacities you need to carry out your plans, including more fully assessing the status of your operational infrastructure, as well as staff, technical, and resource capacities. *Question #5 begins on page 133.*

QUESTION #3

How Will You Achieve Your Goals Effectively?

(EFFECTIVENESS)

Now that you have conducted your data and resource assessments and specified your goals and desired outcomes, it's time to choose effective programs and projects you can use to reach your goals. A community-wide initiative will most likely be planning to implement a coherent set of programs and projects, designed to achieve multiple goals and outcomes. An organization or a program within an organization will most likely be planning to implement a single project or program, which may be designed to achieve a single goal or outcome or multiple goals and outcomes.

In this chapter, we will discuss how to look for and select programs suited to your goals and outcomes, principles for customizing or creating programs if you can't find exactly what you're looking for, and how to make sure your programs are as effective as they can be.

The activities in this chapter will help you:

- Examine potential programs and projects that will help you achieve your chosen goals and desired outcomes;
- Select the best programs and projects for your communities of interest;
- Determine how to customize existing programs to develop a more appropriate fit with your chosen goals and actions;
- Develop your own innovative program or project (or set of programs and projects) to meet your goals and outcomes, if none currently exists;

- Make sure your chosen programs and projects are infused with asset building; and
- Summarize your work to date in a logic model.

This chapter will help you integrate principles of asset building and effective prevention programs into your work. By taking the time to closely link your goals and outcomes with the best principles of asset building and prevention programs, you increase your chances of meeting widely accepted accountability criteria. This means you are choosing the most effective ways to achieve your goals and outcomes and then holding yourself responsible for reaching them. In the process, you may also discover methods, approaches, and resources you need to accomplish your goals.

In addition to your work group, here's what you'll need to get started:

- *Completed worksheets* from Question #2; and
- *Additional time*—if you choose—to read more deeply some of the resources we cite in this chapter, some of which are included on the CD-ROM.

We also recommend that you read Appendixes B and C at this point, if you haven't already. These two appendixes summarize the background, research, and evidence base of the Developmental Assets framework and the Getting To Outcomes process, which form the basis of your current work. They will be helpful to you as you work to identify the logical links between your goals, your projects and programs, and your planned activities.

Your community-wide initiative or program may be doing something similar to what PPYD is doing—using a complementary combination of approaches to achieve goals and outcomes (see page 69). Regardless of your approach or approaches, the next section of this chapter will help you identify whether potential programs are asset building and/or prevention based and, if they are not, how you can infuse clearly identified principles of each approach into your work.

The Asset Approach

The Developmental Assets framework is not itself a program; rather, the framework can help guide us in working toward our overarching goals to create a society in which all young people are valued and thrive. Assets can be the focus of a community-wide initiative encompassing many organizations and participants, or they can be the focus of a single program aimed at achieving a specific purpose. Assets can also be infused into existing initiatives, organizations, and programs that are already working to intervene in or solve problems.

A SNAPSHOT OF THIS STEP IN ACTION

Prevention Partners for Youth Development (PPYD), Onondaga County, New York

Prevention Partners for Youth Development (PPYD) is a community coalition of many Syracuse/Onondaga County organizations, neighborhoods, and individuals, including youth, whose vision is to work together to protect young people and promote their development so they can identify possibilities to achieve their potential. An initial assessment revealed that there were many available resources for younger children up to age 12, so the founding PPYD leadership decided to focus its work on older youth ages 12 to 21. Using Search Institute's surveys and other methods, such as focus groups with youth and adults, the partnership regularly assesses the assets and needs of youth in the county to clarify goals and desired outcomes. Assessment results are used to help achieve one of the partnership's primary goals: to educate and mobilize the community to help build assets for and with youth.

The coalition emphasizes an eclectic approach to address concerns expressed by some founding partners that adhering to only one model of prevention or youth development would limit their work. PPYD primarily uses Search Institute's Developmental Assets framework and Five Action Strategies for Transforming Communities and Society as its key guiding principles. The group's criteria for selecting strategies are that they are evidence-based, will meet the needs expressed in assessments, and will fit with the coalition's mission. They have also borrowed elements of other models, such as Communities That Care and Karen Pittman's review of youth development literature, which yielded five outcomes for youth (known as the five Cs: connection, competence, confidence, character, and contributions).

PPYD's development and evaluation process is also grounded in Getting To Outcomes, meaning that they have used the ten questions in their work as outlined in this book. This eclectic, blended approach is one of the key factors contributing to so many stakeholders remaining at the PPYD table. In addition to educating its own leadership about evidence-based strategies, PPYD also provides technical assistance to community groups to aid them in determining which best practices and interventions are available for them.

While the coalition itself looks for ways to provide supports, opportunities, and services to young people, there is an important emphasis on building the capacity of communities within the county to do the same so that the overall vision of PPYD can be fully realized. PPYD tries to increase its impact by implementing evidence-based youth development practices on many levels including individually (with youth workers and supervisors) and organizationally (through local and state policy and practice standards). PPYD also emphasizes the implementation of culturally competent, evidence-based practices to further promote healthy environments that respect and value youth.

Writing in the report *A Fragile Foundation: The State of Developmental Assets among American Youth* (Search Institute, 1999), authors Peter Benson, Peter Scales, Nancy Leffert, and Eugene Roehlkepartain describe the power of shifting youth development from solely deficit- or risk-oriented to a more positive focus.

When you blend the strength-based approach of asset building with existing, effective problem-reduction and intervention strategies, you increase your likelihood of contributing to the success of all your community's young people.

The report outlined some key concepts that describe important ways to use or infuse assets as you select or design your programs and projects:

- ***All parts of young people's lives need to be asset rich.*** While a supportive and loving family life gives young people an advantage, not all young people have that advantage, and the advantage is weakened if youth have poor school experiences or lack meaningful relationships and structured time in their community. It's important, therefore, to strive to build assets in multiple contexts. In asset language, this is often referred to as the *horizontal accumulation* of assets in multiple settings (e.g., families, schools, faith communities, after-school programs, parks, playgrounds, and workplaces).
- ***The more assets, the better.*** While a constellation of key assets involving family (Asset 1. Family Support), schools (Asset 5. Positive School Climate), youth programs (Asset 18), and religious community (Asset 19) seem to be especially important in helping young people avoid risky behaviors, the entire set of 40 assets has even greater protective power. You will want to be attentive to both the distribution and number of assets as you build your work. Youth who experience a handful of key assets everywhere they go are more protected from risk than other youth, but youth who experience a majority of the 40 assets in all areas of their lives are much more likely to thrive. In the language of Developmental Assets, this is often referred to as the *vertical accumulation* of assets.
- ***Projects and programs that address multiple issues at once are more effective.*** Young people do not experience one asset or one risk at a time in a single setting. The complex relationships among risky and positive behaviors are best addressed through strategies that focus on multiple issues at once rather than just a few. Consequently, collaboration across all community sectors is not just a nice way to think about community—it's essential if we want to tap into the interlocking power of asset building.
- ***Targeted asset building can have a profound impact on some powerful risks.*** One reason there is so much activity around trying to reduce drug, alcohol, and tobacco use among youth is because substance abuse has numerous negative consequences in and of itself and also has a particularly strong influence on the chances of youth engaging in other high-risk behaviors. These include engaging in

early sexual intercourse, antisocial behavior, and violence. If you are considering targeted prevention efforts, you may want to focus specifically on substance use in addition to any other risky behaviors you address.

- ***It's important to build assets both informally and formally.*** Many initiatives, organizations, and programs focus on addressing risky behaviors by formally infusing asset building into institutions and structured programs so that youth feel more connected to schools, clubs, and faith organizations. It's equally important to find ways to build assets informally through everyday acts of caring, support, relationship, and modeling. Together, these two approaches create a continuum of everyday influences that help young people learn and internalize asset lessons. One example of how structured programs and informal asset building can work together is the popular DARE substance abuse prevention program. Despite its broad implementation, the DARE program, by itself, has not been highly effective in preventing substance abuse. However, recent efforts to combine the traditional DARE curriculum with asset-building strategies that engage parents and communities have shown promise (these findings and the associated research are summarized in Search Institute's *Insights & Evidence,* "Tapping the Power of Community: Building Assets to Strengthen Substance Abuse Prevention," March 2004).

In addition to the above, you may want to incorporate two additional concepts: the *chronological accumulation* of assets, in which asset-building experiences are renewed and reinforced for and with young people repeatedly across time; and *broad reach,* which focuses on intentionally extending the reach of asset-building energy to *all* children and adolescents, not just those judged to be "at risk." When developing the specific programs and projects to reach your goals and outcomes, look at ways you can—within your time frame and resources—include components that address these concepts.

LEARN MORE: See Appendix B for more details of the research on Developmental Assets. Useful *Insights & Evidence* reports that discuss the principles, research, and evidence base for Developmental Assets include "Tapping the Power of Community: Building Assets to Strengthen Substance Abuse Prevention," "Unique Strengths, Shared Strengths: Developmental Assets among Youth of Color," and "Boosting Student Achievement: New Research on the Power of Developmental Assets." All three can be found at www.search-institute.org/research/Insights.

Using the Five Action Strategies for Context and Guidance

In the Introduction, we showed you the larger picture of what asset-based community capacity building can look like (see Tipsheet A, page 5). In addition to cultivating community readiness, energy, and commitment, and creating an operational infrastructure that can support your efforts, the central feature of this overall capacity-building model is what Search Institute calls the Five Action Strategies for Transforming Communities and Society. Steps within each of these Five Action Strategies—Engage Adults, Mobilize Young People, Activate Sectors, Invigorate Programs, and Influence Civic Decisions—are needed to transform your community into a place where young people have access to and experience more Developmental Assets. Taken together, the Five Action Strategies provide a practical structure for identifying, encouraging, and linking the important people, places, activities, and programs necessary for a powerful collective effort.

The Five Action Strategies are:

1. **Engage Adults:** *Engage adults from all walks of life to develop sustained, strength-building relationships with children and adolescents, both within families and in neighborhoods.* Examples might include elders attending local high school drama productions and sending photos with notes of encouragement back to participating teens, or aunts and uncles participating in an intergenerational cousins' camp with nieces and nephews (both of these activities happen in Clarkston, Michigan).
2. **Mobilize Young People:** *Mobilize young people to use their power as asset builders and change agents. This means listening to their input and including them in decision making.* Examples might include Latino high school students in Bellevue, Washington, working alongside adults to put on a Latino Student Leadership Conference, or the Screaming Eagles Academic Team at Ohio County High School in Hartford, Kentucky, which is a group of teens with special needs who read to younger children in local elementary schools.
3. **Activate Sectors:** *Activate sectors of the community, such as schools, congregations, businesses, and youth, human service, and health care organizations, to create an asset-building culture and to contribute fully to young people's healthy development.* Examples include the Air Force in Langley, Virginia, providing asset training at its Fatherhood Conference for enlisted men and officers, and in New York, the state's Office of Children and Family Services giving out strategic planning funds to 15 counties intended, in part, to help those coun-

ties integrate the asset model into their local plans for community involvement and service delivery.

4. **Invigorate Programs:** *Invigorate, expand, and enhance programs to become more asset rich and to be available to and accessed by all children and youth.* An example includes efforts among six different Edmonton YMCA branches in Alberta, Canada, where representatives came together to create an "association work group on asset development" to begin infusing assets into their organizations and programs. Their work resulted in a master plan on asset building, which included such activities as asset trainings for staff and integrating assets into parent and guardian trainings.
5. **Influence Civic Decisions:** *Influence civic decisions by influencing decision makers and opinion leaders to leverage financial, media, and policy resources in support of the positive transformation of communities and society.* Examples include providing research, evaluation, training, and technical assistance on asset building to organizations, community groups, and local governments, as PPYD does, or youth summits like those held in Bellevue, Washington. That city's Teen Services Department supports the Youth Link Board (youth and adults who advise the city on policies and budget ideas for youth involvement) and the larger Bellevue Youth Council (student representatives from every public and private middle and high school) to put on a Youth Involvement Conference. Youth plan and run the conference where young people from all area schools take workshops (on such topics as civic rights and job searching) and together develop a youth Action Agenda that is submitted to the city council.

The following graphic illustrates how the Five Action Strategies are all interconnected to provide big-picture context for your work. The two lower circles represent the traditional focus on the "three Ps" of policy, programs, and professionals. But those two strategies are not enough. Communities and society cannot be transformed without also focusing on activating the asset-building capacities of a community's members in all of the settings where the lives of adults and youth intersect. It's the combination of all five strategies that creates the overarching picture of what an asset-building initiative aims to do.

While programs will tend to focus on the "Invigorate Programs" strategy, it will still be useful to look at the other four strategies to get ideas for the kinds of supports to build into the program or who to build partnerships with to enhance the program's impact. For example, a youth-oriented prevention program can look at other action strategies to consider how to involve adults, like parents and neighbors, while also hooking up with local schools. While asset-building

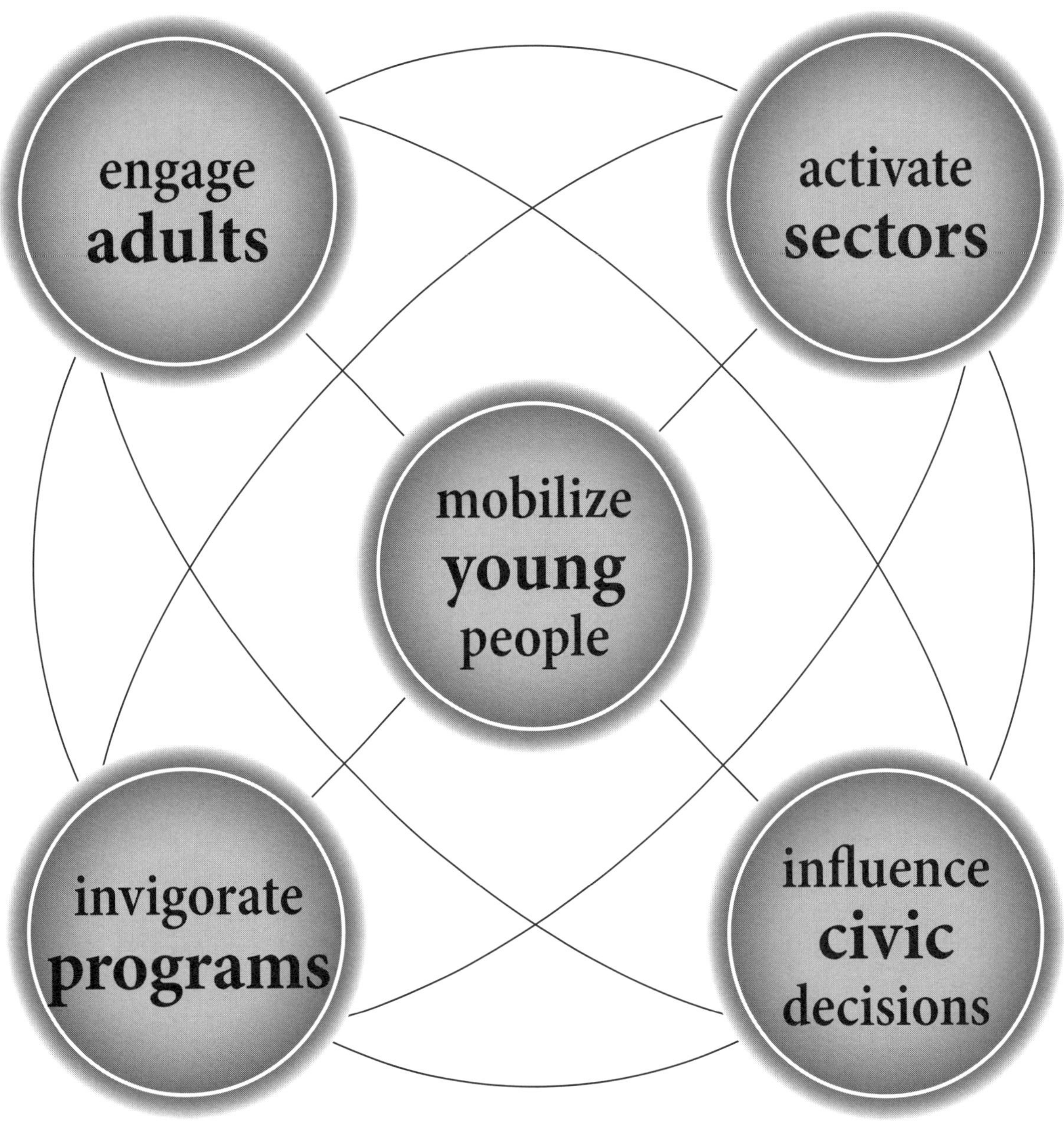

Five Action Strategies for Transforming Communities and Society

initiatives will ultimately be working in all five strategies with multiple projects and programs, you may choose to focus on one or two strategies in the beginning as you gear up.

LEARN MORE: *Assets in Action: A Handbook for Making Communities Better Places to Grow Up* (Search Institute, 2003) describes the fundamentals of how to start, build, and support an asset-building initiative based on the Five Action Strategies.

The Prevention Approach

As we've indicated in the Introduction and in Appendix C, part of the original impetus for developing the ten-step Getting To Outcomes process came from examining successes in prevention programming. The article in Appendix C in particular discusses the evidence base for some of the prevention-oriented strands of Getting To Outcomes. By evidence base, we mean that programs and projects have been evaluated for effectiveness using certain standards and criteria. In general, evidence-based programs are theory driven, with activities related to that theory, and have been well evaluated. If you are able to use an evidence-based prevention program or project to meet your goals and outcomes, you can meet accepted accountability criteria in a number of spheres, such as those associated with the Strategic Prevention Framework developed by the federal Substance Abuse and Mental Health Services Administration (SAMHSA). This can, of course, increase your chances of success.

As with Developmental Assets, there are also some key principles drawn from the study of successful work in drug, alcohol, and tobacco prevention programs that will be useful in researching and selecting the approaches you use to reach your goals and outcomes. While originally coming from substance abuse prevention programs, these key prevention principles are now being applied more widely to a variety of areas, including health, education, violence prevention, and family support. SAMHSA is just one of the federal government agencies beginning to use many of these principles as part of its criteria for evaluating and sanctioning programs as effective. Another organization using these principles is the National Institute on Drug Abuse (NIDA).

Writing in *American Psychologist,* Assets-GTO author Abraham Wandersman collaborated with other researchers to distill from the large body of literature on prevention nine core principles of effective prevention programs:

1. *Comprehensive,* using multiple strategies to address critical domains in young people's lives (family, peers, community);
2. *Varied teaching methods* that both raise awareness and build skills;
3. *Sufficient dosage* (e.g., attendance and participation) to produce and maintain the desired effects;
4. *Theory driven,* based on accurate information and research;
5. *Positive relationships* with both adults and peers;
6. *Appropriately timed* in light of developmental needs and early enough to have a preventive impact;
7. *Socioculturally relevant* by being tailored to community and cultural norms;

STRENGTHENING YOUR YOUTH PROGRAM

In *More Than Just a Place to Go: How Developmental Assets Can Strengthen Your Youth Program,* the authors provide a multitude of ideas about how to integrate asset building into your youth organization's programs. While the resource is tailored to the fourth action strategy (Invigorate Programs), the ideas for creating strong, healthy adult-youth relationships and interactions can also apply to the other action strategies. Consider using some of these ideas from the book, organized by the Developmental Assets categories, as you develop and continue to improve your programs:

1. *Support.* Build support into the entire fabric of your program; start sessions with check-in times; use games and activities to build communication skills; reinforce listening and create opportunities for youth to be listened to.

CD FEATURE: You can find some useful asset-building activities that will help you add to your programs on the CD-ROM included with this book.

2. *Empowerment.* Encourage young people to be leaders, decision makers, and changes makers. Support young people in devising effective strategies to address the issues they care the most about. Give youth meaningful opportunities to volunteer. A Search Institute study of religious youth workers showed that providing opportunities for youth to serve others more easily kept youth voluntarily involved as they got older.
3. *Boundaries and Expectations.* Involve young people in articulating the rules of your program and high expectations for participants, and in looking for ways to build shared responsibility for communicating, reinforcing, and rewarding participants' efforts. Including parents, neighborhoods, and schools in your work will help educate others about how to set and maintain appropriate boundaries and high expectations.

8. *Outcome evaluation* that documents results relative to stated goals and objectives; and
9. *Wel-trained staff* who are appropriately trained in program implementation.

The above list is quoted in Search Institute's March 2004 *Insights & Evidence,* "Tapping the Power of Community: Building Assets to Strengthen Substance Abuse Prevention." It is drawn from "What Works in Prevention: Principles of Effective Prevention Programs" (2003) by Nation, M., Crusto, C., Wandersman, A., Kumpfer, K. L., Seybolt, D., & Morrissey-Kane, E., *American Psychologist,* 58 (6/7), 449–456.

STRENGTHENING YOUR YOUTH PROGRAM, *continued*

4. *Constructive Use of Time.* Well-designed programs naturally build assets by giving young people a broad range of opportunities to enhance their lives. Promote balance by honoring the creative and spiritual facets of young people, as well as sports and academics, across the community, family, and social dimensions of their lives.
5. *Commitment to Learning.* Articulate your support of learning while providing time and opportunity for youth to do homework and study. Find opportunities for reading. Coordinate with schools for tutoring. Listen to young people's experiences about their school climate and encourage them to find ways to contribute to a more caring school climate.
6. *Positive Values.* Set aside time for discussion or values-clarification exercises so young people can identify and explore their values. Encourage them to ask questions. Make shared positive values explicit in your program and school culture.
7. *Social Competencies.* Ensure that staff, volunteers, and teachers have some training in asset-building conflict resolution skills. Offer informal workshops and discussion groups on decision making and help young people expand their ability to see a wide variety of options for positive, healthy choices. Honor and promote diversity and celebrate the cultures of all young people.
8. *Positive Identity.* Help young people experience a sense of personal power and cultivate optimism about the future by including them in decision making, program planning, and empowerment activities. These opportunities should be provided in multiple settings such as the family, school, and community. All of the asset categories reinforce each other in working toward positive identities.

From *More Than Just a Place to Go: How Developmental Assets Can Strengthen Your Youth Program,* by Yvonne Pearson, Kristin Johnstad, and James Conway; Search Institute, 2004.

LEARN MORE: You can find more information on the Strategic Prevention Framework, the National Institute on Drug Abuse principles, and SAMHSA's criteria and model programs at http://modelprograms.samhsa.gov. You can also find useful program, principle, and evaluation information on the Web site of the Forum for Youth Investment at www.forumfyi.org/index.cfm.

Blending the Asset and Prevention Approaches

Many community-wide initiatives and even specific programs are using blended approaches to achieve their goals and outcomes. The Upper Bucks Healthy Communities Healthy Youth Coalition in Pennsylvania is just one example of a larger initiative using a creative, complementary combination of Developmental Assets, proven prevention programs (e.g., the research-based LifeSkills Training Program), and other models, such as Communities That Care, to achieve its goals and outcomes. The St. Louis Park High School 9th Grade Program blends a Developmental Assets approach with what works in substance abuse prevention to reach its goals and outcomes.

To help you see how these various approaches can be complementary and to assist you in blending your own combination of approaches, whether you're an initiative or a program, we've including two charts that show what we call the "crosstalk" between various aspects of different frameworks:

- The first chart shows you how Developmental Assets and Getting To Outcomes complement each other under the key provisions of SAMHSA's Strategic Prevention Framework (see page 79).
- The second chart shows you the compatibility between Developmental Assets and several other well-known frameworks, including Communities That Care, America's Promise Communities of Promise, the Institute for Policy Research's Asset-Based Community Development, the National Civic League's U.S. Healthy Communities Initiative, and the Center for Youth Development's Community Youth Mapping (see pages 80–81).

CD FEATURE: We have also included a detailed chart on the CD-ROM with this book showing the complementarity of Developmental Assets and Communities That Care's risk and protective factors.

SAMHSA Strategic Prevention Framework Tasks

Tasks	Organize the community to profile needs, including community readiness	Mobilize the community and build capacity to address needs	Develop the prevention plan (activities, programs, and strategies)	Implement the prevention plan	Evaluate for results and sustainability
Asset activities	Develop community-wide profile of Developmental Assets, risk behaviors, and thriving indicators	Create cross-sector and intergenerational leadership teams Build shared vision Disseminate vision and profile to the community	In response to vision and profile, blend community-wide asset-building initiative with prevention programs	Launch, monitor, and refine coordinated rollout of prevention programs within a community-wide asset-building initiative	Conduct change-over-time assessments of: youth asset levels, youth risk behaviors, thriving indicators, community indicators
Getting To Outcomes elements	Needs and resources	Capacities	Goals Evidence Fit Planning	Implementation	Outcomes Continuous Quality Improvement Sustain

A Simple Plan for Selecting Programs and Projects

Now that we've given you some background and ideas on key asset and prevention principles that, when integrated into your work, will increase your chances of success, you're ready to move on to finding, selecting, or creating the programs and projects you'll implement to reach your goals and outcomes.

There are several different ways to approach selecting the programs and projects you want to use:

1. *You can use an existing program.* It may be possible for you to simply buy a program that has already been developed in your topic area, such as Project Northland, a school-based substance abuse prevention curriculum designed by the University of Minnesota's School of Public Health, currently in use by a number of HC • HY initiatives around the country.

Developmental Assets and Other Youth Development Frameworks

← Youth focused						Community focused →
	Developmental Research & Programs: **Communities That Care**	*Search Institute:* **Healthy Communities • Healthy Youth**	*America's Promise:* **Communities of Promise**	*Institute for Policy Research:* **Asset-Based Community Development**	*National Civic League:* **U.S. Healthy Communities Initiative**	*Center for Youth Development:* **Community Youth Mapping**
Age Range	0–18	0–20	0–18	Entire life course	Entire life course	Entire life course
Change Methodology	Risk prevention programs and community involvement	Cultural and community change movement	Leveraging partnerships and commitments to provide the five fundamental resources to at-risk youth	Community building through convening community to assess and leverage community resources	Dialogue—building new communicaton structures through training of community leadership in collaboration	Promote youth development while mapping needs to build community
Change Agent	Community involvement but programs implemented by professionals	All	All	All	Community leadership	Youth
Research Action Base	Factors that put youth at risk for substance abuse, delinquency, teen pregnancy, school dropout, and violence Relationship of programs organized around protective factors and risk reduction for healthy youth	Relationship of Developmental Assets to risk behaviors and thriving Dynamics of community and social change	Search Institute, Public/Private Ventures, AED, and resiliency research	Qualitative research: listening to, working with, and observing communities through mapping and building process	Public health research	Qualitative research: listing to, working with, and observing communities through mapping and building process Data collected at the community level; needs assessment
← Risk and protective factors						Community Change →

← Youth focused						Community focused →
	Developmental Research & Programs: **Communities That Care**	*Search Institute:* **Healthy Communities • Healthy Youth**	*America's Promise:* **Communities of Promise**	*Institute for Policy Research:* **Asset-Based Community Development**	*National Civic League:* **U.S. Healthy Communities Initiative**	*Center for Youth Development:* **Community Youth Mapping**
Age Range	0–18	0–20	0–18	Entire life course	Entire life course	Entire life course
Resources Provided	Research Training Program models Needs assessment protocol	Research Training and consulting Networking conferences Publications	Publications Summit design protocols Needs assessment protocol	Capacity assessment Publications	Leadership training Technical planning assistance Capacity assessment	Leadership training for youth Data collection and analysis training
Bridges to Collaboration	Community empowerment Promotion of positive development	Community empowerment Civic engagement Promotion of positive development	Community empowerment Civic engagement Promotion of positive development	Community empowerment Civic engagement	Community empowerment	Community empowerment Civic engagement
← **Risk and protective factors**						**Community Change** →

2. *You can adapt an existing program.* If the right program does not exist for your exact needs or the cost of an existing program is too high, it may be possible for you, without cost, to borrow, model, or replicate successful asset-building projects and programs developed by other initiatives or organizations.

LEARN MORE: You can find out more about asset-building programs and projects from other HC • HY initiatives around the country. Go to www.search-institute.org and click on "communities."

Sometimes adaptations can be simple but extremely effective, such as the one proposed by St. Louis Park, Minnesota, Mayor Jeff Jacobs when local soccer leagues were organizing one year. Usually young people sign up three months in advance to participate in the soccer program, but children from low-income, transient families cannot always predict where they will be that far ahead. The mayor proposed that school districts and soccer leagues come up with flexible ways to accommodate kids who show up to play soccer the day the season starts, but haven't registered in advance. This adaptation did not fundamentally change the basic provisions of the soccer program, but it successfully increased access for a lot of children and increased the program's success in meeting its goals of involving more kids.

3. *You can design your own local innovation.* Consumers, clients, and citizens, as well as practitioners, *can* and *do* develop and put into practice new ideas for effective projects and programs. Local innovations should aspire to meeting generally accepted criteria for effective programs in order to be considered for continued implementation or dissemination. For example, several asset-building initiatives have developed very effective and innovative mentoring programs. While basing them on tried-and-true practices of mentoring, they add a significant twist: instead of adults mentoring youth, young people mentor adults or younger children. The InterNat Project in South Bend, Indiana, pairs teens with senior citizens who want to learn how to use a computer and navigate the Internet. Along the way, typical barriers between the two different age groups dissolve as the real outcome of the program—relationship building—comes to fruition.

One way to ensure that the programs or projects you offer are culturally relevant is to adapt an existing evidence-based program or project that has demonstrated effectiveness with similar diverse communities or groups. If you need to design your own, you can incorporate the key principles or characteristics of those successful programs.

LEARN MORE: Find out how two statewide asset-building initiatives have worked to make programs relevant for Spanish-speaking and indigenous cultures by visiting their Web sites: Alaska (www.alaskaice.org) and Colorado (www.assetsforcoyouth.org).

Balancing the monetary costs of implementing an effective or evidence-based project with an initiative's or program's own resources and capacities is a real challenge and something that you will have to address. The cost of *not* implementing an effective program should also be considered, however. Implementing a less-expensive program or project that doesn't lead to the desired changes could be a waste of time and resources, as well as frustrating for everyone involved. Such a decision could also undercut your efforts to sustain your work over time. You will increase your chances of reaching your goals *and* be better able to demonstrate measurable success by aligning your programs and projects with the principles and criteria we have outlined in this chapter.

In this next section, you're going to go through these simple steps:

1. ***Assess.*** Narrow the range of choices in programs and projects that fit best with your goals and outcomes. This step includes a worksheet for choosing programs or projects within the context of the Five Action Strategies.
2. ***Review.*** Review your choices from the previous step to make sure each of the chosen programs and projects will be effective in helping you reach your goals and outcomes.
3. ***Select.*** Finalize the selection of programs and projects you want to implement to reach your goals and outcomes.
4. ***Build your logic model.*** Organize all your choices so far into a logic model that will form the basis of your work as you move forward. This step includes worksheets for clearly linking all of your goals, outcomes, and programs, and then summarizing everything in a logic model.

We recommend that you convene a work group responsible for this phase to go through this next set of activities and worksheets together. (You may want to look ahead to Worksheet 3.1, Choosing Programs and Projects through an Asset-Building Lens, as your initial discussion guide.) You can have someone write down the main points of your discussion on a white board or flip chart as you go and use them later to help you fill out the worksheets in this chapter.

1. ASSESS

Ask yourself these questions: How will you use the Developmental Assets and the Five Action Strategies to guide the fine-tuning of your goals and outcomes? Which of the eight asset categories and Five Action Strategies best fit your goals and desired outcomes? What is your simple plan for surveying possible available programs and projects most compatible with your goals and outcomes? Can the resource assessment you conducted while working on Question #1 help you here, for example?

You may already have an idea from your experience of working with your asset-building initiative or conducting research and surveys about which assets you plan to focus on, as well as which of the Five Action Strategies you plan to activate. If you need more information to help you select your programs and projects, conduct research in your content area to find promising strategies. You can do this online, through libraries, or through prevention literature specific to your content area. You can also talk to others who have implemented similar programs and projects. To help you narrow your search, review programs that best match the age, ethnicity, and gender of your intended community of interest.

LEARN MORE: If you are looking for evidence-based programs and activities in other areas, the Center for the Study and Prevention of Violence within the Institute for Behavioral Science at the University of Colorado, Boulder, has developed a detailed blueprint summarizing where you can find information about a variety of areas. The blueprint identifies agency and practitioner rating categories and criteria for the American Youth Policy Forum, violence prevention, mental health, substance abuse prevention, education, family therapy, and delinquency prevention (http://www.colorado.edu/cspv/blueprints/). For substance abuse prevention programs, you can look at the SAMHSA Model Programs featured at http://modelprograms.samhsa.gov/. Programs at this site have been tested in communities, schools, social service organizations, and workplaces across America, and have provided evidence that they have prevented or reduced substance abuse and other related high-risk behaviors. For a database and bibliography of out-of-school program evaluations from the Harvard Family Research Project, see http://www.gse.harvard.edu/hfrp/projects/afterschool/evaldatabase.html.

Now you're ready—if you haven't already done so—to identify which programs or projects you think will be the best to use to reach your goals and outcomes. Among the members of your work group, and using your resource assessments from Question #1, discuss what you know about what other initiatives or organizations are doing , to make sure you won't be needlessly duplicating efforts.

To help guide you in narrowing your choices, we've provided Worksheet 3.1 on pages 87–88, Choosing Programs and Projects through an Asset-Building Lens. This worksheet will help you look at your choices in two significant ways: by asset categories and in line with the Five Action Strategies. For an initiative, we recommend that when making your choices, you try to select a mix of projects and programs that activates all five of the strategies and builds all eight of the asset categories.

Instructions for Using the Choosing Programs and Projects through an Asset-Building Lens Worksheet

The process for completing Worksheet 3.1 is as follows:

1. Gather together the group that will be working on selecting your programs and projects.
2. Collect whatever relevant completed worksheets, other data and information you feel you'll need to help you complete this worksheet. This could include your Developmental Asset surveys, needs and resource assessments, or other useful information gathered from the community.
3. Have copies of the completed Developing Goals and Developing Outcomes Worksheets (2.1 and 2.2) from Question #2 on hand.
4. Make as many copies of the worksheet as you and your work group need on which to do your work.
5. In the middle column of Worksheet 3.1, write down a selection of effective and/or evidence-based programs and projects in each asset category that you have determined will fit with your planned goals and outcomes. Note that extremely effective programs or projects can (or should) address all eight categories.
6. In the right-hand column, check off which of the Five Action Strategies you think will be activated in each category. For example, if you develop a mentoring program co-led by youth and adults using local business people as mentors, that program could involve Invigorating Programs, Mobilizing Young People, and Engaging Adults.

7. If you are focusing on certain categories or one or two of the Five Action Strategies to start with, just concentrate on selecting programs or projects for those. You might want to modify this form to include space to write down a time line for when you plan to implement the other asset categories.

2. REVIEW

After your work group has made its choices, do a simple review to check that each potential program or project being considered is compatible with your goals and outcomes. This could be accomplished in the same work session.

Evaluate the list of potential programs and projects according to criteria you consider important. Here are some of the points we recommend you include:

- The chosen programs or projects are asset-oriented, prevention-oriented, or a blend of both approaches.
- The chosen programs or projects fit with your group's values and priorities.
- The chosen programs or projects have strong supporting theories, are evidence-based or proven to be effective.
- The chosen programs or projects are shown to be effective for the same target audience(s) with which you'll be working.
- The chosen programs or projects are shown to be effective for issues or topics similar to those that you will be addressing.
- Your initiative, organization, or program has the capacity to implement what you've chosen.

If you decide to adapt or modify an existing program or project, or design your own local innovation, the principles we've outlined in this chapter can serve as touchstones.

Keep in mind that adapting or modifying an existing program will require some careful thought about how to implement it close to its intended use, using what prevention researchers call program *fidelity.* For example, if it isn't possible to deliver all 12 sessions of a parenting class, you need to know if it's enough to do only 10 sessions.

WORKSHEET 3.1

Choosing Programs and Projects through an Asset-Building Lens

Asset category	Which program(s) or project(s) could be used to build this asset category?	Which of the Five Action Strategies will be activated? (check all that apply)
Support: The program or project fosters caring relationships and a warm climate in which all youth feel welcomed and accepted.		☐ Engaging Adults ☐ Mobilizing Young People ☐ Activating Sectors ☐ Invigorating Programs ☐ Influencing Civic Decisions
Empowerment: The program or project empowers youth to serve and lead, and offers them physical and emotional safety.		☐ Engaging Adults ☐ Mobilizing Young People ☐ Activating Sectors ☐ Invigorating Programs ☐ Influencing Civic Decisions
Boundaries and Expectations: The program or project supports appropriate boundaries for behavior and challenges youth to do and be their best.		☐ Engaging Adults ☐ Mobilizing Young People ☐ Activating Sectors ☐ Invigorating Programs ☐ Influencing Civic Decisions
Constructive Use of Time: The program or project utilizes young people's time for enrichment and personal growth.		☐ Engaging Adults ☐ Mobilizing Young People ☐ Activating Sectors ☐ Invigorating Programs ☐ Influencing Civic Decisions

Worksheet 3.1 continued on next page

Choosing Programs and Projects through an Asset-Building Lens

Asset category	Which program(s) or project(s) could be used to build this asset category?	Which of the Five Action Strategies will be activated? (check all that apply)
Commitment to Learning: The program or project encourages curiosity, learning, and discovery.		☐ Engaging Adults ☐ Mobilizing Young People ☐ Activating Sectors ☐ Invigorating Programs ☐ Influencing Civic Decisions
Positive Values: The program or project articulates, teaches, and reinforces values like honesty, responsibility, and integrity.		☐ Engaging Adults ☐ Mobilizing Young People ☐ Activating Sectors ☐ Invigorating Programs ☐ Influencing Civic Decisions
Social Competencies: The program or project builds young people's life, relationship, and resistance skills.		☐ Engaging Adults ☐ Mobilizing Young People ☐ Activating Sectors ☐ Invigorating Programs ☐ Influencing Civic Decisions
Positive Identity: The program or project nurtures a sense of purpose, worth, and possibilities for the future.		☐ Engaging Adults ☐ Mobilizing Young People ☐ Activating Sectors ☐ Invigorating Programs ☐ Influencing Civic Decisions

CD FEATURE: We have provided some background and a detailed Fidelity Worksheet for you on the CD-ROM included with this book. The worksheet describes steps to follow when considering how to adapt an existing program or project.

3. SELECT

On the basis of your review from the previous steps, you're now ready to select the programs and projects you want to implement to reach your chosen goals and desired outcomes.

Don't worry if you're not entirely sure of all your choices at this stage—working through subsequent chapters in this book may help clarify some issues for you. We've also built in some activities in chapters coming up specifically designed to help you recheck and refine your choices before you implement and evaluate your program(s) and project(s).

4. BUILD YOUR LOGIC MODEL

Now that you have identified your goals and desired outcomes and selected your programs and projects, the final activity in this chapter is to organize all of your ideas into what's called a logic model. A logic model is a flow chart or table that describes what your initiative or program expects to achieve and how it's all expected to work, based on the logical relationships between your goals, desired outcomes, strategies, and assumptions. Although we won't be dealing with evaluation until Questions #7 and #8, clarifying the logic model now helps you have a clearer idea of exactly what you need to eventually measure.

INTEGRATE ASSETS-GTO by working with your work group, initiative or staff members, or vision team on building the logic model together. This process helps build consensus and deeper buy-in among your partners. Consistent use of the logic model as a key communications tool will also help integrate Assets-GTO more broadly in your organization and community.

Develop the Basic Assumptions That Will Tie Everything Together

To more closely tie your chosen programs and projects to your goals and outcomes, specify *how* a planned program, project, or set of programs and projects is intended to lead to the desired changes in the participants. This specification of logical relationships is sometimes referred to as the underlying "theory of change" that forms the foundation of your entire process. By articulating how you plan to get from your goals to your outcomes using your chosen programs, you create a dynamic set of stepping-stones that are all contingent upon one another.

This theory can be as simple as a set of "if-then" statements that describe how your programs and projects will lead step-by-step to achieving your goal(s). Basically, you want to describe a clear structure of events ordered in time. This way, you can more easily see and describe the steps it might take to get you to your desired outcomes. In addition to helping you better assess whether the programs you have chosen are the best ones, having a theory of change is important for the evaluation you will conduct.

Here's one example of what a set of assumptions can look like—a description of a key program from the St. Louis Park High School 9th Grade Program, along with basic activities and the assumptions linking the activities to the strategy. Remember, the overarching goal of the overall program is to increase the total number of assets among all 9th graders (and consequently, reduce substance abuse and school failure). The "if-then" statements are summarized in the "assumptions" at the end of the example:

> ***Service #4:*** Offer "I Time" Program
>
> *Description:* I Time is a specific period of time during the week when the teacher focuses on building relationships and teaching social competencies. Students are instructed in relationship skills, team building, self-care, and other strategies designed to promote assets. Nearly all the 40 assets are covered by specific activities in I Time, and a training guide is provided that includes activities for every skill. Teachers will also use this time to monitor individual student progress and complete school business, such as registration and career information.
>
> 1. Minimum of 38 sessions, each 30 minutes in length; 20 minutes curriculum driven, 10 minutes individual contact.
> 2. Content derived from the Natural Helpers curriculum, with a focus on building Developmental Assets.

3. Skills taught include:
    - Team building
    - Goal setting
    - Long-range plans
    - Careers
    - Dealing with peers
    - Communication
    - Conflict resolution
    - Flash judgments (i.e., diversity training)
    - Self-care

Assumptions: If students are offered I Time, they will acquire skills based on the assets, thereby increasing their number of assets. Relationships between students and teachers will also be improved, resulting in an increased number of assets. If the number of assets increases, then alcohol, tobacco and other drug use, academic failure, and the number of discipline referrals will decrease, and attendance will improve.

Your theory of change should be strong and solid, but don't think of it (or your goals and outcomes) as rigid and unchangeable. The ten questions in this Assets-GTO process are designed to help you learn along the way and be flexible enough to make midcourse corrections in any of those areas as you go without jeopardizing your desired outcomes.

If you are using an existing program or project, a theory of change may have already been worked out for you by the developers. Look for this in any materials that you acquire.

If you are designing your own program or project, then you will need to specify your own theory. If you have difficulty in specifying a coherent theory for the programs you have chosen, this may tell you something important. Perhaps the programs you have chosen are not the best ones; you may need to consider alternatives.

CD FEATURE: Read the 16-page report in the Question #2 folder on the CD-ROM included with this book called "Making Evaluation Integral to Your Asset-Building Initiative: Employing a Theory of Action and Change." This report discusses the basic concepts of logically linking your goals, outcomes, and assumptions in preparation for constructing a logic model.

To help you organize your thoughts, we've provided a Developing Assumptions Worksheet on page 93. Thinking and working through this worksheet will help you develop the assumptions that will tie together your goals, desired outcomes, and proposed programs or projects.

Instructions for Using the Developing Assumptions Worksheet

The process for completing Worksheet 3.2 is as follows:

1. Make enough copies of the worksheet for your group to complete the work.
2. Have on hand copies of the completed Developing Goals and Developing Outcomes, Worksheets 2.1 and 2.2 from Question #2, as well as the just-completed Worksheet 3.1 from this chapter.
3. You can make as many copies of this worksheet as you want. You may want to make one copy for each individual desired outcome you've developed in Question #2 so you can focus on developing one complete set of assumptions and activities for each desired outcome.
4. In the Goals and Desired Outcomes column, fill in what you plan to do at the individual, program, community, and policy levels.
5. In the next column, write down the proposed project(s) and/or program(s) you think will help you reach the desired outcomes.
6. In the last column on the right-hand side, write an "if-then" statement that shows the connection between each program or project and how you expect it to lead to the changes you desire.

We've provided Worksheet 3.3, Building Your Logic Model (page 95), to help you organize your work so far into a single, practical document. You may find that you come pretty close to a final draft of your logic model here. If you're not sure, you'll have a good working draft. We've provided several more chances to refine your goals, outcomes, and programs as you work through subsequent questions. You'll find two examples of competed logic models immediately following the worksheet.

Instructions for Using the Building Your Logic Model Worksheet

The process for completing Worksheet 3.3 is as follows:

1. Convene your work group.
2. Make as many copies of the worksheet as you need to work on.
3. Have on hand completed copies of your Developing Priorities Worksheet 1.4 from Question #1, Developing Goals and Developing Outcomes Worksheets 2.1 and 2.2 from Question #2, as well as completed Worksheets 3.1 and 3.2 from this chapter.

WORKSHEET 3.2

Developing Assumptions

	Goals and desired outcomes	Proposed program or project	Program's assumptions (How will the proposed progam or project lead to the goals and desired outcomes?)
Individual level			
Program level			
Community level			
Policy level			

4. Starting on the left-hand side of the worksheet and working your way to the right, transfer the appropriate information from previous worksheets as indicated.
5. In the final column on the right-hand side, titled "Evaluation," record how you expect to make an impact on the priorities you wrote down in the first column. Try to describe what you anticipate you will be able to measure, based on your resources and the conditions you believe you can affect.

CD FEATURE: On the CD-ROM included with this book, we have provided an additional example of a logic model. You may want to look at it to see how another group has drafted its logic model. Feel free to adapt some of the specifics of this logic model format—also found on the CD-ROM—to your own needs.

To better help you develop your logic model, we've included on the following pages two examples; one is an initiative-level example (Upper Bucks), and one is from a program (Educo).

Looking Ahead to Sustainability

By identifying and selecting appropriate, effective programs and projects early in your process, you have a better chance of implementing programs and projects that will lead to measurable outcomes. Achieving measurable outcomes increases the likelihood of your success, making it more likely that you'll be able to sustain your efforts.

Pay attention to ways you can incorporate the following elements into your developing work—they will further strengthen your chances of sustainability:

- *Adequate structures to support the initiative or program.* This includes aspects of the model for asset-based community capacity building, such as providing tools, training and coaching, and technical assistance.
- *Adequate expertise and buy-in among staff, volunteers, and participants available to sustain the initiative or program.* Training of staff, volunteers, and participants applies here as well, especially for new people as they come on board.
- *Adoption and maintenance of the initiative or program with integrity that adequately meets stakeholder needs.* Here you are building

WORKSHEET 3.3

Building Your Logic Model

Priorities The conditions that must be addressed:	**For whom** Who benefits:	**Goals** This is what we hope to achieve:	**Desired outcomes** We expect these changes by ______	**Strategies** By doing the following:	**Assumptions** Then we think this will happen:	**Evaluation** We will show the impact by:

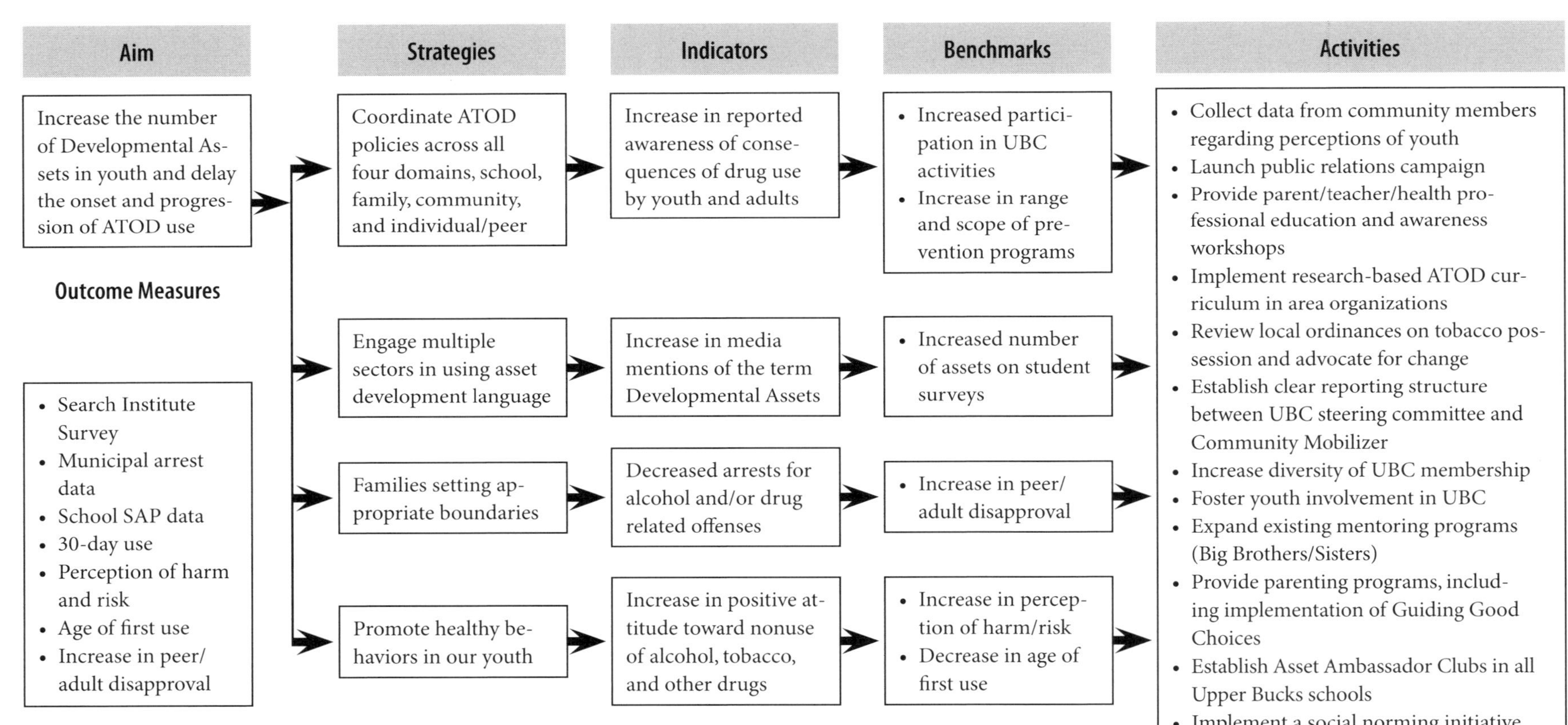

Theory of Change
Formalizing an operating structure for UBC; expanding efforts to mobilize, train, and involve greater segments of the community in positive youth development and substance abuse prevention activities; implementing evidence-based prevention programs; guided by theories that blend both individual and environmental approaches; and applying multiple strategies in multiple settings will lead to the delay and progression of ATOD use among Upper Bucks County youth.
Aim
Strategies
Indicators
Benchmarks
Activities
Increase the number of Developmental Assets in youth and delay the onset and progression of ATOD use
Outcome Measures
• Search Institute Survey
• Municipal arrest data
• School SAP data
• 30-day use
• Perception of harm and risk
• Age of first use
• Increase in peer/adult disapproval
Coordinate ATOD policies across all four domains, school, family, community, and individual/peer
Engage multiple sectors in using asset development language
Families setting appropriate boundaries
Promote healthy behaviors in our youth
Increase in reported awareness of consequences of drug use by youth and adults
Increase in media mentions of the term Developmental Assets
Decreased arrests for alcohol and/or drug related offenses
Increase in positive attitude toward nonuse of alcohol, tobacco, and other drugs
• Increased participation in UBC activities
• Increase in range and scope of prevention programs
• Increased number of assets on student surveys
• Increase in peer/adult disapproval
• Increase in perception of harm/risk
• Decrease in age of first use
• Collect data from community members regarding perceptions of youth
• Launch public relations campaign
• Provide parent/teacher/health professional education and awareness workshops
• Implement research-based ATOD curriculum in area organizations
• Review local ordinances on tobacco possession and advocate for change
• Establish clear reporting structure between UBC steering committee and Community Mobilizer
• Increase diversity of UBC membership
• Foster youth involvement in UBC
• Expand existing mentoring programs (Big Brothers/Sisters)
• Provide parenting programs, including implementation of Guiding Good Choices
• Establish Asset Ambassador Clubs in all Upper Bucks schools
• Implement a social norming initiative
• Host annual community meeting to share UBC activities
• Host annual fundraiser for UBC Mini-Grant program
Upper Bucks Healthy Communities Healthy Youth Coalition (UBC) Logic Model
October 2005–October 2006

PROGRAM: Teen Leadership Program **AGENCY:** Educo Colorado

PROGRAM GOAL: **Youth develop a personal environmental ethic, show an awareness of personal leadership styles/goals, are interpersonally competent, and have a sense of purpose.**

TARGET POPULATION: **Youth from lower-income families**

How does your program provide service		How much service do you provide?	What difference does this program make?		
What RESOURCES are dedicated to this program?	**What SERVICES are provided?**	**What AMOUNTS OF SERVICE are provided?**	**What are the BENEFITS TO PROGRAM PARTICIPANTS? (Outcomes should be in logical, sequential order and follow an if – then logic.)**		
• 1–2 Staff • 1 volunteer from the community • Development time from the Program Director • Certifications of staff (Wilderness First Responder, Wilderness First Aid, CPR) • Weekly staff training • Multiple sources of restricted income • Special public land use • Permits • Outdoor equipment • Food and other supplies • Administration facility • Recruitment: presentations in community-based programs and schools • Outside referrals	An after-school community program that focuses on building participants' 1. Interpersonal competence, 2. Leadership skills and 3. Environmental awareness through a variety of outdoor activities (e.g. rock climbing, snowshoeing, and backpacking). The program culminates with a weekend backpacking trip where participants can demonstrate their skills. Participants also receive the opportunity to participate in a weeklong summer expedition.	• 12 youth per group attend each semester • Two semester programs each lasting 4 months • 12 weekly meetings • One full day outing each month • The program culminates with a weekend backpacking trip and the opportunity to participate in an extended trip during the summer.	1. Youth acquire basic skills for expedition behavior.	1. Youth show interpersonal competence.	1. Youth feel a sense of purpose in life. 2. Youth develop personal leadership style.

Section VII - OUTCOME MEASUREMENT ASSESSMENT PLAN

List outcomes from previous page that you plan to measure here. **Outcomes**	What cornerstone are you measuring? **Cornerstone**	How will you measure whether you achieved the outcome? **Indicators and Targets**	What questions tell you this information? **Question #**	Where and how will you get your information? **Data Source and Collection Methods**
Initial Outcomes 1. Youth acquire basic skills for expedition behavior.	a. Leadership	a. 90% of youth feel comfortable demonstrating 3/5 wilderness skills by the end of the program. (Comfortable defined by 4 or 5 rating on 5-point scale.) 1. LNT 2. Planning for trip 3. Tents 4. Camp stoves 5. Figure eight knot	a. P/P – 1	In-person pre and post surveys from participating students. Staff observations. Parent survey in person at the end of the course. Information is collected at the beginning of the course and at the end of the course. Data is analyzed and aggregated manually at the end of the program. Data is then manually entered into an Excel spreadsheet.
	b. Leadership and Sense of Purpose	b. 75% of youth can list 4/7 LNT ethics by the end of the program. 1. Plan ahead and prepare 2. Travel and camp on durable surfaces 3. Dispose of waste properly 4. Leave what you find 5. Minimize campfire impacts 6. Respect wildlife 7. Be considerate of other visitors.	b. P/P – 5	**Program Director's Responsibilities and Time Tables** **Level 1:** First week of course: Administer P/P pre At Graduation: Administer P/P post Administer PS Two weeks after graduation: All info must be entered into program document.
	c. Leadership	c. 75% of youth demonstrate an increase in planning and decision-making skills by 1 point.	c. P/P – 4 PS – 3 SO – 6	**Level 2:** All above and add: Second week of course: Fill out SO – pre At Graduation: Fill out SO – post

Section VII - OUTCOME MEASUREMENT ASSESSMENT PLAN, *continued*

List outcomes from previous page that you plan to measure here. **Outcomes**	What cornerstone are you measuring? **Cornerstone**	How will you measure whether you achieved the outcome? **Indicators and Targets**	What questions tell you this information? **Question #**	Where and how will you get your information? **Data Source and Collection Methods**
				Level 3: All above and add: Three months after course completion send out PPT and PPS. *Legend:* *P/P – pre & post participant survey* *PS – Parent Survey* *SO – Staff observations* *PPT – Post-post test* *PPS – Post-post survey*
Intermediate Outcomes 2. Youth show interpersonal competence.	a. Compassion b. Leadership c. Compassion and Sense of Purpose	a. 40% of youth show an increase in their self-confidence by the end of the course. b. 75% of youth show an increase in personal responsibility by 1 point. c. 75% of youth increase their appreciation for or awareness of impact on nature by 1 point.	a. P/P – 6, 8 PS – 3 SO – 3 b. P/P – 4 PS – 3 SO – 5 c. PS – 3 SO – 4, 7	In-person pre and post surveys from participating students. Staff observations. Parent survey in person at the end of the course. Information is collected at the beginning and upon completion of the course. Data is analyzed and aggregated manually at the end of the program. Data is then manually entered into an Excel spreadsheet.
Longer-Term Outcomes 3. Youth feel a sense of purpose in life. 4. Youth develop a personal leadership style.	a. Compassion and Sense of Purpose b. Sense of Purpose c. Leadership and Sense of Purpose	a. 10% of youth show an increase in compassion for themselves by the end of the course. b. 50% of youth feel a sense of belonging by participating in an after-school program by the end of the program. c. 75% of youth demonstrate the connection between their program experiences and their everyday lives.	a. P/P – 3 b. P/P – 3 Parent – 3 c. PS – 2, 4	In-person pre and post surveys from participating students. Parent survey in person at the end of the program. Information is collected at the end of the course. Data is analyzed and aggregated and manually entered into an Excel spreadsheet.

congruence between identified stakeholder needs and the integrity of your implementation process. This could be as simple as making sure that recommendations from young people are acted upon.

Proactively identifying efforts you think are worth sustaining becomes an important part of your process, too. Maine's statewide Communities for Children and Youth initiative has paid considerable attention to incorporating all of the elements identified in this step at a very high level. The overall goal of the initiative is to build assets for and with all youth while improving prevention and health promotion programs, specifically substance abuse prevention. To accomplish these goals, the initiative is working to reorganize the state's prevention/health promotion infrastructure to better support communities at the local level. The initiative has taken a lead role in identifying the evidence-based practices that should be used, pulling together the key stakeholders and resources within the state that can help implement the initiative's plan, and developing a detailed time line for implementation of the initiative's goals both at the state and local levels.

Maine's project describes several important goals:

- Ensuring that every community across the state has the opportunity to participate in its own needs and resources assessment, along with developing its own cross-disciplinary prevention plan that incorporates evidence-based principles;
- Cultivating a skilled prevention workforce across the whole state with both core competencies and relevant specialty training;
- Implementing culturally component prevention programs, policies, and practices;
- Making sure that leadership is provided by members of specific cultural subpopulations when they conduct their own needs, resources, and readiness assessments (the project also makes grants to these communities to support their efforts); and
- Including trainings on cultural competence and the infusion of cultural competence into other training topics.

Before Going on to the Next Chapter

Now you have a completed logic model tying together a coherent set of goals, outcomes, programs and projects that are asset-oriented, effective, and aligned with proven principles. This not only gives you a clearer picture of where you're headed and how you'll get there, but also increases your chances of successfully reaching your outcomes while meeting widely accepted accountability criteria. Your logic model also gives you a concise communications tool to use to tell your story so far.

In Question #4, you'll conduct an assessment to help you make sure your chosen projects and programs fit the context of your organization's and community's other efforts. In Question #5, you'll conduct an assessment to make sure you have sufficient capacities to implement with high quality the program(s) and/or project(s) you've chosen.

QUESTION #4

How does your work fit with existing programs and community-wide initiatives?

(FIT)

Now you're ready to take the next steps to ensure that what you're planning to do is going to fit in well with what's already going on in your community. If you're working at the initiative level, you want to make sure that your set of asset-building programs and projects fits into the larger picture of other programs and projects already being offered by other organizations in the community. If you're working at the program level, you also want to make sure your program or project will work well in your community, but your examination may have a more narrow focus, comparing your potential offering with other similar, existing programs. In either case, you want to make sure that what you plan won't waste resources by duplicating what someone else is already doing. If you haven't done so already, you might need to take some time to find out if there are any potential road blocks to implementing your programs or projects, as well as determine whether your community is ready to receive what you're offering.

All of these considerations come under the heading of determining whether what you plan to do will "fit" within your community. The definition of community here depends on your particular scope. If you're an initiative, it may be a big picture—the entire state, city, or region where you live. Your projects or programs could operate across a collection of different aspects of the community, such as neighborhoods or school districts, or you may be speaking directly to a specific segment of the community, such as schools. If you're a program, you might be delivering your services to an entire community or just one segment, but you might also be looking at how your work potentially fits within your own personal organizational community—your coworkers/staff, participants, volunteers, and funders. New staff or changes in funding can affect fit, too, requiring a step back to redirect or retrain. Finally, you want to be aware of similar types of programs occurring or evolving in other parts of the larger community or within the network of service and program providers related to what you're doing.

Taking the time to identify potential barriers, make sure you're not duplicating efforts, and assess the readiness of your community to participate in your plans will advance the likelihood of your success. Understanding the fit between what you want to do and what the community is ready for and likely to accept can also help you further refine your goals. You can more clearly define how to match what you're offering with the genuine concerns and issues in the community, which will result in better participation and broader community support.

You probably already know a lot about what works for your community, which will be useful to you in this chapter's work. Bringing your initiative, coalition, or program to fruition in the first place most likely involved developing an understanding of your community's personality, culture, characteristics, values, and beliefs. You may have started your work *because* your understanding of your community helped you see how asset building could catalyze or enhance a developing interest in supporting youth in new ways. By now, you also probably have a good understanding of the values, principles, and priorities of all the stakeholders at the table, as well as the programs and services they provide.

As we stated in the introductory comments before Question #3, you may not need to spend a lot of time on this step if you already have a good idea about how well your plans will fit within your community. You can still use some of the suggestions in this chapter to check the accuracy of your choices so far and continue preparing for implementation.

If you need to spend a little more time determining fit, what you've done in the previous three chapters has already laid the foundation for the work you'll do in this chapter. Your vision, priorities, goals, outcomes, and program choices will all help you determine where your efforts can complement existing community ones or where you can create the innovations that will address your goals.

The steps in this chapter will help you:

- Understand what we mean by the term "fit";
- Determine the readiness of your community to accept your plans;
- Double-check to make sure you're not duplicating existing services;
- Determine if any barriers or roadblocks exist to your plans and come up with ways to deal with them; and
- Fine-tune—if necessary—your selection of programs and projects.

Here's what you'll need to get started:

- *From Question #1.* Completed Resource Assessment and Developing Priorities Worksheets (1.2 and 1.4). You may also want to have the results of your asset surveys and other data available, depending on the questions you're still exploring;
- *From Question #2.* Your completed Developing Goals and Outcomes Worksheets (2.1 and 2.2);
- *From Question #3.* Your completed Logic Model (Worksheet 3.3); and
- Any other information you've gathered in the development and/or implementation of your initiative, organization, programs, and projects that may be useful.

Applying the Lessons of Fit

Making sure there's a good fit between what you want to do and what the community wants you to do is important for increasing your chances of success, as well as using your resources wisely. Every community is different. Some initiatives embrace urban or suburban environments; others are more rural. Schools or youth organizations in one community may be eager to embrace and infuse the asset framework into their work; a school district in another may have too many other pressing priorities to take on what is perceived as "another" task. Programs and projects successfully applied in one culture may not work well in others without significant adaptations that are relevant to that culture. One of your tasks is to make sure that the goals, outcomes, and programs you are proposing will work within the context of your community.

Fit can be thought of on a variety of levels. You are developing an understanding of the larger issues of values and culture within your community and the characteristics of its citizens. You want to understand who will be providing the programs and projects you're developing and who will participate in them. If you haven't done so already, this may mean getting to know the missions of the agencies and organizations that are involved in your coalition or of those that are potentially interested. What are the priorities of your key stakeholders, including local policy makers and funders? What are the potential roadblocks to successful implementation of your plans? And how ready is the community to engage in the work you are proposing?

Gathering this knowledge and information will help you more easily see the alignment within your community between asset-building principles and existing efforts: the "natural fit" that ACY identified. Are there already partnerships, organizations, or programs in place that see themselves doing the same kind of work? If so, you'll want to collaborate with them while finding new ways to weave asset building into other efforts. If there isn't a lot of natural fit, what sorts of steps will you need to take, as CYT did, to build the necessary alignment between your work and what exists in the community (see snapshot below)?

You'll also want to be aware of potential barriers or roadblocks that might lead to resistance or conflict. Sometimes the roadblocks can be hard to anticipate. For example, when they offered to provide food at an established Juneteenth celebration in the Douglass community in Dallas, Neighborhood Matters! volunteers were unexpectedly met with stiff resistance from a group of elders who had traditionally prepared the food for this event. A community

A SNAPSHOT OF THIS STEP IN ACTION

PROGRAM LEVEL—
The Cannabis Youth Treatment Program, Santa Barbara, California

INITIATIVE LEVEL—
Assets for Colorado Youth statewide initiative

PROGRAM LEVEL—The Daniel Bryant Youth and Family Treatment Center in Santa Barbara, California, houses a continuum of state-, city-, and federally-funded adolescent drug prevention and treatment programs. The programs range from a recently funded eight-week Cannabis Youth Treatment (CYT) Program through more established 90-day and 180-day outpatient programs. All three target 12- to 18-year-olds. While the programs share a location and some referrals in downtown Santa Barbara, the mix of different funding streams between CYT and Daniel Bryant's outpatient programs dictates different reporting requirements.

As it got up to speed, CYT faced start-up, client enrollment, staff training, and a certification process all at the same time. Staff were using the original ten-step Getting To Outcomes process to help identify issues and solutions, including priority actions needed to make the program fit into the larger Santa Barbara community context, as well as within the continuum at Daniel Bryant. CYT was actively developing referral relationships with other federally funded drug and alcohol treatment programs in the area, building partnerships with Youth Service Specialists who do mentoring and youth support programs in the schools (also officed in the same building), and working out an after-care plan with Daniel Bryant that youth could transition into once they finished CYT.

As staff worked through Question #4 on fit, two significant implementation barriers were identified: (1) a significant number of youth were showing up for the program without any parents, and (2) staff were having a hard time getting adequate locator information at intake. Since the program's federal funding required 80% follow-up, contact with parents and confirmed locator information were deemed crucial to the program's success. Staff proposed a variety of solutions, including asking courts that ordered youth to treatment to order parent involvement as well, providing waivers for youth who were having significant problems with family, holding open houses to invite parent participation, member helped broker a solution—the two groups collaborated, with the elders providing their traditional meal and the Neighborhood Matters! volunteers supplying dessert later in the evening. By being aware of potential roadblock issues, you'll be able to work with others to bolster their existing strength-based programs or projects and more intentionally integrate asset building into organizations and programs.

It will be especially important to deeply involve youth and members of local cultural communities in the development of your programs and projects. It is impossible to completely understand the culture of a specific community from outside that community. To ensure relevance and fit, you need to involve members

A SNAPSHOT OF THIS STEP IN ACTION, *continued*

translating intake forms into Spanish that could be sent home, or having Spanish-speaking staff try to get intake information over the phone. Staff also proposed making contact with youth and families more positive than punitive, including building a mailing list and sending out information to families once a month or sending birthday cards to youth.

INITIATIVE LEVEL—Begun in 1997 with a $10 million grant from The Colorado Trust, Assets for Colorado Youth (ACY) was formed in partnership with Search Institute to introduce the asset approach to organizations and communities all across the state. A range of 45 agencies received funding to do community mobilization, build partnerships, and work in communities of color.

The initiative was designed to operate on a number of levels while building Developmental Assets for all Colorado youth. Multiple grantmaking strategies helped build the asset movement itself as both the initiative and grantees shared lessons back and forth about their use and implementation of the asset framework.

ACY collaborated with the OMNI Institute in 2003 to conduct an in-depth evaluation that examined the initiative's role as a catalyst, the impact on Colorado youth, and the transformations or new practices that came out of the organizations and individuals who championed the asset work. One of the main findings: that asset integration occurred more fluidly among organizations for which the asset framework was perceived as a natural fit with the work they were already doing. According to the OMNI report, "For many of the organizations that expressed this natural fit, asset integration was less about changing existing programs and more about bringing assets to the forefront of the work already being conducted."

The lessons learned from CYT, ACY, and other asset-building efforts—combined with your knowledge of your community—can help you make sure there's a good fit between your goals and the needs of your community.

LEARN MORE: You can learn more about Assets for Colorado Youth and download summaries and copies of their evaluation reports at www.assetsforcoyouth.org.

of the communities you hope will participate in your efforts. Also ask people in those communities to lead and shape programs and projects. This ensures that their historical sense, traditions, beliefs, and practices will guide and shape the development of your overall plans. This is what the Tri-Ethnic Center for Prevention Research calls making a process more "culture-embracing," which authentically encourages the development of creative cultural strategies. You can do this by formally inviting youth and members of local communities to participate in your efforts or by becoming involved in the activities of youth and local communities. You can also accomplish a lot through relationship building and informal networking—talking with young people over coffee or lunch or setting up an information and resource table at the local mall or community fair as a way of getting to know people.

How to Determine Fit

Now we'll help you more deeply mine the data you've already collected from your asset and resource assessments, as well as further refine the goals, actions, and outcomes you've developed. Through your preliminary mapping and measuring activities, you probably already gained an idea about whether your community is ready for the programs and projects you're planning. You may find that your community has a strong desire for change and is ready to embrace asset building to achieve its goals. It may also be that a number of people are excited about asset building, but wider capacity building and some organizing efforts are needed before you can move forward.

Depending on the size and structure of your initiative or program and your current level of knowledge about fit and readiness, you can consider going through these questions and ideas in a single meeting involving your workgroup, stakeholders, vision team, or youth board. If your group wants or needs several meetings to do the work, feel free to adapt this process to make it work for your needs.

A Simple Plan for Determining Fit

In this next section, we're going to go through some simple steps:

1. ***Readiness.*** How to recognize whether your community (e.g., initiative, sector, organization, neighborhood) is ready for the programs and projects you're planning. This activity includes two worksheets you can use to assess the readiness of your community or program for asset building and one worksheet to help you articulate potential roadblocks to your plans, then figure out some solutions before moving ahead.

2. ***Review.*** How to review your previous resource assessments to make sure you won't be duplicating existing efforts and clearly articulate how your plans will be distinctly useful in the community.
3. ***Select.*** If you've not already zeroed in on the programs and projects you want to implement, this step gives you another chance to hone your choices.

#1. READINESS. Determine if your community is ready for the programs or projects you're proposing.

Understanding whether your community is ready to move ahead on the programs and projects you're planning will help you determine if your plans are appropriate and likely to succeed. If you discover that some segments of the community are more ready than others, it may work best to start your work with those groups. Someone else in the community may have already started something similar, and it would enhance your efforts and theirs if you worked together. On the other hand, you may need to come up with brand-new ways of tackling the important priorities you see, and this may mean coming up with the resources to support your innovations. If you discover that any barriers or roadblocks exist, you may need to step back and spend some time helping selected segments of your community get ready to participate in your plans.

For the purposes of the Assets-GTO ten-step process, it's suggested that you start examining community readiness by mining your existing data, surveys, and other assessments to discern the degree of awareness within your community of your priority issues or problems; the level of community members' knowledge of the issues; the level of willingness within your communities of interest to accept your proposed strategies; and the present level of assets and capacity that will make it possible for changes to occur.

There are a number of useful ways to conduct your community readiness analysis. Your choice of approach will depend, in part, on the size, experiences, and characteristics of your community, as well as what sorts of programs and projects already exist. Generally, you are trying to discover your community's level of awareness of and action around priority issues, which may range from no awareness at all, to some recognition and willingness to offer support, to active engagement. Different segments of the community may be in different stages of awareness and action on different issues. Has your community or school been aware and organized around youth alcohol, tobacco, and other drug use for a long time, for example, or have some recent events just brought these issues into the open, jolting the community into action without a clearly identified plan as yet? You can sit down as a work group and develop a list of issues and ideas that you want to find out more about. You can also form a team of four to six people within your group who are interested in zeroing in on the specific information you need.

Here are some suggestions and tools to help you get started:

- ***Use the information you already have.*** Use the trends you discovered from the surveys, data collection, resource assessment, and priorities summary from Question #1 to help you develop a set of questions you want to explore in the greater community to assess awareness and readiness. A program can look into the community as part of its assessment, too, as the St. Louis Park High School 9th Grade Program did when it determined that some of the asset-building resources it needed were already present because of the Children First initiative. For example, if you identified high rates of alcohol use among teenagers as a problem, you'll want to know more about how police enforce the laws on underage drinking and whether parents also perceive underage drinking as a problem. What do teenagers themselves think about the issue? Are there already programs available in the community to address this issue? Where have they been successful and where do barriers still exist?
- ***Have informal conversations to learn more.*** Informal conversations and networking with young people, diverse community members, key stakeholders, and providers about the relevance and applicability of your proposed programs and projects could yield a lot of useful information. You may be able to discover some of the historical reasons certain interventions have failed or discover a core group of citizens (whom you can support) who are ready to tackle a specific issue.
- ***Conduct key informant interviews.*** Interviewing key members of the community using a specially designed series of questions may further yield trends regarding the priorities, goals, and outcomes you're planning. A key informant is someone who understands and cares about the issues, but may or may not be a leader or decision maker. A semi-structured interview using a series of questions designed to gather specific information is conducted systematically with your chosen informants. You identify who your key informants are and you ask each of them the same set of questions. This presents a good opportunity to work in culturally sensitive ways, too, either by partnering with natural community leaders to conduct interviews or by learning the ways in which you need to adapt language, questions, and interviewing style to make your conversations more effective. Be sure to involve youth in the quest for information. Youth will bring their own

"insider" perspective to developing both the questions and answers about what's important for young people, what the level of awareness is about a particular issue, and what should be done about it. Their perspective will also be helpful if you have them go out into the community and ask their own questions.

We have provided two worksheets on pages 112–113 and 115–125 that you can use to help determine fit by learning more about your community's overall readiness for asset-building strategies. The first one is called Assessing Community Readiness for Asset-Building Programs and Projects (4.1). The second worksheet is called Healthy Community Rating (4.2). Both of these worksheets will help you and the members of your work group assess whether you think the community is ready for your asset-building programs and projects and to what degree, at both the initiative and program levels. A third worksheet on pages 127–128 will help you determine what roadblocks might exist and help you think through possible solutions before continuing on.

LEARN MORE: The Tri-Ethnic Center for Prevention Research at Colorado State University has developed a model for community readiness that you may find useful to understand, assess, and build community readiness in culturally sensitive ways. It can be found online at www.triethniccenter.colostate.edu. The nine stages of this model are consistent with similar community readiness models sanctioned by the federal government for use in drug abuse prevention as well.

Instructions for Using the Assessing Community Readiness for Asset-Building Programs and Projects Worksheet

This worksheet will help those of you working within your planning group get a picture of how *you* view where the community stands. The process for completing Worksheet 4.1 is as follows:

1. Identify who should fill out this worksheet for you. You may want to extend your inquiry beyond the current work group. You can begin by having your work group discuss these questions, then fan out to get information from others in the community to compare your perceptions.
2. Determine what sort of information you may need to answer the Yes/No questions. This information may help you develop ideas about what steps you can take to reach each stage of readiness.

WORKSHEET 4.1

Assessing Community Readiness for Asset-Building Programs and Projects

	Yes	No	What steps can we take toward this?
1. Is there a history of commitment to children and youth in our community?			
2. Is there a history of successful collaboration among programs and/or community-wide action?			
3. Are there other community-wide issues, initiatives, efforts, or programs that will vie for citizens' time and efforts?			
4. Is a variety of sectors and/or programs involved in assessing the feasibility of an asset-building initiative?			
5. Are young people actively involved in launching an asset-building initiative or program?			
6. Have you or your fellow asset champions worked to create a shared vision for your community?			
7. Are the people, programs, and organizations involved passionate and excited about the Developmental Assets framework?			

Worksheet 4.1 continued on next page

Assessing Community Readiness for Asset-Building Programs and Projects

	Yes	No	What steps can we take toward this?
8. Are the individuals, programs, and organizations involved becoming empowered to build assets for and with young people?			
9. Do the people involved represent the diversity of your community (in terms of age, ethnicity, gender, income, religious beliefs, and so on)?			
10. Are the people involved beginning to use the language of Developmental Assets without being prompted to do so?			
11. Have you addressed issues of inclusiveness and diversity?			
12. Do you have access to funding, resources, or other financial support?			
13. Do you have the sense that your community is ready to rally together behind your children and youth?			

3. If you find areas in which you don't believe the community is ready, fill in the column on the right-hand side of the worksheet with ideas about what steps you can take. Use the material we've provided on developing the community's asset-building capacity and the Five Action Strategies to help you develop some actions for improving community readiness.

Instructions for Using the Healthy Community Rating Worksheet

This worksheet is designed to help you determine how well your community, its organizations, and its residents embody the characteristics of an asset-building community. This rating sheet can provide a new picture of how well your community is doing at being an asset-building community. Besides guiding your team toward priorities and next steps, it also suggests areas for productive reflection on the basis of people's opinions about their community.

The members of your work group, initiative, organization, or program staff, volunteers, and participants can fill this out from their perspectives; you can also plan on fanning out to ask members of the community to fill out this worksheet to get a broader perspective. You can use this rating sheet in a variety of ways, including as mailed questionnaires or survey-based telephone interviews. The information you gather using this worksheet will be more meaningful and helpful if you ensure that a relatively large and diverse sample of the community is asked to complete the survey.

Tallying

Once the rating sheets are completed, use the tally sheet provided to compile your results. Use tally marks to determine how many respondents agree or disagree with each of the statements in the three sections. Then use the boxes at the end of each section to guide further thinking about asset building in your own lives, neighborhoods, organizations, and broader community. As you discuss the results in your work group or evaluation team, consider the following questions:

- Which section has the most "agree" and "strongly agree" responses?
- Which has the fewest?
- Why is this so?
- How do we know?
- What can we do to improve?

WORKSHEET 4.2

Healthy Community Rating

For each of the characteristics listed here, decide whether you strongly agree (SA), agree (A), disagree (D), or strongly disagree (SD) with each statement and circle the corresponding letter(s). If you don't know, mark an X in the margin next to that characteristic and think about how you can find out.

I. Individual Commitment and Action

1. Most residents take personal responsibility for the well-being of the community's children and youth.

   SA A D SD

2. Most residents make time to build Developmental Assets for and with all children and youth who come into their spheres of influence.

   SA A D SD

3. Most residents respect and value young people for who they are and for who they are becoming.

   SA A D SD

4. Most residents learn and practice trustworthiness and relationship-building skills.

   SA A D SD

5. Most residents take steps to increase their involvement in organizational and community actions on behalf of young people.

   SA A D SD

II. Organizational Commitment and Action

6. Most groups and organizations throughout the community mobilize their internal asset-building capacities to create asset-promoting policies, systems, and structures.

   SA A D SD

7. Most groups and organizations make assistance and support readily available to everyone in the community.

   SA A D SD

Worksheet 4.2 continued on next page

Healthy Community Rating

8. Most groups and organizations train workers and administrators in the asset framework and in asset-building strategies.

   SA A D SD

III. Community-wide Commitment and Action

9. The community incorporates shared values, boundaries, and expectations regarding youth in its sense of identity.

   SA A D SD

10. Developmental needs and assets of youth are a regular topic of conversation throughout the community and are articulated as a community priority.

    SA A D SD

11. Youth needs and challenges in the community are recognized and addressed from a positive youth development perspective.

    SA A D SD

12. Youth are a visible, active, and positive force in community life.

    SA A D SD

13. Most neighborhoods are places of caring.

    SA A D SD

14. Most neighborhoods are places of support.

    SA A D SD

15. Most neighborhoods are places of safety.

    SA A D SD

Tally sheet for Worksheet 4.2

I. Individual Commitment and Action

1. Most residents take personal responsibility for the well-being of the community's children and youth.

Strongly agree (SA)	Agree (A)	Disagree (D)	Strongly disagree (SD)
Total	Total	Total	Total

2. Most residents make time to build Developmental Assets for and with all children and youth who come into their spheres of influence.

Strongly agree (SA)	Agree (A)	Disagree (D)	Strongly disagree (SD)
Total	Total	Total	Total

Worksheet 4.2 tally sheet continued on next page

Tally sheet for Worksheet 4.2

I. Individual Commitment and Action (continued)

3. Most residents respect and value young people for who they are and for who they are becoming.

Strongly agree (SA)	Agree (A)	Disagree (D)	Strongly disagree (SD)
Total	Total	Total	Total

4. Most residents learn and practice trustworthiness and relationship-building skills.

Strongly agree (SA)	Agree (A)	Disagree (D)	Strongly disagree (SD)
Total	Total	Total	Total

Worksheet 4.2 tally sheet continued on next page

Tally sheet for Worksheet 4.2

I. Individual Commitment and Action (continued)

5. Most residents take steps to increase their involvement in organizational and community actions on behalf of young people.

Strongly agree (SA)	Agree (A)	Disagree (D)	Strongly disagree (SD)
Total	Total	Total	Total

The statement in this section we can most effectively focus our plans on is:
How can we find out more?
Possible steps toward progress:

Worksheet 4.2 tally sheet continued on next page

Tally sheet for Worksheet 4.2

II. Organizational Commitment and Action

6. Most groups and organizations throughout the community mobilize their internal asset-building capacities to create asset-promoting policies, systems, and structures.

Strongly agree (SA)	Agree (A)	Disagree (D)	Strongly disagree (SD)
Total	Total	Total	Total

7. Most groups and organizations make assistance and support readily available to everyone in the community.

Strongly agree (SA)	Agree (A)	Disagree (D)	Strongly disagree (SD)
Total	Total	Total	Total

Worksheet 4.2 tally sheet continued on next page

Tally sheet for Worksheet 4.2

II. Organizational Commitment and Action (continued)

8. Most groups and organizations train workers and administrators in the asset framework and in asset-building strategies.

Strongly agree (SA)	Agree (A)	Disagree (D)	Strongly disagree (SD)
Total	Total	Total	Total

The statement in this section we can most effectively focus our plans on is:
How can we find out more?
Possible steps toward progress:

Worksheet 4.2 tally sheet continued on next page

Tally sheet for Worksheet 4.2

III. Community-wide Commitment and Action

9. The community incorporates shared values, boundaries, and expectations regarding youth in its sense of identity.

Strongly agree (SA)	Agree (A)	Disagree (D)	Strongly disagree (SD)
Total	Total	Total	Total

10. Developmental needs and assets of youth are a regular topic of conversation throughout the community and are articulated as a community priority.

Strongly agree (SA)	Agree (A)	Disagree (D)	Strongly disagree (SD)
Total	Total	Total	Total

Worksheet 4.2 tally sheet continued on next page

Tally sheet for Worksheet 4.2

III. Community-wide Commitment and Action (continued)

11. Youth needs and challenges in the community are recognized and addressed from a positive youth development perspective.

Strongly agree (SA)	Agree (A)	Disagree (D)	Strongly disagree (SD)
Total	Total	Total	Total

12. Youth are a visible, active, and positive force in community life.

Strongly agree (SA)	Agree (A)	Disagree (D)	Strongly disagree (SD)
Total	Total	Total	Total

Worksheet 4.2 tally sheet continued on next page

Tally sheet for Worksheet 4.2

III. Community-wide Commitment and Action (continued)

13. Most neighborhoods are places of caring.

Strongly agree (SA)	Agree (A)	Disagree (D)	Strongly disagree (SD)
Total	Total	Total	Total

14. Most neighborhoods are places of support.

Strongly agree (SA)	Agree (A)	Disagree (D)	Strongly disagree (SD)
Total	Total	Total	Total

Worksheet 4.2 tally sheet continued on next page

Tally sheet for Worksheet 4.2

III. Community-wide Commitment and Action (continued)

15. Most neighborhoods are places of safety.

Strongly agree (SA)	Agree (A)	Disagree (D)	Strongly disagree (SD)
Total	Total	Total	Total

The statement in this section we can most effectively focus our plans on is:
How can we find out more?
Possible steps toward progress:

Finally, the worksheet on pages 127–128 entitled Working through Roadblocks will guide you in determining if there are any turf issues, minimal organizational capacities, or other potential problems that might hinder your efforts to move ahead. It's wise to forecast what some of these challenges might be and generate possible solutions for them. You may not know the solutions now, but you will be able to update the worksheet at any time in the future.

Instructions for Using the Working through Roadblocks Worksheet

The process for completing Worksheet 4.3 is as follows:

1. This may be a worksheet you want to do as a group. The collective wisdom of your work group's understanding of your community may help you nail down potential roadblocks as well as creative solutions.
2. Make as many copies of the worksheet as you need to write on.
3. Fill in the columns that are relevant for you.

#2. REVIEW. Confirm which initiatives, projects, and programs are already operating in your community and what's already working.

From your information review, conversations, interviews, and assessments, you should be getting a clearer picture of your community's level of awareness of the issues you've identified and whether there is a sense of readiness about taking action within the community and relevant sectors or among organizations. This should help lead you into an examination of what interventions are currently being brought to bear on the priorities and goals you've identified. You may already have sufficient information to provide a clear picture of what's going on in your community at this point. If so, you will only need to spend a short time looking at the review points we cover. But if you need to fill in some blanks, our suggestions might help you finish your review of existing initiatives or programs that address the goals you've developed, especially now that you know more about effective programs from Question #3.

For discussing or reviewing the key points in this section, you'll want to have on hand your resource assessments, your list of selected evidence-based projects and programs, and your logic model.

Consider the following:

- ***Is your resource assessment complete?*** Now that you know more about your community, fill in any new information on the Resource Assessment Worksheet (1.2) from Question #1 about what initiatives, programs, and projects are already operating.

WORKSHEET 4.3

Working through Roadblocks

Roadblocks	Issues	Solutions
Turf and competition: Although your effort is attempting to build coordination and cooperation, some organizations and groups may become competitive and territorial.		
Bad history: Previous efforts in your community may not have gone well and have given people the attitude that they've tried this before and it doesn't work.		
Failure to act: Too much planning can hurt an initiative or program. Be sure to do both planning *and* action.		
Dominance by, or lack of, professionals: Initiatives should involve and empower residents, not just professionals and people in power. Programs, on the other hand, need well-qualified staff as well as volunteers.		
Poor links to the community: Meetings, planning, and action in initiatives and/or programs can become inaccessible to certain groups in your community.		
Minimal organizational capacity: Unclear vision, goals, objectives, and plans can hurt an effort.		

Worksheet 4.3 continued on next page

Working through Roadblocks

Roadblocks	Issues	Solutions
Funding: Too much funding and too little funding can hurt efforts. Initiatives and programs started without funding and as grassroots groups often have more genuine community interest at the outset. But underfunded efforts have trouble producing desired results.		
Failure to provide and create leadership: An effort has two leadership tasks—to provide competent leadership for the initiative or program and its tasks, and to create new leadership in the community, when necessary, to support the effort's ongoing work.		
Costs outweigh benefits: Busy people drop out of efforts when the costs (especially time) outweigh the benefits of being involved.		
Other:		

- ***Can you identify what's already working well?*** Using what you now know about effective programs, work to increase your knowledge of what's already going on within your particular location as well as within the communities you wish to serve. Are there evaluations available on the effectiveness or evidence base of local programs, or do you have all the information you need from your conversations, interviews, and youth assessments? If you haven't already done so, complete the far right-hand column on your Resource Assessment Worksheet (1.2).
- ***Can you clearly state how your programs and projects will offer something unique and useful if similar activities and programs exist?*** Will your program or project meet certain needs in your communities of interest that aren't currently met by the existing efforts? Can you enhance the efforts of existing programs, organizations, or initiatives, or will you need to design something new to reach your goals and outcomes? Does your proposed program enhance (e.g., a tutoring component being added to an existing after-school program), provide an opportunity for a new collaboration (e.g., high school students begin mentoring younger children), or contradict (e.g., distributing condoms in a school district served solely by an abstinence-only curriculum)? You can work together with other program providers to make sure that what you are proposing strengthens or enhances what already exists in your community. It's also important information for you if what you are proposing to do contradicts other programs.

Knowing the existing resources in your community will also help you define new ways to connect and work with stakeholders who may not yet be involved with your efforts. This may help address any perceived competitive or turf issues as you move forward.

#3. SELECT. Determine what programs and projects are going to fit your community.

By this point, you know what you want to do, you know whether your community is aware of the same issues, whether it is ready to address those issues, and what interventions for dealing with those issues are already operating. Now you're ready to draw final conclusions about whether your chosen goals, outcomes, and potential programs and projects will fit well within your community.

Consider these points:

- Determine whether the programs, projects, and methods of delivery involved will be suitable for your communities of interest either at the initiative, sector, or organizational level. If not entirely suitable, you will need to think about whether the program can still be successful.
- Determine whether adaptations are needed for the proposed program or project to achieve a better fit, and clarify how to make these changes while still ensuring that the program will produce the intended outcomes.
- Determine the cost and feasibility of any adaptations you're considering. For example, what will be the cost of translating an entire curriculum into another language?

As you fine-tune the selection of your goals, outcomes, and project(s) or program(s), keep in mind that it could make the most sense to look for ways to infuse Developmental Assets into existing work rather than trying to start new programs or projects.

INTEGRATE ASSETS-GTO more deeply by looking for new ways to consistently build capacity in your community and among organizations and programs to conduct asset building. You can do this through the continued development of your operational infrastructure as well as through deeper use of the Five Action Strategies. Can you share with other organizations the good ideas you've learned about how to mobilize adults and engage youth from your research into your community's programs and resources? Have you developed new and stronger ties with youth and different cultural communities that could lead to new partnerships and events? The newly emerging Cannabis Youth Treatment Program profiled at the beginning of this chapter benefited during start-up from the experience of staff at the Daniel Bryant Center, where the program was housed. Assets for Colorado Youth (ACY) made sure the lessons learned by one organization were shared by all those participating in asset building statewide.

Consider the following indicators of successful Developmental Assets integration identified by ACY and used in its evaluation of grantee organizations to see how well they were able to achieve asset integration. While these are cast in more program-specific language, they could also be applied at the community level. For example, the asset message can be incorporated in materials for, and presentations to, parents or the community at large. Use these indicators as idea generators for ways to infuse Developmental Assets into your community, initiative, organization, or program:

- How staff incorporated the asset approach into their work at the organization;
- The establishment of new programs or modification of existing programs;

- The incorporation of the asset message into staff trainings and orientations;
- The integration of the asset message into materials and other resources used and developed;
- The incorporation of the asset framework into policies and procedures, such as requiring that all new staff receive training in the assets or that there be a youth representative on decision-making councils or boards;
- Youth involvement in the development of asset-building efforts at the organization; and
- The fit of the asset framework with the community/population served by the organization.

Looking Ahead to Sustainability

The Imagine That Improvisational Theatre Troupe in Spartanburg, South Carolina, had been in existence for more than ten years when it lost the majority of its funding. This arts program had been especially successful in promoting awareness of the program, recruiting volunteers, and serving multiple youth in diverse settings. Because the company had established strong ties to schools, churches, parents, businesses, and other nonprofit agencies, the community quickly organized to ensure that the troupe would continue. Local newspapers and television stations were tapped to run stories about the loss of funding, and the parents of the participants organized and met with community leaders, including board members of a larger arts organization and a local foundation. A plan was developed for how the community would continue to support the arts program. The arts organization offered to house the program at no cost, and the local foundation encouraged the arts program to apply to it for support, emphasizing how the program fit within the foundation's funding priorities. In addition, the parents and other community leaders decided the arts program should apply for nonprofit tax status to ensure self-sufficiency and sustainability over time.

Taking the time to assess the fit between your plans and your community's needs strengthens your overall efforts and makes good use of everyone's resources. Congruence and efficiency bolster sustainability. Getting to know more about the existing organizations, programs, and supports in your community also shows you where to engage multiple agencies, organizations, and community sectors that have a shared stake in what you're doing if you're conducting an initiative, or how to best situate your individual program if that is your focus. These connective efforts further strengthen everyone's work on behalf of young people. In the case of Imagine That, taking time to develop the fit between the program and the community made it possible for the program to continue even when its funding was significantly cut.

By taking such steps, you can:

- *Continue to secure community buy-in as you reach out to new participants;*
- *Ensure the continuation of your chosen programs and projects by having multiple stakeholders share in their implementation and success;*
- *Demonstrate to other entities you engage in the future the efficacy of your plans because of the successful, collective efforts of you and your stakeholders.*

Integrating your work into existing efforts ensures sustainability. Working actively with your partners to build your collective efforts also allows you to monitor the fluctuating context of the community and readjust goals, plans, and projects or programs, when necessary.

Before Going on to the Next Chapter

If you haven't already, now is the time to refine your logic model and update the draft on which you've been working. Make sure everyone in the work group has a current copy. You may also want to report back to people who participated in your Healthy Community Rating Survey, telling them the results of what you found and giving some indication of how you are using those results.

In Question #5, you will examine your current capacities as you look ahead to implementing your plans. This will be the final step in assessing and reviewing your capacities and choices before moving on to implementation and formalizing your evaluation plans.

QUESTION #5

What capacities will you need to implement your program or asset-building initiative?

(CAPACITIES)

As you move forward to reach the particular goals and outcomes you have now developed, you need to have the capacity to successfully implement your chosen projects and programs. Generally, capacity refers to the different types of resources a community, initiative, organization, or program uses to put its plans into motion and sustain them. You can use the Developmental Assets framework and relevant aspects of the Framework for Asset-Based Community Building (which we first showed you in the Introduction, page 5) to strengthen your programs and projects.

For an initiative, asset building is aimed at activating the entire community's capacity to support all young people by calling on individuals, organizations, and networks to contribute to the accumulation of many Developmental Assets in multiple contexts and across time. For an organization or program, asset building can be used to activate the capacity of both, as well to better support young people. In both arenas, initiatives and programs seek to fully equip themselves with the all tools they need to conduct their work—infusing assets, building and maintaining the infrastructure needed to complete the work, developing collaborative partnerships, and finding the appropriate resources to carry out programs and projects (such as staff, volunteers, and funds).

It's important to assess your capacity before you implement your plans because having adequate capacity directly relates to *how well* your projects and programs will do. If there is not enough capacity to carry though a project or program as intended, then it's unlikely you will achieve your desired outcomes. You want to know what capacities the community, initiative, or organization already has and which ones you need to develop to undertake a project or program with high quality. Some programs may be too difficult or resource intensive for an organization to deliver with quality, for example. In cases where the community, initiative, or organization does not possess adequate capacities, you will need to develop clear plans to obtain or access them elsewhere, modify projects and programs so that they require fewer resources, or choose different projects and programs that require fewer resources.

In previous chapters, you've selected the projects and programs you want to use to carry out your goals. This chapter is designed to help your initiative, organization, or program determine whether you have sufficient human, technical, resource, and structural capacities available to successfully carry out those chosen projects and programs. You may already know these details, in which case you can use this chapter to double-check your status. If not, this chapter will help you understand the key issues and decisions related to capacity.

The activities in this chapter will guide you to:

- Understand the fundamental capacities and infrastructure you need to support your efforts;
- Determine whether you have the appropriate levels of community or organizational capacity, as well as the specific staff, technical, resource, and collaborative partnerships, to implement and sustain your projects and programs; and
- Develop a plan for building the capacities you still need to implement your plans.

Here's what you'll need to get you started:

- Your logic model.
- Any information that will help you understand your initiative, organization, or program structure, the current experience levels of your staff and volunteers, as well as the fiscal resources you have to launch and conduct your programs or projects. This information may be resident within the members of your work group, or you may have some of it in written form such as reports or budgets.

A Framework for Unleashing the Capacity of an Asset-Building Community

In his preliminary report on the Howard County Connections initiative in Maryland, Search Institute's Director of Family and Congregation Initiatives, Gene Roehlkepartain, observes that "building Developmental Assets is the work of the community—its young people, adults, organizations, and institutions. Thus, a community's asset-building infrastructure should be designed not to *do*

A SNAPSHOT OF THIS STEP IN ACTION

St. Louis Park High School 9th Grade Program

St. Louis Park High School staff and administrators chose several key asset-building strategies to help them tackle substance abuse, academic failure, attendance, and discipline problems—build more meaningful relationships, communicate high expectations, and increase opportunities for youth participation in school. The evidence base for selecting these program elements was research demonstrating that these Developmental Assets in particular were associated with reductions in the specific problems that were raising concerns.

To make it more likely that teachers and other staff would be able to build meaningful relationships with students, administrators and staff implemented the following actions:

- Reducing class size so teachers could have more time with more students.
- Reorganizing the 9th-grade teachers into "blocks" consisting of three core teachers (English, social studies, and science) who all work with one group of 80 students. The teachers who work together in a block meet weekly with a social worker and talk about how each student is doing. Every student is discussed so that no one is overlooked.
- Requiring every 9th-grade student to meet individually with a counselor. This gives each student a chance to identify her or his own needs and strengths.
- Introducing a new curriculum called "I Time," 30 minutes every week in which teachers and students participate in icebreakers, team-building activities, and education in communication and social competencies.

Other components of the program worked on getting parents more involved as positive partners with the school and developing peer relationships among students.

Several capacities were needed to put these program components into place. First of all, the staff recognized that time was a key factor in relationship building—students, teachers, and staff simply needed more time together. To reduce class size and restructure the 9th-grade class into blocks, the high school successfully garnered funds from the school district and other grant sources. Financial resources also helped pay for the development of a new curriculum, as well as additional staff and teacher time. But teachers and staff needed training on how to implement some of the new program components. Training also helped reduce some of the initial objections teachers had to what they perceived as going back to old models of homeroom teaching, something they had previously fought to eliminate.

the community's asset building or to control what the community does, but to inspire, equip, and unleash the people, places, and systems of the community to engage in asset-building action."

The overall infrastructure we're referring to here is the Framework of Asset-Based Community Building (Tipsheet A) that we introduced you to in the Introduction on page 5. This model shows you a picture of one way to organize the initiative leadership, systems, and processes that stimulate, support, and develop the capacity of youth and adults, organizations, networks, and systems to build Developmental Assets.

The first set of components we've identified within this model as useful in cultivating community readiness, energy, and commitment include shared vision, common purpose, personal and collective efficacy, public will, and social trust. If you are already working under the auspices of a functioning initiative, you have probably already begun developing many of these important components. While your net will be cast wider if you are doing all of this at the broad community or initiative level, at the organizational or program level you may still be creating a vision and common purpose within your organization or in partnership with several other organizations to conduct your program or project. You may also be cultivating readiness, energy, and commitment within your organization—and particularly among staff and volunteers—to carry out your plans.

While nurturing the energy, enthusiasm, pride, and commitment of community residents and leaders is a primary objective of an initiative, it's easier to implement your goals if you have an *operational* infrastructure to help link, promote, and support your efforts. This more formal structure helps you better support the work of the community, especially in the next phase of the model, which includes the Five Action Strategies (Engage Adults, Mobilize Young People, Activate Sectors, Invigorate Programs, and Influence Civic Decisions). Nurturing energy, enthusiasm, pride, and commitment among staff and volunteers is equally important within an organization or program. And while some aspects of the operational infrastructure may already be taken care of for a program by its parent organization, you may benefit if you pay particular attention to what your program needs. For example, a mentoring program for young people will need engaged adults to participate. The St. Louis Park High School 9th Grade Program, in a way, needed to influence civic decisions to ensure its sustainability. Staff made sure the program's successes were publicized, leading to wider support among parents and out in the community. When it came time to ask the school district for ongoing funds, the district and school board knew the program was achieving success and it was easier to support it.

The core functions of an operational infrastructure include:

- *Planning, decision making, and governance* that guide both the mission and maintenance of your work. For example, St. Louis Park staff made sure teachers had time built into their schedules to come together and discuss how the program was working and what changes needed to be made along the way to make it work better. In the St. Louis Park asset initiative, Children First, an ongoing vision team meets regularly to talk about these big-picture issues.

- *Accessing resources* (financial, personal, skills, etc.) needed to support your capacity-building efforts in the community, organization, or program. This means having adequate funds, but it also means making sure whoever is delivering your program has the training to help them do a good job. At the initiative level, it means tapping into the resources of the wider community (e.g., donated staff time, meeting rooms, copying, skilled facilitators, or volunteers) to help you get things done.
- *Convening, networking, and organizing* committed leaders (both adults and youth) who have the passion to spread the word and help make the vision a reality. You want to create opportunities for these champions to learn from, support, and inspire each other. At the program level, this could mean making sure staff, administrators, and parents are all brought together regularly to hear how the program is going, make plans, and just have a chance to inspire one another. Keeping parents regularly informed in St. Louis Park got them so fired up, they went from being passive receivers of information to ardent and active supporters who helped secure more funding. Larger initiatives often take time to celebrate their participants, leaders, and champions at special events or simply at every regular meeting.
- *Communicating* broadly to the community or organization members to inspire and support engagement by distributing information, making presentations, and tapping the media to raise awareness about asset building and other local efforts. Many initiatives regularly send out press material, work out arrangements to run regular asset-oriented articles in local newspapers, or set up speakers bureaus. The success of the St. Louis Park High School 9th Grade Program started getting attention in the local media and evaluators started collecting press clippings as one way to measure the program's impact.
- *Providing tools, training, and technical assistance* that increase the capacity of individuals and organizations to engage in, deepen, and sustain their asset-building efforts. Initiatives regularly give asset trainings to local organizations and citizens. In conjunction with its biennial citywide youth summit, the city of Bellevue, Washington, also does an asset training for community adults. The St. Louis Park High School program provided regular trainings for staff, teachers, and administrators as new pieces of the curriculum were developed or refined.
- Initiating and/or coordinating *formal documentation, assessment, and evaluation.* Both initiatives and programs learn to track and document their efforts. Remember that using many of the worksheets in this book can help you with this stage.

- *Celebrating and recognizing* efforts and progress.
- *Managing and coordinating* schedules, budgets, and other administrative tasks, as needed.

CD FEATURE: If you want to do a deeper analysis of your asset-building efforts by assessing your community's capacities, you can use the worksheet titled Asset-Building Community Mobilization Grid found on the CD-ROM included with this book. This can help you at the initiative level. If you want to know about the specific asset-building capacities within your organization, you can also use the worksheet titled Checklist for Examining Asset Building in Your Organization. This can help you at the program level.

The Catalyzing Influence of Asset Champions and Collaborative Partnerships

There are obviously many important aspects to consider when trying to create or expand initiatives, as well as implement projects and programs. We want to direct your attention to two in particular that are worth some special focus.

The first is *leadership*. Initiatives and communities all benefit from the variety of leadership that emerges in the course of an asset-building initiative or project. Asset building often starts on a very personal level with individuals who hear about the asset framework, understand it, learn more about it, and feel passionate enough to start promoting it to others. The impact of these asset champions is magnified by the fact that these people are generally already deeply involved in their community.

Keep in mind, though, that these asset champions are not necessarily the people who are traditionally thought of as community leaders, although they may be. We are talking about a range of natural community guides or messengers with different cultural backgrounds, people of different ages and professional backgrounds, strategic and operational thinkers, and people who bring both passion and analytical skills to the table. As part of your efforts to successfully implement your projects and programs, you want to recruit and cultivate these competent, committed individuals who can help you.

Assets for Colorado Youth discovered these characteristics common to asset champions:

1. They spread the asset model and philosophy intentionally through both formal and informal means;

2. They were identified by more than one person or organization as the source of their asset-related inspiration;
3. They served as the hub—or point of connection—for networks or partnerships;
4. They served as a resource to others. Asset champions supported and encouraged others to move from awareness of the assets to their application in work and personal lives; and
5. They demonstrated a sustained commitment to, and passion for, the asset framework—they stuck with it over time.

As you assess the capacities of your projects and programs, take a look at what sort of leadership is present. While many initiatives and programs rely on asset champions to kick-start their work, there is also a need for those leaders who will step in to take the work beyond the launch stage. Part of your role will be to recognize and cultivate these leaders as your work continues. You can determine if you have this type of leadership already present, or whether such asset champions are out in the community that could be recruited for your efforts. You may also want to incorporate training into your efforts to cultivate the capacities of your asset champions and leadership so they are better able to intentionally spread the word.

The second area that deserves some special attention is *collaboration*. Achieving collaborative partnerships requires effort and time, but it pays off by helping you maximize resources, reducing duplication, and creating successful efforts that are more than the sum of their parts. At the program level, high school students may collaborate with the local elementary school to offer an after-school homework club. At the organizational level, several youth-serving organizations may collaborate on implementing a common agenda or jointly promoting a drug awareness campaign throughout the community. At the community level, an initiative might work with youth organizations, school PTAs, local media, and businesses to create a big first-day-of-school event.

You may have already identified asset champions or developed fruitful collaborative partnerships as you've created your initiative or program. You also may have discovered that some roadblocks exist to involving leaders or partners. Some of the people you'd like to involve may not have the time to devote to your efforts, or perhaps a charismatic leader who helped jump-start things has moved on to a new job, leaving efforts flagging. Other organizations in your community may feel that resources are spread too thin to develop a new program, or there might be a perception that your efforts will hamper theirs. This is when it is time to slow down and build the relationships you'll need to continue your efforts. Look for people who support you—both individuals and in organizations—and start by involving those folks first. Perhaps you can develop a good working relationship with one key person in an organization you're trying to cultivate, then let *her or him* begin to influence the organization on your behalf from within. It will also help if you can be specific with people about what you want them to do and how long you want them to be involved. Specific commitments are often easier to accept than open-ended ones.

Prevention Partners for Youth Development (PPYD) in New York created a successful infrastructure for supporting its work by incorporating many of the elements we've highlighted. Working from a clear set of community-wide goals and priorities, the coalition organized itself into a multilevel planning structure that took charge of making sure that every level of every organization associated with the coalition was equipped to activate and strengthen different sectors. The coalition's leadership recognized that the community at large and the participating organizations would all need to have adequate structures and capacities to better incorporate evidence-based information and implement best practices. In this way PPYD provides the body (coalition) that coordinates and supports the movement of these various parts by attending to the content (youth development theories and practices) and to the processes (relationship and team building) simultaneously.

Some examples of how this works include:

- PPYD's original steering committee, which got its efforts going, evolved into its current Executive Council, which is now responsible for creating and sustaining the larger picture of a county-wide youth development agenda.
- To more concretely integrate youth development principles into the community, PPYD developed a Community Capacity-Building Workgroup, open to all community members who work with youth, which operates in tandem with a Training Team (composed of citizens with specific expertise) to educate service providers, community organizations, and interested stakeholders like parents and teachers.
- To make sure organizations do more than just learn about youth development principles, PPYD provides training and consultation to help invigorate programs, engage adults, and activate sectors to assist organizations in building their own capacities. PPYD also mobilizes young people by providing training for them as well as promoting opportunities for youth participation and civic engagement.

Youth participation in PPYD is especially important to its success; the initiative creates opportunities for young people to be decision makers, cotrainers, consultants, and evaluators. To further build the capacity of the initiative, staff has youth development expertise, which they share as trainers available to participating community organizations.

A variety of structures and organizational models have emerged in the asset-building movement, but no single type is effective in all communities. What works in your community will depend on the realities of your community: politics, existing resources and networks, personalities of initiators, and the interests of funders and other partners. In fact, the creation of your own model or structure is empowering to your stakeholders and fosters a sense of shared ownership and commitment. You don't need to have all the leadership, infrastructure, and collaboration issues thoroughly worked out in order to move forward with your projects and programs. At this point, it's simply good to be aware of the current status of your capacities in these areas to help you decide how to move forward. Knowing your status will also help you evaluate your results later.

Specific Staff, Technical, and Resources Capacities to Consider

In addition to assessing and building the overall capacities you'll need to implement your chosen projects and programs, there are other important factors to assess. The capacities in this next section represent what research has shown to be important in planning, implementing, and evaluating prevention programs. They include more specific issues such as staffing, technical expertise, and finances and resources.

Staff and Volunteer Capacities

There are a variety of considerations with regard to potential staffing needs when you plan for the implementation of your projects or programs, whether they stand alone or are part of a larger initiative:

- *General Staffing Issues*
  Your initiative or program may have paid (either part-time or full-time) staff or volunteers or a combination of both. In addition to understanding how many people and what types of staff and/or volunteers are required to implement your projects or programs, it's beneficial for staff and volunteers to have a general set of skills that research has shown will enhance your chances of success. These basic skills, which rest on a foundation of commitment and feelings of ownership, can apply to many different types of programs and projects and include leadership, communication, conflict resolution, decision making, and meeting facilitation.
- *Staffing Issues Specific to a Particular Program or Project*
  Depending on what you've chosen to do, you may need staff with certain qualifications, such as a particular degree or type of prevention

experience, to best implement your program or project. There is some evidence to show that staff with formal education can more easily conduct program planning and implementation if specific prevention programs are involved. If a program (evidence-based or otherwise) requires that staff have certain qualifications in order to run it effectively, we recommend that these requirements be followed. Under-qualified staff (even those who have been trained in the program's specifics) may make the program less effective. Some programs also recommend gender or ethnic matching or balance in staffing to increase effectiveness.

Some specific points to consider regarding staff and volunteers include:

- *Adequate Training*
  The majority of the studies that have looked at the effects of teacher or staff training have shown that training enhances knowledge, attitudes, intentions, and comfort level with a new program, which improves the delivery of that program.

  The type of training that seems to work best is "active" learning, in which the participants have the opportunity to practice or role-play the program or activity and then receive feedback on how they did. Training that involves only "passive" activities, such as just watching a video or only reading printed program materials, has been associated with poorer program delivery.

  Training is important even in cases where you have designed your own local innovations. Figure out which sets of skills are required and provide active training for staff in those areas.

  It will be especially important to provide cross-cultural training, as well as training that includes cultural context and knowledge regarding youth in particular. Young people will feel more supported, and are more likely to achieve greater potential, when trusted adults work with them to help them understand their own cultural heritage better as well as the cultures of others.

Check with the program developers to see if they have developed any training materials to support the program.

Staffing/Volunteer Level and Composition

- *For model programs.* Similar to training, it is highly recommended to follow program guidelines on the number of staff and/or volunteers required for program implementation. Asking too few teachers, trainers, staff, or volunteers to do more than was initially planned by program developers will result in inadequate implementation.

- *For local innovations.* It is difficult to know the exact number of staff and/or volunteers to recommend. However, when considering the tasks that need to be completed, besides the obvious program implementation and service delivery tasks, you might go back and look at some of the other questions in this book to help you determine what the appropriate staffing levels should be. You could also look at similar programs to guide you. Will you want staff to conduct an evaluation of the program or project as well as implement it? When other tasks such as evaluation, continuous quality improvement, and sustainability are all "tacked on" to an already full load of program delivery, it is not likely that these tasks will be done well—unless the capacity is available. You will need to plan for this. As mentioned in the Snapshot at the beginning of this chapter, St. Louis Park High School developed its "I Time" curriculum, then built in training time for teachers to learn how to use it.
- *For any program.* It's important for cultural competence to have staff who reflect your community and clientele. This may mean hiring staff and recruiting volunteers from different communities, not just training the ones you have.

Technical Expertise Capacities

Certain types of technical expertise may be needed for successful community initiative implementation and/or program delivery, including:

- *Application of program materials.* It is recommended that you obtain all of the program materials you need from the original source, even though you may have to pay for them. Materials that are obtained from other sources such as photocopies from other staff may be cheaper in the short run, but they may also be incomplete and out of date since program developers are constantly updating their materials.
- *Access to and utilization of personnel with appropriate evaluation skills.* Having someone available who knows about evaluation can be very helpful in implementing a sound evaluation plan. Questions #7 and #8 will provide you with a great deal of evaluation knowledge and numerous tools, but you may still want additional expertise for more complicated evaluations. It may be possible for you to partner with

experienced evaluators from a local university or to recruit organizational and program participants with the expertise you need.

CD FEATURE: There is additional material (first referenced in Question #2) called "How to Hire an Evaluator" on the CD-ROM included with this book.

- *Access to technical expertise.* There may be people in the community willing to volunteer their expertise to help you develop your plans or train your participants. Public relations companies in both Seattle and Portland, for example, provided paid and volunteer time to help asset-building initiatives in those cities develop their social marketing plans.

Fiscal and Resource Capacities

Adequate funding is just one aspect of what is needed to ensure the successful implementation of a project or program, especially since many evidence-based programs can be expensive to purchase and then require additional resources for training and technical assistance. There are many ways to pursue funding, including grants, gifts, matching funds, sponsorships, fund-raising events, and special sales. It will probably be important to pursue a variety of funding streams at the same time.

It's also important to develop other resource capacities to ensure your success. These could include cultivating volunteers, engaging and sustaining adult and youth participation, or finding specific technical expertise you may need from the community, such as educators and business leaders. You could also consider developing partnerships across many sectors, including faith-based organizations, local governments, law enforcement, juvenile justice institutions, neighborhoods, schools, business, and youth-serving organizations. These partnerships will give you not only the human capital you need to successfully implement your plans, but also access to resources other than money that will help you in your work, such as printing, transportation, meeting rooms, food, and so on.

Instructions for Using the Capacities Checklist

On pages 145–146, we've provided a short checklist that summarizes the key capacities we've outlined in this chapter. We suggest you go through this checklist to get a quick look at whether you think your community, initiative, or organization has the capacities needed to implement your chosen projects and programs.

WORKSHEET 5.1

Capacities Checklist

Do we have . . .	**Yes**	**No**	**Not sure**	**Simple steps we can take to unleash this capacity**
1. Our basic operational infrastructure?				
2. An understanding of our community's asset-building capacity?				
3. An understanding of our initiative's or organization's asset-building capacity?				
4. Asset champions?				
5. A variety of leaders?				
6. Collaborative partners?				

Worksheet 5.1 continued on next page

Capacities Checklist

Do we have . . .	Yes	No	Not sure	Simple steps we can take to unleash this capacity
7. Staff and/or volunteers who can implement our chosen programs or projects?				
8. The training needed to implement our chosen programs or projects?				
9. The technical expertise we need to implement our chosen programs or projects?				
10. The money we need to implement our chosen programs or projects?				
11. The other resources we need to implement our chosen programs or projects?				
12. The staff, expertise, and resources we need to adapt or modify our chosen projects and programs?				

CD FEATURE: If you see areas you think need deeper analysis before you continue, we've provided more detailed Capacity Assessment Worksheets on the CD-ROM included with this book. The capacity worksheets will help you review general and program-specific staff capacities, levels of technical expertise, fiscal and resource capacities, as well as structural linkages and collaborative partnerships. These more detailed worksheets will help you identify where you may still need to build some capacities and develop plans for doing so.

INTEGRATE ASSETS-GTO by building in regular orientation and training time for new staff, employees, volunteers, and participants to become familiar with your ongoing work. Orient them to the view that the Assets-GTO process is an integral part of the organization's ways of operating, and make sure they have the basic information about your initiative, program, or project to help them do a good job.

Looking Ahead to Sustainability

By building and maintaining the infrastructures and capacities needed to plan, do, and grow your work, you increase the likelihood that you'll be able to sustain your work. This means paying attention to the nuts and bolts of doing things like governance, decision making, documenting, managing, communicating, coordinating, and celebrating, as well as supporting the people involved by providing recognition, training, and support. Simply having regular meetings, compiling good records, and keeping communication channels open will help maintain the infrastructure.

To further support your work and build sustainability:

- *Look for ways to build formal and informal relationships among leaders, champions, and stakeholders within your initiative or program to strengthen your work;*
- *Look for ways to build formal and informal relationships across community groups, other organizations, and institutions; and*
- *Develop plans for increasing resources dedicated to your initiative, program(s), or project(s), as well as ways of securing ongoing, yet flexible, resources for your work.*

The Upper Bucks HC • HY Coalition (Pennsylvania) has established a specific goal in its long-term substance abuse prevention plan to develop strategies for program sustainability "by enhancing and strengthening the collaboration of the member institutions, associations, and citizens to more effectively leverage financial and human resources to prevent and reduce substance abuse among youth." Among its objectives:

- Expanding membership in the coalition to include faith-based organizations, police departments, municipal governments, and neighborhoods that include government-subsidized housing;
- Expanding youth involvement by holding a youth leadership summit and training Student Asset Ambassadors;
- Giving presentations and disseminating an electronic newsletter; and
- Developing a sustainability plan in which 100% of the coalition members will have agreed upon a role to support continued financing of programming provisions after the initial grant has ended.

Catalyzing leadership and asset champions builds sustainability. You want to recruit adults and youth who can be part of shaping and implementing your vision while developing enough capacity within your initiative or program to withstand leaders moving on. Shared leadership promotes community ownership and helps sustain your efforts by letting people know they have important roles to play.

Before Going on to the Next Chapter

You've now reviewed and refined your plans, goals, and outcomes, making sure that you'll be using effective projects and programs, that your work will fit within the context of your community, and that your initiative or program will have the capacity to carry out your plans. Now you're ready to move on to developing your process and outcome evaluation plans as you prepare to actually launch and implement your chosen project(s) or program(s).

In Question #6, you'll be identifying the individual program components you plan to implement and describing the actions needed to deliver each component—this is your actual implementation plan. Question #7 takes you through your process evaluation, which helps you make sure you put your plans into action with high quality. Question #8 guides you through the actual outcome evaluation of your project(s) and program(s).

PART THREE

Launch, Monitor, and Evaluate

You are now moving into the final stages of preparation to actually launch and measure your initiative project(s) or program(s). The next three questions will help you *plan* and *do* at the same time. The chapters are designed as a unit, with planning and implementation sections in each. We will walk you through the steps to prepare you to launch your project(s) or program(s), then monitor their progress, and, finally, measure the outcomes of what you've done.

The questions in this section are:

Question #6. What is your plan? (PLAN) This question guides you through bringing together in writing the projects and programs you've identified, tying them directly to your goals and outcomes, determining the components of the projects and programs you'll deliver, specifying the activities of each component, and looking ahead to your process and outcome evaluation so you'll know what you'll be doing before, during, and after your launch. *Question #6 begins on page 151.*

Question #7. How will you assess the quality of implementation? (PROCESS) This question will help you plan and conduct a process evaluation designed to ensure a high quality of project or program implementation. The process evaluation will help you identify how well you put your plans into action. This question also helps you examine and reflect on the implementation process itself, so you can strengthen and improve your programs and projects as you go. *Question #7 begins on page 173.*

Question #8. How will you determine if the program or asset-building initiative is working? (OUTCOMES) This question will help you finalize your outcomes, select the monitoring and measuring tools you'll want to use during and after your implementation, and make some decisions about how you'll report your findings. This stage is where you'll attempt to document whether the projects or program(s) led to positive effects among your participants in the ways you intended. *Question #8 begins on page 193.*

QUESTION #6

What is your plan?

(PLAN)

If you haven't done so already, you're about to launch the project(s) and/or program(s) you've been developing. Although planning sometimes seems to take attention away from initiative projects and programs, good planning improves implementation, which, in turn, leads to improved outcomes. So it's worth spending time up front. This chapter will help you bring together in writing the projects and programs you've identified, tie them directly to your goals and outcomes, determine the components of the projects and programs you'll deliver (such as a mentoring or life-skills training as a piece of the larger goal of decreasing substance abuse among teens), specify the activities of each component (i.e., break down how each component will be staged and delivered, such as which schools and involving how many teens), and look ahead to your process and outcome evaluation so you'll know what you'll be doing before, during, and after your program and projects launch.

At the end of this chapter you should be ready to launch your program(s) and/or project(s), but we've designed Questions #6, #7, and #8 to work together as both a planning *and* doing unit. So before you actually start, you'll want to look ahead to the planning sections in Questions #7 and #8 to make sure you have finalized your outcomes, developed your benchmarks, and selected the monitoring and measuring tools you'll use during and after implementation. Taken together, the planning sections in these three chapters will allow you to launch, monitor, and evaluate your program(s) and/or project(s).

Keep in mind that the more carefully you plan, the more likely you are to yield the fruits of your labors from answering the previous questions. We realize, however, that it may not seem possible, given the capacities your initiative or program has, to devote sufficient time and energy to filling in *all* of the detailed worksheets we have provided in this and upcoming chapters. We suggest you find a way to capture important baseline progress as you implement, monitor, and evaluate your program(s) and project(s)to ensure the integrity of process and outcomes.

The steps in this chapter will help you to:

- Identify the individual components of your program(s) or projects;
- Link the appropriate components to your goals;
- Break down, plan, and track each component into detailed activities;
- Make sure you've accounted for any additional resources or supports you need to achieve high-quality delivery of your plans; and
- Anticipate the process and outcome evaluation steps that need to occur before, during, and after the implementation of your program(s) and project(s).

Here's what you'll need to get started:

- Your completed logic model;
- The results of any previous assessments that may be relevant to this stage of your planning;
- Copies of any specific program materials; and
- Copies of the logic models for Educo's Teen Leadership Program and the Upper Bucks HC • HY coalition from Question #3 (pages 96–99) for examples of both program- and initiative-level details.

Final Steps to Prepare for Implementation

The following steps will help you clarify the details of your program(s) or project(s) and prepare you to evaluate the impact of your work. Most of this chapter will walk you through the use of a constellation of planning and recording worksheets that starts on page 156:

- *Worksheet 6.1, Projects and Programs.* This worksheet is designed for those of you working at the initiative level. This worksheet will help you clearly connect your goals to each of the Five Action Strategies you're targeting and then concretely connect the goals and strategies to the project(s) and program(s) you've selected.
- *Worksheet 6.2, Components.* This worksheet is for both initiative and program leaders to specify the broader components being employed to reach your goals and outcomes. You'll start this worksheet in this

A SNAPSHOT OF THIS STEP IN ACTION

Prevention Partners for Youth Development (PPYD), Onondaga County, New York

The vision statement for Prevention Partners for Youth Development is: "PPYD envisions a community that works together to protect youth and promote their development so they can identify possibilities to achieve their potential." To achieve this vision, the coalition's participating leadership, youth-serving community organizations, and volunteers agreed on the following five goals:

1. Building communities' capacity to promote the healthy development of youth;
2. Disseminating new knowledge and training on evidence-based research and practices;
3. Consulting with organizations and communities on implementation and evaluation issues;
4. Offering opportunities for networking and collaboration; and
5. Advocating for systems change to create more caring, respectful, and responsive environments for youth, including involving youth in decision making.

For each of these goals, the coalition then developed a set of components, or "deliverables," to carry out these broad goals. All of the coalition's work is intended to increase collaborative opportunities among the participating groups, so components and activities were all designed to provide those opportunities. For example, here are the major components used to work toward goal #1, building communities' capacity to promote the healthy development of youth:

- Convened regular monthly Community Capacity-Building Work Group meetings to connect community members to plan, implement, and evaluate evidence-based youth development practices in community settings;
- Conducted a Community Youth Mapping Initiative, which resulted in a report used in setting community priorities and planning in Syracuse/Onondaga County;
- Put theory into practice by assisting a local teen center, called the CANTEEN, to obtain funding, as well as helping youth design, implement, and evaluate their own programs at the center, which eventually averaged approximately 100 participating youth a day; and
- Utilized youth consultants and adult staff from successful local programs to transfer their knowledge and practice to other programs.

The coalition also leveraged funding from the New York Office of Children and Family Services and the United Way of Central New York to create a youth-development training curriculum for supervisors and administrators that included a six-month follow-up consultation with an evaluation component. Other fruitful collaborations included PPYD's work with a local funder to implement a Youth Philanthropy Project using youth from the Spanish Action League and Fowler High School as decision makers, as well as consultation with the Onondaga County Parks and the Department of Aging and Youth to involve 120 youth in the development of a new skate park.

PPYD uses a variety of tools to evaluate the impact of its work, such as satisfaction surveys and measuring participation rates, as well as examining the integration of youth development principles into other organizations.

chapter and finish it in Question #7. You will *plan* your components in this chapter, using the first four columns (component, goals linked to components, services anticipated, and participants anticipated). In Question #7, after you have implemented your project(s) and program(s), you'll use the remaining four columns of this worksheet to *record* dates delivered, the actual number of participants, the percentage of actual participants based on your expectations, and whether the component was delivered as planned.

- *Worksheet 6.3, Activities Details.* This is another planning and recording worksheet. In this chapter, you'll *plan* the actual activities needed to deliver your program components and anticipate who will participate, as well as determine when you'll actually do the activities, resources needed and their source, who will make sure things get done, and where the activities will take place. In Question #7, you'll *record* the completion date of each activity.
- *Worksheet 6.4, Summary Checklist.* This worksheet is designed to let you take one last big-picture look at all the details you've developed in this chapter and make sure all the bases have been covered.

We will describe what goes into each section and how to fill in each level, as well as provide examples. Working through these worksheets will help you get progressively more detailed in your planning and then do a final review to confirm all the tasks that will be necessary to complete before you implement your program(s) or project(s).

Start by Listing Your Project(s) and/or Program(s)

If you are creating or working with an initiative, the first worksheet for you is found on page 156, the Projects and Programs Worksheet. This worksheet is designed to help an initiative summarize its portfolio of programs and projects in one place, then provide guidance in clarifying which goals, as well as which programs and projects, are tied to which of the Five Action Strategies you're targeting. If you are planning a program only, you may find this worksheet helpful in thinking through the larger context of your program and how it fits into your organization's larger goals, but you may go on to begin with the next worksheet, if you wish.

The second worksheet, called the Program or Project Components Worksheet 6.2 on pages 160–161, is designed to help you track the main elements of each individual program or project you are planning to implement. If you are planning an initiative, you will want to fill out one Components Worksheet for each of your programs and projects; if you are planning a program, you will fill out one Components Worksheet for that program.

Instructions for Using the Projects and Programs Worksheet

You will want to have your logic model at hand, as well as the list of programs and projects you have selected from Question #3, whether you have purchased or adapted an existing program or designed a local innovation.

The process for completing Worksheet 6.1 is as follows:

1. Make as many copies of the worksheet as you need to write on.
2. Have your logic model and any other useful planning documents in hand.
3. Starting at the top, fill in the name of the person completing the form (this may be helpful to someone else who reads the material later and has questions); the name of the initiative, organization, or program (this might be helpful if you're sharing these sheets among stakeholders as reports or planning documents); and a concise summary of the initiative or community project under which this work is being done.
4. Fill in each goal for your initiative in the left-hand column. For example, if you were going to use the PPYD activities we just described on page 153 to fill in this worksheet, here you would write in the first goal we cited—"building communities' capacity to promote the healthy development of youth."
5. Fill in the corresponding Action Strategies in the middle column of the worksheet. Building on our PPYD example, you might see that engaging adults, mobilizing youth, and activating sectors are the three most relevant strategies.
6. Fill in the right-hand column with the program(s) and/or project(s) you plan to implement to achieve your goal. If you have multiple programs and/or projects for achieving a single goal, you can either use one worksheet for each goal, or you can summarize multiple strategies and programs under a single, overarching goal. Please feel free to modify the worksheet to make it fit your unique situation. Continuing to build on our PPYD example, one project related to mobilizing youth is conducting youth mapping across the county.
7. When completed, this worksheet will lay out the big picture of your initiative and/or the larger context of your program. Then you will move on to Program or Project Components on pages 160–161.

WORKSHEET 6.1

Projects and Programs

Name of person completing the form:
Initiative/Organization/Program: Summary:

Goal	Related Action Strategies	Project or program

Next, Break Down Your Projects and Programs into Individual Components

Now that you've identified your specific projects and programs, you want to identify and describe the main components of each one. By components, we mean the next level of detail about what you will actually do to deliver your programs. In the case of the Upper Bucks HC • HY initiative, for example, the larger goal is to reduce substance abuse among youth through a variety of education programs. The broad education program plan was broken down into a series of training and education packages provided to youth. These are the initiative's components, which include such projects as providing a LifeSkills Training course and expanding a mentoring program. Eventually, initiative organizers broke down each component into the series of activities required to implement their plans, including scheduling and conducting classes (you will do this in the next worksheet).

Worksheet 6.2 can be used by both initiative and program leaders to describe components, which goals are linked to each, and which services and how many participants are anticipated. As we previously mentioned, you will record some information about what really happened during implementation on this sheet in Question #7.

All these details will become part of the information you use to measure your progress. For example, you need to know if you have delivered enough sessions of a particular program to enough participants to achieve the intended outcomes of the program.

Instructions for Using the Program or Project Components Worksheet

The process for completing Worksheet 6.2 is as follows:

1. Make as many copies of the worksheet as you need to write on. An initiative will need multiple copies in order to detail the components of each of its planned programs and projects.
2. Have your logic model and any other useful planning documents on hand; for initiatives, you'll need your completed Worksheet 6.1, Projects and Programs.
3. Fill in a concise written summary of your program or project. Remember—taking the time to articulate details such as your summary not only helps you be clear about what you are doing, but such summaries can be used to communicate your goals to staff,

volunteers, and others. It is also useful to have the summary appear in future reports, since it will orient your audience to the program and its purpose. This will be especially helpful when introducing new staff or volunteers to the program or in your general communications about your activities. For example, a new program in the Bellevue (Washington) School District is "aimed at boosting student achievement among Latino students." This simple statement would be your program summary.

4. In the far left-hand column, write in the specific components of your program or project. In choosing how specific you need to be when identifying program components, think about what will be useful to monitor throughout the implementation of your program or project. You do not need to identify every single detail of running the program, such as copying worksheets; rather, think of primary components such as how many education sessions, one-on-one counseling sessions, school assemblies, or series of public service announcements (PSAs) you'll provide. Using our school district example, some sample components would include (1) presenting a Latino Student Leadership Conference, (2) forming a parent advisory committee, and (3) offering Spanish lessons for teachers.
5. Moving to the right, write in the goals that relate to each component in the next column. The goals will come from those you have specified in your logic model. If the component does not logically support your stated goals, you should think about how valuable the component is to your stated goals and consider whether or not to include the component. You may have to do a short review to make sure you tie the right components to your goals. You may have one overarching goal for a whole collection of components, or you may have multiple goals tied to multiple components.

   For example, the overarching goals for Educo's Teen Leadership Program are "youth develop a personal environmental ethic, show an awareness of personal leadership styles/goals, are interpersonally competent, and have a sense of purpose." Educo offers a variety of components to fulfill these overarching goals, including an after-school community program that culminates with a weekend backpacking trip.
6. In the next column, fill in the services you anticipate providing, sometimes also called *outputs.* Outputs are the direct products of program components and usually are measured in terms of work

accomplished. The anticipated services might be the number of hours or sessions you plan to deliver or the number of PSA ads aired in a media campaign. Outputs or services should be stated in precise terms. For example, a road sign that reads "Los Angeles this way" is not as helpful as a sign that reads "Los Angeles 100 miles." Like distance and destination signs on a highway, outputs indicate that your program is going in the direction that you intended.

Some examples of outputs include:

- The number and length of teacher or youth training sessions needed to implement your program (e.g., four sessions of 3 hours each);
- The number of meetings or events required to fulfill the goals of the program (e.g., ten weekly meetings); and
- The amount of materials distributed (e.g., three handouts, four worksheets, and one workbook to each participant).

Using Educo as an example, the Teen Leadership Program provides two semester programs each lasting four months. There are 12 weekly meetings, one full-day outing each month, and a weekend backpacking trip at program's end.

7. Next, fill in how many participants you anticipate for your program. In the Educo example, the goal is 12 youth per group for each semester.

There is also space provided at the bottom of the worksheet for you to write down any notes about progress, problems, or lessons learned as you go.

In the upcoming process evaluation you'll do in Question #7, the anticipated services or number of participants will be compared with the actual services delivered and the number of people who participated. If you are not achieving your expected goals, the difference between anticipated and actual outputs may be one important area to examine to find out why. By monitoring program outputs throughout the course of the program, you will also be able to gather information to make improvements while the program is active.

Now You're Ready to Plan Activities for Each Program or Project Component

Now that you've thought through the program and project components, each one needs to be broken down into the next level of detail. To plan the specific

WORKSHEET 6.2

Program or Project Components

Name of person completing the form: **Name of Initiative/Program:**	Date:
Program or project title: ***Summary:***	

Program/ project component	Which goals are linked to each component?	Services anticipated (hours/sessions)	How many participants anticipated?	Dates delivered?	How many actual participants?	% actual/ anticipated	Implemented as planned?

Worksheet 6.2 continued on next page

WORKSHEET 6.2 *continued*

Program or Project Components

Program/ project component	Which goals are linked to each component?	Services anticipated (hours/sessions)	How many participants anticipated?	Dates delivered?	How many actual participants?	% actual/ anticipated	Implemented as planned?

Progress, problems, and lessons learned

activities—the things you'll actually do to deliver the programs or projects—for each of your components, you'll be using Worksheet 6.3, Activities Details on page 164. Here, think about the individual *activities* that need to be completed in order to make each component successful. Each component is made up of several activities. To be able to track your results, it's important to list each of the activities necessary to implement the components of your program or project.

For example, to implement Educo's Teen Leadership Program, the organization needs to plan out all the details of what it takes to teach young people the wilderness skills they'll need to have successful, short outdoor experiences, culminating in full-day and weekend trips. We'll use some of the details of Educo's program as we explain how to fill out this next worksheet.

Instructions for Using the Activities Details Worksheet

The process for completing Worksheet 6.3 is as follows:

1. Make as many copies of the worksheet as you need to write on.
2. Have your logic model, other filled-in worksheets, and any other useful planning documents in hand.
3. Starting in the far left-hand column, write in the component on which you're working. This information can be transferred from the previously filled out Components Worksheet 6.2. From our Educo Teen Leadership Program example (p. 97), one component would be "an after-school community program."
4. Moving to the right, write down your key activities and details in the next column. Here you will fill in all the actions and activities you'll need to accomplish to implement your program or project, such as identifying, enrolling, or recruiting participants and recruiting and training volunteers. You'll also list the needed presentations and meetings and the steps you'll need to take to monitor the program while it's running. You can include promotional activities, such as creating and posting flyers to advertise the program or key steps you want to take to collaborate with other organizations, such as schools and service agencies. This step could also include staff trainings or when transportation and food might be needed. You may have already described some of these activities in your logic model or other planning documents.
5. Continuing to the right, now you'll fill in who participates in your program or project. Using the Educo example, the program is

targeted for youth from lower-income families. Their logic model indicates that Educo anticipates 12 youth per group will attend each of two semesters.

6. Next, fill in the scheduled dates of your program. Deciding the approximate dates for the completion of each activity will help a timeline emerge if you don't already have one. You can also use these dates to assess whether your program is being implemented in a timely fashion.
7. In the next column, fill in specifically who will be responsible for the various activities you've listed, including staff, volunteers, management, or any other personnel. Looking at who is responsible for all of the activities may reveal some staff or volunteer gaps that will help you develop some recruitment plans or tap potential partnerships for the additional people you need.
8. Next, fill in the kinds of resources you'll need to complete the program. Here you want to specify what resources you anticipate needing for each activity and where they'll come from. This may include money, as well as specific supplies needed, like food, markers, or paper. Will you need to purchase materials with grant funds or can you get them donated by local businesses or citizens? Use this step to double-check the specific amounts you put in your initial budget or budget request to make sure they're still correct. This information may also help you see needed changes.

   If you look at the Educo logic model, you'll see that they have actually indicated resources as the first column of information listed. Resources include staff and volunteer time, development time, the certifications they'll need for staff to teach the required wilderness skills, staff trainings, income, permits, equipment, and supplies. They've also listed recruitment and referrals as resources they need to meet their goals.
9. Finally, fill in—if relevant—where your program will be delivered. Here you will describe where you plan to hold the various activities and note whether certain locations require significant lead time to reserve or have other requirements, such as permits.

Remember, the final column on this sheet, "Dates of completion," will be filled in once your program is done in Question #7. You can also make notes as you go, in the space provided at the bottom of the worksheet, about partnerships developed or needed, progress made, problems encountered, and lessons learned in the course of designing and implementing your program.

WORKSHEET 6.3

Program/Project: ______________________________

Activities Details

Components	Key activities and details	Who participates?	Scheduled dates	Who is responsible?	Resources needed/source	Location/ details	Date of completion
Component							
Component							

Partners, progress, problems, and lessons learned

Other Elements to Consider

There are many details to consider when implementing a program or project. It's helpful to talk to other initiatives or organizations that have implemented either the program you've chosen or one similar to get ideas on important components and activities to anticipate and track. In the meantime, we want to point out several points to review as you prepare to implement your program, project, or portfolio of programs and projects.

Collaboration: Many funders *require* that collaborations be part of any project they support, so chances are you have participating partners in your initiative or program. If you haven't already established some strategic, collaborative partnerships with other groups, agencies, and/or organizations, now may be a good time to do so. Collaborations can be desirable because they may increase the potential effectiveness of programs or initiatives, reduce duplication, and broaden the base of those who participate. Collaborations can also help create new opportunities for obtaining funding and other forms of support.

Integration: Every effort should be made to integrate the current program or project with other programs and services and to identify any initiatives with which you share a common mission. This helps to ensure that resources are maximized and services are not unnecessarily duplicated within a community. You spent some time looking at this issue in Question #4, but now may be a good time to make sure you haven't missed something. Information that you gathered about other programs, services, and projects in your Resource Assessment (Worksheet 1.2) could be useful here.

Budget for Program: You may have already developed a budget for the specific program(s) or project(s) you'll be implementing. If not, now is the time to nail down the details. To supplement your own experience and expertise, you may be able to get budget information from program developers as part of the package you secure, or you may be able to get information from other organizations who have implemented the same program. If you have developed a local innovation, you may be able to get advice from organizations that have run similar kinds of programs to gain at least a rough idea of what your budget will need to be. The more details you can anticipate and estimate, the better your plan will be.

Budget for Initiative: Initiatives incur overall expenses as well. A number of asset-building initiatives have found it difficult to support themselves in the long run if they allocate too much too early for staffing and space. Identify what initiative partners can provide. In-kind goods and services ranging from office space and computer and phone use to printing and meeting space can help keep start-up and operating costs manageable. Initiative activities can be planned using the same ideas and questions as the budget for programs.

Culturally Appropriate Efforts: You have no doubt accounted for cultural and community factors as you have worked through the steps of your planning process. Continued awareness of, and attention to, cultural issues in all the planning, implementation, and evaluation stages of programs and initiative projects are important to your ultimate success. This goes beyond token acknowledgment of cultural and community factors and includes incorporating ethnic/cultural characteristics, experience, norms, and values of the communities you hope to involve during implementation. Ideally, a diverse group of community members has helped you develop and customize your plans in ways that will be relevant for the communities you want to serve. You also want to have staff and volunteers representative of your key communities involved in your program or initiative projects or, at the very least, have trained your staff and volunteers in cultural competency relative to your key communities. Your implementation plans may also include making sure that presentations and/or printed materials are translated into the appropriate languages or that the foods you serve are appropriate.

A Final Summary Checklist

What must be done to prepare for this program or set of initiative programs and projects? The Summary Checklist Worksheet 6.4 on pages 168–169 presents a series of prompts to ensure that the necessary activities and tasks are completed prior to beginning implementation. The checklist is not exhaustive, but summarizes all the points we've covered in this chapter. For some programs or projects, there may be additional tasks that must be done before starting, and the checklist is easily customizable. For example, you will need to conduct background checks on potential mentors for a mentoring program. You can modify the checklist document from the CD-ROM to customize it for your needs.

It may be helpful to organize the summary by component, creating an individual checklist for each separate part of a program or for each project of an initiative. For instance, in the case of an initiative planning to launch a public awareness and media campaign, you may want to produce a checklist for each component of the campaign to make sure you've covered all the media bases.

Instructions for Using the Summary Checklist

The process for completing Worksheet 6.4 is as follows:

1. You might want to do this one as a group, or you can divide the work among several people who can each be responsible for completing a checklist for an individual component. Then you can all bring your work back together and see if you've covered all the bases.

2. First, develop the core list of activities tasks that best represents your program or project.
3. Write in yes (or Y) for the tasks that have been sufficiently addressed.
4. For each task that has not been completed, write no (or N), and provide a short summary of a plan for addressing it in the future, as well as a projected completion date.
5. Fill in "not applicable" (or NA) if the task listed is not relevant to your effort.

You may wish to modify this worksheet to suit your unique situation, depending on whether you are running an initiative or a specific program.

INTEGRATE ASSETS-GTO by using the planning steps in this chapter as part of your initiative's or organization's overall strategic planning. The work you do to closely tie your strategies and activities to your goals strengthens your long-term planning. Do the "if-then" statements you drafted in Question #3 still make sense? Take some time to review and affirm the connections among your goals, planned outcomes, and your chosen programs and projects to make sure you're still headed in the right direction.

Looking Ahead to Sustainability

The important transition that occurs in Question #6 is that you begin to more smoothly manage both planning and doing. A balance of both is necessary to maintain momentum in your asset-building efforts. If you spend too much time planning, energy and enthusiasm can wane in the absence of action. If you spend too much time doing, on the other hand, you may wind up in motion that doesn't lead toward your goals. We like to say that you can think of *planning* as stepping with the left foot and *doing* as stepping with the right foot. Integrating planning and doing allows you to draw on the contributions of both planners and doers in your initiative, organization, or program.

To further build sustainability into your efforts at this stage, continue to think about strengthening important aspects of your initiative or program, such as:

- *Continuing to recruit effective leaders who will take appropriate actions to sustain the initiative or program.* Effective leadership will help you proactively respond to a changing environment so you can make needed adjustments while still maintaining your vision and goals.

WORKSHEET 6.4

Summary Checklist

Y/N/NA	Key activities	If no, plan for completion	By when
	Resources obtained		
	Person responsible identified		
	Staff trained		
	Duties assigned		
	Location identified		
	Time line written		
	Collaborative partners identified		

Worksheet 6.4 continued on next page

Summary Checklist

Y/N/NA	Key activities	If no, plan for completion	By when
	Cultural issues addressed		
	Program materials developed		
	Barriers or roadblocks considered		
	If preexisting program, all components are included OR adapted with good justification.		
	If building a new program, components are in line with principles of effective programs.		
	Other:		

- *Continuing to cultivate asset champions (youth and adults) who will guide and inspire your community change movement.* These may not be the usual community leaders or people performing in the usual formal roles, although they can be. Asset champions can help you continue to broaden the initiative or program reach through flexible, informal, catalyzing ways.
- *Continuing to develop adequate policies and procedures that will help you sustain your initiative or program.* By establishing measurable goals and procedures for evaluating your progress, you will have a way of systematically reflecting on your work that helps inform your actions as you move toward your goals.

The advantages of cultivating diverse leadership to help deepen sustainability and continuity are coming to fruition in the Healthy Communities Coalition (HCC) of Lyon and Storey counties in Nevada. HCC has a legacy of strong leaders networking within organizational hubs of community action, such as Central Lyon Youth Connections in Dayton and Community Chest, Inc., in Virginia City. Both of these organizations have served as a "training ground" for younger leadership under the tutelage of longtime human service professionals and community activists like Michelle Watkins and Deborah Loesch-Griffin, referred to as the Founding Mothers of HCC. These two codirectors are experts at local community coalition building, youth mobilization, and development of the larger vision of HCC's future role in statewide policy change. As seasoned leaders, they have been able not only to help strengthen HCC but also share the lessons they've learned in other professional arenas. They provide consistency to the initiative's operations while inspiring and mentoring younger, emerging leaders who will someday be able to transition into managing HCC.

Making sure you are clear about the contributions of both planners and doers—and integrating their ideas into your work—will help you build sustainability. One of your roles is to attract many different people to the many different tasks of asset building by remaining invitational. Keep inviting and informing. Find ways to revisit your vision, but keep going.

Before Going on to the Next Chapter

Now you've finished planning all the components and activities of your program(s) and/or project(s). If you have not already developed process and outcome measures, we recommend you do the following before formally launching your work:

- Do the planning portion of Question #7 on pages 173–183 to identify what process evaluation measures you'll monitor while your program(s) or project(s) are running.
- Do the planning portion of Question #8 on pages 193–207 to identify what outcome evaluation measures you'll use to assess how well the program(s) or project(s) worked after you're done.

Now is also a good time to reflect on and celebrate just how much work you've accomplished so far. You've gone all the way from a broad assessment of concerns and resources in your community, through the development of priorities, goals, and outcomes, then created a set of projects and programs linked to your goals. And you've detailed the components of your planned projects and programs; now you're ready to begin doing them.

In the remaining chapters in this section, you will plan and do at the same time, implementing your plans, evaluating the integrity of your process, and measuring your outcomes.

QUESTION #7

How Will You Assess the Quality of Implementation?

(PROCESS)

Now it's time to put your planned program(s) and/or project(s) into action. As you move ahead, you'll be measuring two facets of your work. One will be the *quality* of your implementation efforts. The emphasis in this chapter will be on ensuring a high quality of program and/or project implementation through a process evaluation. A process evaluation will help you identify how well your plan was put into action. The second facet you'll eventually measure is whether your program(s) or project(s) actually caused the improvement or outcome you intended. Outcome evaluation will be the focus of Question #8.

A process evaluation assesses the degree to which your programs and projects are implemented as planned. It includes an examination of:

- The degree to which activities specified in the logic model are implemented as planned;
- The quality of the activities implemented and midcourse corrections;
- The targeted number of people you hope to involve versus the actual number of participants who become involved; and
- The degree to which your targeted group members (youth and/or adults) participate as planned. This could mean evaluating the duration or intensity of your participants' experiences or their perceptions about the quality of their experiences.

Information from a process evaluation allows you to examine and reflect on the implementation process itself. You can use this process to help you monitor your program in progress while also gathering information to strengthen and improve the program as you continue.

How well a program or project is implemented is critical to obtaining positive results. Understanding what is working well and what's not working well helps you ensure that you are achieving your priorities, goals, and strategies. A well-planned process evaluation is developed *prior* to beginning a program or project and continues throughout its duration. The first part of this chapter will help you prepare your process evaluation, and the second part will guide you through using the tools and timetables you select to monitor your programs and projects while they're running. Eventually, some of the process measures you gather in this phase of your work will help support the outcome evaluation you'll begin in Question #8.

Remember, when we talk about "programs and projects," we mean any structured, intentional activity you are conducting. This could mean a port-

A SNAPSHOT OF THIS STEP IN ACTION

St. Louis Park High School 9th Grade Program

As part of the reporting requirements under its State Incentive Grant (SIG), the St. Louis Park High School 9th Grade Program had to conduct both process and outcome evaluations. Project staff began to develop and implement aspects of the project as early as 1998 and funding was received in 2000. The SIG grant supported the program through 2003. (The Minnesota Institute of Public Health, in cooperation with Youth Frontiers and Search Institute, is now marketing a version of the program called Building Assets—Reducing Risks.)

Project staff and evaluators used observations and a combination of individual and group interviews to measure the integrity of the program's implementation. A summary of both process evaluation findings and conclusions drawn from what was discovered in these interviews and observations was part of the program's final evaluation report.

Among the many findings:

- The start-up phase for the SIG grant was strong. The project was "up and running" fairly quickly in comparison to other projects of similar nature and scope.
- Teachers viewed the SIG grant project as a response to their concerns about the 9th-grade class, rather than something imposed upon them externally.
- Enforcement of school boundaries improved due to the implementation of a new schoolwide policy.
- The Parent Advisory Committee increasingly offered input regarding program implementation. Early meetings were characterized by parents receiving project updates; later ones involved staff actively seeking parent input.
- Leadership on the project stabilized in year two.

folio of asset-building projects and programs nested within the larger context of your coalition or initiative, or a more specific, individual program implemented by your organization. The process evaluation can be applied at both levels.

The activities in this chapter will help you:

- Develop a well-planned process evaluation *prior* to beginning your program or project;
- Map out what questions you'll ask, what tools you'll use, what your evaluation schedule will be, and who will be responsible for each task;
- Implement your process evaluation;
- Make careful midcourse corrections; and
- Prepare to conduct your outcomes evaluation.

A SNAPSHOT OF THIS STEP IN ACTION, ***continued***

Among the conclusions drawn from the process evaluation:

- A team approach was used for the project's leadership, which proved effective regarding program operations and services rendered to students.
- Students, teachers, and staff reported gains in a number of social and academic areas that they attributed, in part, to the 9th Grade Program. According to the project's findings, that meant the program was moving "in the right direction" in terms of reducing risk for 9th-grade students.
- Once staff began to see some changes, they started proactively addressing the issue of sustainability by seeking funds to continue—and even expand—the 9th Grade Program. Substantial funds were not initially forthcoming, which was discouraging.
- A factor that emerged as a clear contributor to the success of the program was the dedication and commitment of the staff involved, including teachers, student services staff, and administrators. Their ability to work together as a team, placing the needs of the students first, despite significant challenges and dwindling resources, had to be recognized. If this program were to be replicated, critical to success would be the choice of high-caliber staff.

One problem that emerged was the impact of budget constraints. Budget cuts at the school district, state, and federal levels made funding programs less accessible and more competitive, leading to uncertainty about the program's future. Budget limitations also delayed the planned readministration of the *Profiles of Student Life: Attitudes and Behaviors* survey from the fall of 2002 to the spring of 2003, affecting the program's evaluation design. These roadblocks were taken into account as the program moved forward.

Here's what you'll need to get started:

- Your completed logic model;
- Your partially completed Program or Project Components Worksheet (6.2); and
- Your partially completed Activities Details Worksheet (6.3).

Before You Implement: Organize Your Process Evaluation

Generally, the two most important process evaluation questions you will ask are (1) *Was the program or project implemented as planned?* and (2) *Was the program or project implemented with high quality?* Answering these two basic questions will provide useful data that will help you develop your short-term and long-term plans for improvement.

In the short term, tracking the different aspects of a program's implementation yields information about the components and activities that are working well and the ones that are having no impact or a negative impact on the program's success. This information then allows staff and volunteers to make mid-course corrections right away to keep the program on track. For example, New York's Prevention Partners for Youth Development (PPYD) conducts process evaluations with its coalition members through an annual survey and regular assessments at meetings and training events to see if the coalition's networking goals are being met.

In the long term, a process evaluation helps explain the final evaluation results. To ensure positive outcomes, you need not only an appropriate program with a solid rationale or theory that's based on the underlying issues you're trying to address, but also high-quality program implementation. In the St. Louis Park example cited above, for example, committed, high-caliber staff was identified as something that contributed to the program's success and an element necessary for replication.

Knowing whether or not the implementation was done with quality can tell you whether the selected program or project and its underlying theory of change are appropriate. For example, if the process evaluation indicates high-quality implementation but the program does not produce positive outcomes, then it is likely that there is a theory-of-change problem; your program does not produce the outcomes you expected.

In addition, the process evaluation provides information about the successful components and activities so they can be repeated in the future, as well as information about which activities need to be modified or discontinued. This is helpful when attempting to repeatedly conduct the program or project. A process evaluation can help to demonstrate a level of program or project progress to others, like the media or larger community, before the outcome evaluation has a chance to show results. For example, as part of its process evaluation, St. Louis Park High School program staff tracked media coverage of its activities to help gauge their impact.

The process evaluation can tell you something else very important—what's *not* working. Determining what aspects of your program are not working, honestly facing them, and communicating that information effectively without compromising the entire initiative, project, or program is very challenging for program staff. However, identifying weaknesses and making changes as a result is the mark of a great project over a good one.

The first step in preparing to do your process evaluation is to develop a short plan that will include:

1. What process evaluation questions will be addressed;
2. What tools will be used;
3. Your data-gathering schedule; and
4. The person or persons responsible for gathering the information.

Different types of data will answer different types of questions, and the information you need can be gathered at different times in the process.

The simple table on page 178 shows different process evaluation questions, their corresponding data collection activities, when you most likely will employ them, and the resource requirements of each.

In Tipsheet E, Ways to Gather Process Evaluation Information, on pages 179–181, we've provided a summary of some of the evaluation activities shown in the table on page 178. The tipsheet describes in more detail what some of these activities are, how to do them, and why they're important.

Develop a Simple Process Evaluation Plan

The Process Evaluation Plan, Worksheet 7.1 on page 184, will help you organize a simple plan for your process evaluation. The process evaluation questions shown in the table on page 178 are reprinted in this worksheet for you. You can modify them if you have other questions or more questions you wish to explore or if you want to use different terminology.

If you're working in an initiative, you will likely want to fill out a worksheet for each program or project; for a program you will likely need to fill out only one copy.

Process Evaluation Questions and Activities			
Process evaluation questions	**Evaluation activities**	**When conducted**	**Resource requirements**
1. *What are the program or project characteristics?*	Organizational assessment	Before	Expertise: low Time: low
2. *What are the program or project participants' characteristics?*	Demographic, asset, and risk factor assessment	Before/during	Expertise: moderate Time: moderate
3. *What is the participants' satisfaction?*	Focus groups Satisfaction surveys	During/after	Expertise: high Time: moderate Expertise: low Time: low
4. *What is the staff's perception of the program or project?*	Focus groups Interviews Program debriefing	During/after	Expertise: high Time: moderate Expertise: moderate Time: moderate Expertise: low Time: low
5. *What were the individual program or project participants' dosages?*	Monitoring individual participation	During/after	Expertise: low Time: moderate
6. *Did the program or project follow the basic plan for service delivery?*	Monitoring outputs	During/after	Expertise: low Time: low
7. *What were the program or project components' level of quality?*	Fidelity monitoring: staff Fidelity monitoring: observers	During/after	Expertise: moderate Time: moderate Expertise: moderate Time: high

*Not all these process evaluation questions will be relevant for every program or initiative.

Tipsheet E

WAYS TO GATHER PROCESS EVALUATION INFORMATION

You'll no doubt use a variety of methods for collecting your process evaluation data. Here's some additional information about a few key ones we've mentioned in this chapter.

Program Participant Characteristics

What they are: Demographic, asset, thriving, risk, and protective factor data. Demographics include variables such as age, sex, race/ethnicity, and native language.

How to do it: You have probably already gathered much of this information in the course of planning for and establishing your initiative, or as a routine part of running your organization, project, or program. Often, these types of questions are asked as part of an outcome assessment survey. Information can be gathered during an interview with each participant, as well.

Why it's important: So you'll know if your program or project is serving the youth and adults you'd planned to engage.

Satisfaction Surveys

What they are: Information such as how much the participants enjoyed the program, whether they got something out of it, and whether they learned what they expected to learn.

How to do it: The easiest way to collect this data is to administer brief surveys to participants as part of the program at the end of each session or activity. This is better than waiting until the end of the entire program or project because sometimes participants forget details from earlier sessions. Surveys can also be handed out at the end of a program with self-addressed, stamped envelopes so participants can complete the survey and return it later. This method, however, adds expense (cost of postage) and often yields a lower rate of completed surveys.

For a community coalition or initiative that provides training or other awareness-building activities, attendees might be asked not only about their satisfaction with the event, but also about their level of understanding about Developmental Assets and/or the local initiative before and after an event. Sometimes initiatives can work a few of these questions into ongoing surveys being conducted by other groups. For example, the Children First initiative approached the city of St. Louis Park, asking to include a short survey of questions about respondents' awareness of Developmental Assets and the initiative, and their level of intentionally doing asset building, along with the city's periodic citizen satisfaction survey, which asks questions about water and other municipal services.

Why it's important: Typically, participants who enjoy the program and find its learning useful will attend more often and be more engaged.

Tipsheet E continues on next page ▶

Focus Groups

What they are: In-depth interviews with a small number of carefully selected people brought together to provide their opinions. Unlike the one-way flow of information in a one-on-one interview, focus groups generate data through the give-and-take of group discussion.

How to do it: You want to have a variety of participants involved from your program or project to ensure good representation in your responses. In a focus group, there should be a limited number of questions asked, and the structure of the interview should be in a funnel: Each major topic should start with broad questions, then get more specific. Be sure to tape-record the focus group or have a designated note taker. The data can be analyzed by looking for the number of instances certain themes appear in the transcripts or notes.

Why it's important: Focus groups are an excellent method to learn about attitudes and get suggestions for improvement. Data from focus groups often yield "qualitative" (i.e., text) data as opposed to surveys, which usually yield "quantitative" (i.e., numerical) data. Qualitative data usually have rich descriptions of a topic area, such as satisfaction with a program. Listening as people share and compare their different points of view provides a wealth of information—not just about what they think, but also why they think the way they do.

Gathering Staff Perceptions of a Program

What they are: Staff perceptions about what worked and didn't work during the implementation of a program or project.

How to do it: Three methods for gathering data on staff perspectives are: focus groups, interviews, and program debriefing. In addition to what we've already mentioned about focus groups, an *interview* can be a good way to get detailed information about program implementation from staff. While interviews with staff involve a similar type of questioning as a focus group, in an interview you're talking with one person at a time.

A program debriefing is a straightforward way for staff to quickly meet immediately after a program component such as a session has been conducted and answer two questions: (1) what factors facilitated implementing this program component? and (2) what factors were barriers to implementing this program component?

Why it's important: Program staff are often in an excellent position to comment on how well a program is being implemented. Although they, like anyone else, may be biased, they still can provide a clear view from "the trenches" that can be vital for program improvement.

Tipsheet E continues on next page ▶

Fidelity Monitoring

What it is: A way to track how well your implementation matched the program developers' intentions.

How to do it: If you are using an existing best practice or evidence-based program, often these programs come with their own tools to assess fidelity. Check with those responsible for disseminating the program to see if they have these types of instruments. If such an instrument does not come with the program materials, call the program developer to see if an experimental tool is in the works or if perhaps other purchasers of the program have created one.

If you are using a homegrown program, a local innovation, or a best practice or evidence-based program that does not have a fidelity instrument, you can develop your own process using the materials on the CD-ROM that is included with this book.

Why it's important: Generally, the closer you can come to implementing a program as it was intended, the better chance you have of achieving your goals and outcomes. You want to be careful in implementation, but at the same time, you don't want to be slavish to something that's not working.

CD FEATURE: On the CD-ROM included with this book, you'll find several simple satisfaction surveys, information on how to conduct a focus group (in Question #1 folder), and a Project Insight Form for tracking staff responses in a program debriefing. You can also refer to the Fidelity Worksheet first referenced in Question #3.

Instructions for Using the Process Evaluation Plan

The process for completing Worksheet 7.1 is as follows:

1. Consider doing this worksheet as a team. Depending on who will be involved in implementing your programs or projects, you could also invite other individuals with additional expertise to join the team and develop the plan.
2. Have your logic model and any other relevant worksheets and documents on hand that you'll need to fill out your plan.
3. Make as many copies of the worksheet as you need to write on.
4. Starting with the first question, fill in which tools you plan to use, your anticipated schedule for getting the information, and the person or persons who will be responsible for gathering the data for each of the questions. Repeat this process for each question.

Keep in mind that you can also customize or add to your plan other process evaluation questions that fit your needs. For example, here are the six main questions the St. Louis Park High School 9th Grade Program used as the basis for its process evaluation:

1. *How are resources allocated and used to implement activities?* This included individual and group interviews to measure staff hours, skills, experience, and training required, budget required, and how accurately the implementation followed the original planned allocation.
2. *How is the work plan implemented?* This included an examination of consistency, participation rates in key services/activities, attitudes regarding participation in key services/activities, perceived magnitude of change, and perceived quality of work plan implementation.
3. *What obstacles or barriers were encountered as each activity was implemented?* This included dealing with such things as budget cutbacks, changes in the evaluation plan, and additional training of staff needed to effectively use the "I Time" curriculum.
4. *How did any broad changes in the school district or community change the context in which activities were implemented?* This included monitoring the school district's response to the program as well as observing the larger context of the community through both local media and scanning the monthly Children First newsletter.
5. *How are the preliminary evaluation findings used to improve implementation of activities throughout the project?* Individual conversa-

tions among the project coordinator, principal, and high school dean provided regular opportunities to discuss findings and solve problems as the project continued.

6. *What is the perceived impact of the project on students?* This information was gleaned not only from staff, administrators, and teachers, but through group interviews with students and parents as well.

What Comes Next: Conducting Your Process Evaluation During and After Implementation

Now you're ready to evaluate whether the program(s) or project(s) you developed in Question #6 were implemented according to your plan. This type of process evaluation is usually the most straightforward to conduct.

Monitoring the degree to which the program or project plan was followed involves developing a careful description of what was actually done; what, if anything, was left out; and how many people were reached or included in each component. Documenting whether or not the components were carried out as intended is essential in evaluating a program. If the program is not carried out as designed, then it's probably not reasonable to expect that the desired outcomes and goals will be accomplished.

The Program or Project Components Worksheet you partially filled out in Question #6 on pages 160–161 (Worksheet 6.2) is designed to now help you assess several aspects of program and project implementation and can be useful in a variety of situations. You have already filled out the columns on components, which goals are linked to those components, the services you expect to deliver, and how many participants you anticipate. Now we'll walk you through finishing the worksheet, including completion dates, tracking how many participants were actually involved with your program or project, how the percentage of participants influenced the quality of your implementation, and whether your program or project was completed as planned.

If you filled out several of these worksheets, simply follow the same instructions for each one, but our instructions are written for a single program or project for simplicity.

You may find that while you refer to various sections of various worksheets only periodically during the course of running a program or project, the Program or Project Components Worksheet should be used *all* of the time. Keep in mind that information is most useful when recorded during or immediately after each class or activity. Otherwise, important ideas that could help improve the chances of achieving results might be overlooked or forgotten.

WORKSHEET 7.1

Process Evaluation Plan

Process evaluation questions	Evaluation tools/method	Anticipated schedule for completion	Person responsible
1. What are the program or project characteristics?			
2. What are the program or project participants' characteristics?			
3. What is the participants' satisfaction?			
4. What is the staff's perception of the program or project?			
5. What were the individual program or project participants' dosages?			
6. Did the program or project follow the basic plan for service delivery?			
7. What was the program or project components' level of quality?			

Instructions for Finishing the Program or Project Components Worksheet

You have previously filled in the individual program or project components and the anticipated number of participants for each. The steps for completing the worksheet you started in Question #6 are:

1. Have on hand your partially completed Worksheet 6.2 from Question #6.
2. Fill in the remaining columns of the worksheet with these data:
   - *Date:* Record the dates of completion for each component in the appropriate column. In the "date" column, describe the period that the information in that row represents. Data may be aggregated across different time spans.

     The type of date(s) recorded here may vary. For instance, it may be helpful to summarize the number of actual one-on-one sessions on a weekly or monthly basis. For group programs that are delivered in a limited number of sessions (e.g., ten), attendance should be recorded for each session.
   - *Actual program participants:* You've already filled in the anticipated number of people you expected to participate in your program. Now you want to fill in the actual number of participants—sometimes called the program output(s)—in the appropriate column.

     If, for example, 100 children were expected to participate in your weekend library-reading program, but only 80 children participated, 100 children would be the "anticipated output" and 80 children would be the "actual output." Staff or volunteers can keep records or attendance logs of who attended to get this information. Or if you planned a community event to raise awareness about asset building and expected 200 adults and youth to attend, but only about 150 adults actually came, "200 adults and youth" is the anticipated output and "150 adults" is the actual output.
   - *Percentage output (% actual/anticipated):* One important part of understanding how well a program worked involves understanding how much of the program was actually received by participants. It is useful to think of programs like medications—in terms of dosage. If you are giving a ten-session training program to high school students and some students attend only seven of the sessions, those students do not receive the same dosage as those who attended all ten sessions.

     Similarly, if you planned for ten sessions but for some reason gave only eight, the program may not have been powerful enough to accomplish your desired goals and objectives. The *dosage* of a program can be expressed as the *% output.* This number represents a comparison of the anticipated outputs and actual outputs of a program. Dividing the actual output by the anticipated output and multiplying that number by 100 produces the *% output.* For example, if you anticipated ten people for a parenting session and only six attended, your equation would look like this:

$$6/10 \times 100 = \% \text{ output} = 60\%$$

The level of information recorded here will vary from program to program. In some cases, it may be useful to record data on a day-by-day basis. In other cases, it may be more efficient to present data by summing up information over weeks or months.

- *Implemented as planned:* The final column asks for a consideration of how well the components of the program were implemented. You are asked to rate the implementation as "high," "medium," or "low." If, for whatever reason, major changes take place in the actual implementation of a component (e.g., certain roadblocks or practical considerations make it necessary to change the design), a rating of "low" would be appropriate. If the implementation of the activity was very close to or exactly as it was planned, the rating would be "high."

In the section at the bottom of the page marked *Progress, problems, and lessons learned,* you can make any notes you believe are relevant about successes, challenges, barriers, changes to the program, or other lessons learned with regard to various activities.

Now you want to make sure that the individual activities you planned for each component were also completed in a timely fashion. Remember that each of your components is made up of several activities. Having listed each of the activities necessary to implement your program or project, you now want to make sure you successfully implemented them as part of your process evaluation.

Instructions for Finishing the Activities Details Worksheet

The process for completing Worksheet 6.3 is as follows:

1. Have on hand your partially completed Worksheet 6.3 from Question #6.
2. Fill in the *Date of completion* in the final column on the right-hand side. This will be the date the activity was actually completed.

3. In the box *Partners, progress, problems, and lessons learned,* record notes about relationships with partners, successes, challenges, roadblocks, changes to the program or project, and other lessons learned with regard to the completion of your activities.

What kind of results can you draw from a process evaluation? Results that can help you understand both what worked and what didn't work. Gleaning information in both of these areas will help you build a stronger program or project. For example, you may uncover evidence that your after-school basketball and homework-help program, held afternoons in the school gym, is not getting as many adult volunteers as you'd hoped. After conducting interviews and surveys, you find out that many of the adult recruits do not feel comfortable holding tutoring sessions in the gym isn't working well. You may also find out that adults involved in the program don't like all the paperwork they have to fill out. Discovering these kinds of specific opinions gives you a chance to redesign or fine-tune your program, which will increase your chances of success.

CD FEATURE: If you wish to track details of some of the other elements we discussed in Question #6 as part of your process evaluation, including recruiting target groups, developing collaboration partners, and levels of program integration, we have provided more background information and worksheets on the CD-ROM that comes with this book.

How Are You Doing So Far?

From the worksheets you've completed in this chapter, you should now be getting a general picture of how things are going so far. Another way to capture similar information more anecdotally is to use the "Progress, problems, and lessons learned" boxes provided on the bottom of several of the worksheets. In addition to the other data you're collecting, noting observations and reviewing these areas on a regular basis can help you keep track of how a program or project is doing or what needs to be tweaked to meet the needs of your participants. Surfacing and dealing with any roadblocks or problems that come up give you opportunities to make timely improvements now and to improve the future implementation of similar programs or projects, both for your own initiative or organization and for others who might use it. How often you address these topics may vary, but it is important to do it frequently and to keep a written record of how they are addressed. Understanding your successes also helps you make necessary changes or know what to build on when you repeat your efforts or even design new programs and projects.

If you want to capture some of these observations and trends into a summary, we've provided Worksheet 7.2 on page 189, How Are Our Evaluation Efforts Going? You can use this sheet as often as you'd like to do a short, written check-in on how you think your process is going so far. It may also be useful to have several people associated with your efforts fill in this worksheet and then compare notes. You can do this among a variety of participants working in different aspects of your initiative or among a variety of staff working in your program.

Instructions for Using the Evaluation Efforts Worksheet

The process for completing Worksheet 7.2 is as follows:

1. This may be a good worksheet to fill out as a team at a regular meeting. Use it at regular intervals to help your evaluation team reflect on and improve your efforts.
2. Make as many copies of the worksheet as you need to write on.
3. Write in the answers to the questions.
4. If you have completed this worksheet at least once, you could use the answer to Question #5 from the previous worksheet (about where to concentrate) as the beginning point for each review to help you track your progress. (You can also use this worksheet but substitute the word "initiative" for "evaluation" if you are looking at the impact of implementing a broader mix of projects and programs.)

Examples you could cite of your evaluation going well might be stating that data gathering is occurring at all points planned so far or, as in the case of the St. Louis Park High School 9th Grade Program, noting that the annual fall survey had to wait until spring because of budget constraints. One way of celebrating what's going well is simply to let staff, volunteers, and participants know how things are going, if that's appropriate. Question #5 on aspects of evaluation for short-term concentration may help you prioritize the most immediate steps you need to take to ensure a high-quality process.

INTEGRATE ASSETS-GTO by using additional copies of the worksheets in this chapter as forms for reporting to your staff, volunteers, participants, and stakeholders. The results of your process evaluation will also help you identify places where you need to build or strengthen your capacity, such as Educo discovering that they needed more staff or more staff time dedicated to their evaluation efforts to yield more information.

WORKSHEET 7.2

How Are Our Evaluation Efforts Going?

1. Aspects of our evaluation efforts that are going well:	2. How should we celebrate what's going well?
3. Aspects of our evaluation efforts that are not going so well:	4. What should we do about them?
5. Aspects of our evaluation to concentrate on during the next 3–6 months:	

Looking Ahead to Sustainability

Your process evaluation will yield concrete data about how well you're implementing your programs and projects, but it can also provide an opportunity for you to reflect on how well things are going. Go back to your vision and see if you are staying on course. Use this as a time to ask your stakeholders if *they* think you are on course. If you think you've strayed from your original vision, talk about ways to refocus your efforts.

To further build sustainability into your efforts at this stage, think about:

- *Actively sharing your goals, chosen strategies, and gathered information* with stakeholders;
- *Continuing to invite new people* and their fresh insights into your process; and
- *Reviewing and finetuning the methods you use* to assess your program or project implementation to continually ensure the integrity of your work.

How do these sustainability ideas look in practice? Since its inception in 2000, Project Cornerstone in California's Santa Clara Valley has built an inclusive movement by mobilizing diverse sectors of a multicultural community. The project's goals are grounded in its vision and mission, as well as in this clearly articulated statement of inclusivity:

> Project Cornerstone is committed to identifying and enhancing the assets of *ALL* children and youth in Santa Clara Valley. This shall include, but not be limited to, characteristics such as ancestry, color, creed, disability, economic status, gender, gender identity, incarceration or probationary status, immigration status, language, parenting status, race, religion, sexual orientation.

The project's 100 partner organizations have achieved significant results in promoting asset building among individuals, organizations, and systems to impact "the 3 Ps"—policies, programs, and personal behavior. These results have been achieved through a variety of projects, including:

- Forming *Diversity Teams* early on to fan out and conduct Outreach and Listening Campaigns, holding focus groups with Latino, Vietnamese, African American, Filipino, and GLBT (gay, lesbian, bisexual, and transgender) communities, as well as with youth in the juvenile justice system. The results of these focus groups helped maintain visibility and momentum for some of the project's ongoing plans;

- Providing *community trainings* in the asset approach for, among others, nearly 100 representatives from diverse faith communities, including Buddhist, Catholic, Jewish, Muslim, and Protestant community leaders; and
- Facilitating *Community Conversations,* a way for partners, organizations, and people in neighborhoods, clubs, and faith communities to share and discuss the results of the latest asset survey. Project Cornerstone provides the guidelines and materials; community participants are asked to provide the location, outreach, and facilitator. Besides sharing the survey results, these conversations help engage a variety of stakeholders in the local, hosting organization as well as in Project Cornerstone.

By constantly talking with its community, Project Cornerstone continually affirms the relevancy of its vision and mission while inviting new participants to the table all the time.

Making sure you're paying attention to implementation quality and integrity that adequately meets stakeholder needs will help you build sustainability. You will not only increase your chances of success, you will also earn the trust and confidence of your partners, which will have a wider impact in other efforts. You will also have a chance to stay on top of any midcourse corrections that may be needed to keep your efforts on track.

Before Going on to the Next Chapter

Now you've finished your process evaluation. Next, you'll move on to the planning section of Question #8 on pages 193–207 to identify what outcome measures you'll use to evaluate how well the program or project worked. Remember, in Question #8 as in the previous two chapters, we'll walk you through how to *plan* and *do* at the same time. You'll prepare your outcome evaluation plan, conduct it, and learn how to analyze and report on your results.

QUESTION #8

How will you determine if the program or asset-building initiative is working?

(OUTCOMES)

By this point you have likely determined the scope and scale your intervention will involve, namely, whether it's a broader asset-building initiative or a more narrowly defined program or project. Evaluating the entire scope of activities within an asset-building community initiative will be much more time intensive than evaluating one program. Initiatives typically comprise a portfolio of projects, including individual programs, community events, and plans to make larger-scale policy and community changes. Developing discrete, measurable outcomes for a community initiative presents a challenge, but if you've followed some of the previous steps in which we helped you break down your larger strategies into components and activities—and combine what you've learned with the steps in this chapter—you should have a pretty good idea about how to describe realistic measurable outcomes even at the community level.

By the time you've implemented your initiative, program, or project, you will probably have a pretty good idea about how well things went. In the preceding chapter, you measured and evaluated the *process* of your work. But the name of the game in Assets-GTO is to know fully and systematically what happened and what difference you made. By conducting an *outcome* evaluation, not only will you know if you've achieved your original goals—and really made a difference in the lives of young people—you also will know what's worth doing again and what needs improvement. By documenting your outcomes, you get a bonus—you also satisfy partners and funders. In this chapter, you will finalize plans to measure, evaluate, and report the outcomes of your work.

Simply put, an outcome evaluation determines whether an initiative, program, or project achieved the desired changes or outcomes. You first developed your outcome statements in Question #2, and since linking them with goals in your logic model in Question #3, you may have changed or refined your outcome statements during the course of your work. Working through this chapter will give you an opportunity to fine-tune your outcome statements one last time before you implement.

Outcomes can be assessed at various levels, including:

- Short-term or immediate changes (e.g., knowledge changes, such as youth learning basic outdoor skills);
- Intermediate changes (such as youth showing increased interpersonal competence);
- Long-term outcomes (such as youth feeling a sense of purpose in life).

An outcome evaluation of asset-building efforts assesses the degree to which the initiative or program made a difference in the lives of youth, adults, or aspects of the community. Just like your process evaluation, a well-planned outcomes evaluation is developed *prior* to beginning your program or project and continues throughout the duration of your work.

We have developed a series of steps to help you plan, implement, and report the results of your outcome evaluation. These steps are relevant to evaluation whether you are conducting a larger-scale initiative or an individual program or project. As noted at the beginning of this section, you will want to finish the planning section of this chapter along with the planning sections in Questions #6 and #7 before implementing your program(s) and/or project(s).

The activities in this chapter will help you:

Phase 1: Plan an Outcome Evaluation

A. Finalize your outcome measures

B. Choose an evaluation design to fit the program or initiative

C. Choose methods of measurement and data collection

D. Determine the target audience(s) for your measures

E. Determine when you will collect the data

Phase 2: Implement an Outcome Evaluation

F. Gather the data

G. Analyze the data

H. Interpret the data

Phase 3: Report the Results of Your Outcome Evaluation

Here's what you'll need to get started:

- Your logic model from Question #3 (Worksheet 3.3);
- Your plan for your initiative, program, or project from Question #6 (Worksheet 6.1); and
- Your plan for your process evaluation from Question #7 (Worksheet 7.1).

A SNAPSHOT OF THIS STEP IN ACTION

"Imagine That" Improvisational Theatre Troupe, Spartanburg, South Carolina

A countywide needs assessment in Spartanburg, South Carolina, determined that there were few existing youth programs that were innovative, youth-led, and focused on building youth strengths. After seeing an improvisational theater troupe from Utah, the local Youth Advisory Board decided to develop an innovative program called Imagine That, which would train high school youth to provide alcohol, tobacco, and other drug use prevention outreach to community members using improvisational theater. Imagine That is an educational and skill-building program for youth; participants learn creative theater techniques and methods and then use them to present performances in various settings in the community, such as group homes, churches, and alternative schools.

The program's main goals, as summarized in its logic model, focus on increasing assets and protective factors, as well as reducing risk factors related to alcohol, tobacco, and other drug use among participants and audience members. Several of the desired outcomes measured are: increased perception of risk of harm from alcohol, tobacco, and other drug use; improved beliefs and attitudes toward healthy behaviors; increased sense of competence; and changes in attitudes toward negative behaviors.

The evaluation plan for Imagine That is twofold and includes assessing changes in both youth participants and audience members. The plan includes pre- and post-test assessments, as well as follow-up surveys for each youth participant and a post-only survey for the audience and parents of the participants. To determine the longer-term effectiveness of Imagine That, additional methods, such as structured interviews, are used to obtain qualitative information about this innovative program. In addition, there is an emphasis on gathering follow-up data to determine the long-term effectiveness of participating in Imagine That.

Upcoming sections of this chapter will describe the various tools used by Imagine That and others that you may find useful to customize your own outcome evaluation plan.

Phase 1: Plan an Outcome Evaluation

A. Finalize your outcome measures

Outcomes are the changes that occur as a result of an initiative, program, or project. You initially developed your outcome statements in Question #2 (page 61) and organized them into your logic model in Question #3 (page 95). As we stated then, common outcomes for program-level interventions are typically changes at the individual level, such as new knowledge, attitudes, and skills. Remember, though, that positive changes in knowledge, attitudes, and skills do not always lead to changes in behavior. For instance, even if students believe that smoking is dangerous to their health, and they know how to resist peer pressure to smoke, they may still become or remain smokers.

In addition to measuring individual-level behavior, there are also outcomes at other levels that you may want to assess. For example, if you are doing a large-scale initiative designed to change school or community conditions, outcomes may include changes in school environment, improved community collaboration among human service agencies, or an increase in asset-building efforts within a particular program. In addition, policy-level changes may also be critical in reaching your ultimate goals. For example, perhaps a school develops a policy that advocates youth being recruited to become meaningful partners in decision-making structures by having them join boards or committees. This policy shift in and of itself is one kind of outcome, but as participating youth become increasingly empowered and develop a deeper commitment to school and academic achievement, you can measure that longer-term impact as an outcome as well.

When finalizing your initiative-level outcome measures, remember:

Initiative-level outcomes could include:

- Changes in the policies or practices of a youth-serving organization to build assets;
- Changes in systems to create a positive organizational climate for asset building;
- Changes in funding streams to prioritize asset-building initiatives throughout the community;
- Changes in how organizations and agencies mobilize their own internal asset-building capacities;
- Changes in grant-making policies to require applicants to include asset-building methods in their programs; and

- Changes in community awareness about the asset-building movement.

Evaluating a program with a starting and stopping point, structured activities, and the same participants over time is often more straightforward than evaluating a large-scale community initiative. When finalizing your program-level outcome measures, remember:

Program-level outcomes could include:

- Changes in youth and/or adult knowledge of how to build assets for and with youth;
- Changes in the frequency and intentionality of asset building by both youth and adults;
- Changes in the level of assets of youth (any or all eight categories);
- Changes in negative behaviors, such as drug use;
- Changes in youth self-efficacy or self-esteem; and
- Changes in the knowledge of administrative, program, and supervisory staff about how to infuse asset building in their work.

Before moving on to selecting the instruments you'll use to measure your outcomes, now is the time to do one last quick review of your outcome statements to make sure you've covered all the bases. Here's a quick checklist to help you:

Have you created outcomes that:	**Yes / No**
Affect actual behaviors?	
Affect larger groups of people?	
Are short term and longer lasting?	
Are realistic?	
Are specific?	
Have at least one measure for each?	
Use the shortest measure possible?	
Are formatted appropriately?	

B. Choose an evaluation design to fit the program or initiative

Now you're ready to develop the overall architecture of your outcome evaluation, your *evaluation design*. This evaluation design will help you reach the best understanding of your initiative's or program's effectiveness. At this stage, you are determining the optimum timing, breadth, depth, and frequency of your evaluation. The evaluation design you choose will help determine the degree to which you can have confidence that it was your initiative or program that created any positive outcomes (i.e., demonstrating a cause-and-effect relationship).

Here we describe five common evaluation designs:

1. **Post only.** This design allows you to examine specific results of your participants at the conclusion of the program or project. However, it's considered the weakest evaluation design. Post only is frequently used when it's necessary to determine the presence or absence of a characteristic (e.g., blood alcohol level when measuring intoxication) or to determine if a standard is achieved (e.g., passing a driving test). Because you gather no baseline information before you implement your program or project, this design isn't as useful as one in which changes can be measured in order to examine whether the intervention was related to the outcome.
2. **Pre-post.** The minimal standard in the field is to have participants complete a survey (or other measurement tool) prior to their participation in the program or project and then complete the same survey (or tool) at the end of the program or project. With this design, change can usually be calculated by comparing your baseline data (i.e., a measurement taken before the project or program) to the data gathered after the project or program is completed. The measurement that's done twice (before and after) must be the same measurement done in the same way in order to be comparable. Also, you need to allow enough time for your program or project to demonstrate outcomes.

   Although this design is an improvement over the post only, you still can't have complete confidence that it was your program or project that was responsible for the outcomes. There may be many other reasons a target group changes that have nothing to do with your program, such as changes in local enforcement policies or laws, other new programs, or media campaigns.
3. **Retrospective pre-post.** This is a special case of the pre-post design in which participants at the end of a program or project rate themselves then and now. The results are based on participants remembering back to what they were like before the program or project

started and making a rating based on that memory. This design has certain advantages:

- Only administering the measure once reduces the burden to the participant and the cost of the evaluation;
- It may result in more honest answers as the participants have presumably come to trust the program staff and have a better understanding of the concepts; and
- There is no need for names or codes to track participants over time, which better ensures confidentiality.

However, this design has all the drawbacks of the standard pre-post plus a new one: It may be difficult for participants to remember accurately what they were like before the program started.

4. **Pre-post with a comparison group.** The way to have more confidence that your program or project was responsible for the changes in outcomes is to assess a group similar to your target group that did *not* participate in the program, called a comparison group. In this design, you assess both groups before, deliver the program to one group (called the intervention or program group), and then measure both groups after. The challenge is to find a group before your program or project begins that is similar to your program group in demographics (e.g., gender, race/ethnicity, socioeconomic status, education) and in the situation that makes them appropriate for the program (e.g., both groups are adolescent girls at risk for dropping out of high school). The more alike the two groups are, the more confidence you can have that the program or project was responsible for the changes in the outcomes of the program group. A typical example of a comparison group situation is when a program is given in a school to one 8th-grade homeroom class and not to another similar 8th-grade homeroom class.
5. **Pre-post with a control group.** In this design, participants are randomly assigned to the intervention group or to a control group. Random assignment means that each person has an equal chance of winding up in either group (e.g., flip a coin to assign each participant to a group). Sometimes you can randomly assign larger groups like entire schools if you're working with a large enough number of participants.

   A control group is a comparison group that is the result of random assignment. This is the best-known way to ensure that both groups are equal. This design gives you the most confidence to claim that your program or project caused the changes that were found. However, because of the high cost of such a design, it's unlikely that you'll be involved in conducting this design unless you're part of a large-scale effort, such as a well-financed university project or a grant-funded demonstration program.

Your final step at this stage will be to select the evaluation design that's going to work best for you. You have to balance costs, the level of expertise to which you have access, and ethical considerations with the level of confidence in the results the design will give you. Although the pre-post design with control group gives you the most confidence that your program was responsible for the changes in outcomes, it's also the most difficult to implement, costs the most, and raises ethical issues about giving some people a beneficial program while withholding it from others at random.

You can use the evaluation design comparison chart below to help you weigh the pros and cons of the five different approaches.

Comparisons of the Five Common Evaluation Designs

Methods	Pros	Cons	Cost	Expertise
Post only	Easy to do, provides some information	Cannot measure change	Inexpensive	Low
Pre-post	An easy way to measure change	Only moderate confidence that your program caused the change	Moderate	Moderate
Retrospective pre-post	Easier than the standard pre-post	Only moderate confidence that your program caused the change *and* it may be hard for participants to recall how they were at the start	Inexpensive	Low
Pre-post with a comparison group	Provides good level of confidence that your program caused the change	Can be difficult to find group that is similar to program group	High; doubles the cost of the evaluation	Moderate to high
Pre-post with a control group	Provides excellent level of confidence that your program caused the change	Difficult to find group willing to be randomly assigned; ethical issues of withholding beneficial program from control participants	High; doubles the cost of the evaluation	High

C. Choose methods of measurement and data collection

Once you choose your design, you'll need to decide how to collect your data. There are strengths and weaknesses to various data collection methods. We recommend that you include a combination of data collection methods and tools to create the best possible picture of your initiative's or program's effectiveness. Ideally you want to collect both qualitative and quantitative data:

- *Quantitative methods answer who, what, where, and how much.* Emphasizing numbers, these methods, often using a survey instrument, target larger groups of people and are more structured and standardized than qualitative methods; this means the same procedure is used with each person.
- *Qualitative methods answer why and how and usually involve talking to or observing people.* Emphasizing words instead of numbers, qualitative methods present the challenge of organizing the thoughts and beliefs of those who participate into patterns of themes. Qualitative evaluations usually target fewer people than quantitative methods.

Tipsheet F, Data Collection Methods at a Glance, which starts on page 202, summarizes many of the standard methods used for collecting data, the pros and cons of each, cost, time to complete, the usual response rates, and what kind of expertise may be needed to use each tool. These methods are most often used when evaluating specific programs and projects, but you may find some of them useful to measure aspects of change at the community initiative level as well.

Search Institute surveys such as the Developmental Assets Profile (DAP) and Me and My World can be useful measurement tools in your evaluation, particularly because they are asset focused. In addition, there are two other models for measuring change at the community level we'd like to describe. There is no one "right" way to evaluate outcomes; you'll need to review the various methods available and decide which are best suited to your community and evaluation plans.

Community-Change Measure #1: Tracking of Actions

In this process, data are collected on the *changes in programs, policies, and practices within a community that are a result of your group's efforts.* Groups who have used this process have found it easy to understand and helpful both to explain their actions to their local community and to generate future support. The kind of data collected in this measure can easily be summarized into graphs, which are useful for local newsletters and media reports as well as planning for

Tipsheet F

DATA COLLECTION METHODS AT A GLANCE

Methods	Pros	Cons	Cost	Time to complete	Response rate	Expertise needed
Interviews—face-to-face and open ended	Gather in-depth, detailed info; info can be used to generate survey questions	Takes much time and expertise to conduct and analyze; potential interview bias possible	Inexpensive if done in-house; can be expensive to hire interviewers and/or transcribers	About 45 min. per interview; analysis can be lengthy depending on method	People usually agree if it fits into their schedule	Requires good interview/conversation skills; formal analysis methods are difficult to learn
Open-ended questions on a written survey	Can add more in-depth, detailed info to a structured survey	People often do not answer them; may be difficult to interpret meaning of written statements	Inexpensive	Only adds a few more minutes to a written survey; quick analysis time	Moderate to low	Easy to analyze content
Participant observation	Can provide detailed info and an "insider" view	Observer can be biased; can be a lengthy process	Inexpensive if done by staff or volunteers	Time consuming	Participants may not want to be observed	Requires skills to analyze the data
Archival research	Can provide detailed information about a program	May be difficult to organize data	Inexpensive	Time consuming	Participants may not want certain documents reviewed	Requires skills to analyze the data
Focus groups	Can quickly get info about needs, community attitudes, and norms; info can be used to generate survey questions	Can be difficult to run (need a good facilitator) and analyze; may be hard to gather 6 to 8 people together	Inexpensive if done in-house; can be expensive to hire facilitator	Groups themselves last about 1.5 hours	People usually agree if it fits into their schedule	Requires good interview/conversation skills; technical aspects can be learned easily

Tipsheet F continues on next page ▶

Methods	Pros	Cons	Cost	Time to complete	Response rate	Expertise needed
Observation	Can see a program in operation	Requires much training; can influence participants	Inexpensive; only requires staff time	Quick, but depends on the number of observations	Not an issue	Need some expertise to devise coding scheme
Self-administered surveys	Anonymous; inexpensive; easy to analyze; standardized, so easy to compare with other data	Results are easily biased; misses info; dropout is a problem for analysis	Moderate	Moderate, but depends on system (mail, distribute at school)	Moderate, but depends on system (mail has the lowest)	Little expertise needed to give out surveys; some expertise needed to analyze and interpret the data
Telephone surveys	Same as paper and pencil but allow you to target a wider area and clarify responses	Same as paper and pencil but miss people without phones (those w/low incomes)	More than self-administered	Moderate to high	More than self-administered	Need some expertise to implement a survey and to analyze the data
Face-to-face structured surveys	Same as paper and pencil, but you can clarify responses	Same as paper and pencil but requires more time and staff time	More than telephone and self-administered surveys	Moderate to high	More than self-administered survey (same as telephone survey)	Need some expertise to implement a survey and to analyze and interpret the data
Archival trend data	Quick; inexpensive; a lot of data available	Comparisons can be difficult; may not show change over time for many years	Inexpensive	Quick	Usually very good, but depend on the study that collected them	No expertise needed to gather archival data, some expertise needed to analyze and interpret the data

Tipsheet F continues on next page

Methods	Pros	Cons	Cost	Time to complete	Response rate	Expertise needed
Record review	Objective; quick; does not require new participants	Can be difficult to interpret; often is incomplete	Inexpensive	Time consuming	Not an issue	Little expertise needed; coding scheme may need to be developed

CD FEATURE: If you need more information about some of the data collection methods shown in the chart, please refer to the CD-ROM included with this book. You will find background material on surveys (including use of Search Institute surveys), archival trend data, observation, record review, focus groups, unstructured interviews, open-ended questions on a self-administered survey, and participant observation.

program staff looking at the trends over time. For example, a substance abuse prevention community coalition in Spartanburg, South Carolina, used this data not only to show its impacts to funders but also to successfully address criticism from a local newspaper that members were "just sitting around and talking."

The Tracking of Actions process involves maintaining event logs of community changes. Community changes are new or modified programs, policies, or practices in the community facilitated by the asset initiative. Examples of community changes include: getting a youth-led committee established at the local high school that will have actual responsibility for setting school policies; getting an ordinance passed that bans alcohol at the local minor league baseball stadium; or creating a high school–middle school buddy program to help middle schoolers transition to high school. These changes must have been planned and facilitated by your group to qualify as community changes. Event logs documenting each of these changes are monitored and converted into a cumulative chart from month to month (with flat lines indicating no activity) so that trends can be assessed over time.

On these logs, statements of community changes should include information about the impact on the community such as the number of schools changing policies. Changes that have not yet occurred, which are unrelated to the group's goals, or which the initiative had no role in facilitating, are not considered community changes for the initiative.

To be included, community change must meet all of the following criteria:

- The events must have actually occurred, not just be planned;
- The events must include community members external to the initiative or program or outside the committee or subcommittee advocating for change;
- The events are related to the initiative's or program's chosen goals and specific outcomes;
- The events involve new or modified programs, policies, or practices of governmental bodies, agencies, businesses, or other sectors of the community; and
- The events are facilitated by individuals who are members of the initiative or program or are acting on its behalf.

We will show you how to conduct a Tracking of Actions process beginning on page 209 when we introduce and discuss Worksheets 8.1 and 8.2.

Community-Change Measure #2: Key Leader Survey

The second community-level change measure we want to describe is called a Key Leader Survey.[1] This involves surveying people within a community who are perceived as representative of their communities for changes in awareness, interest, and involvement around the Developmental Assets model.

Key Leader Surveys have a long history, and many studies have shown that use of these individuals as representatives of their community is justified. Key leaders are valuable resources of information because of their position, expertise, and familiarity with the community. They have an excellent vantage point from which to observe the impact of asset-building initiatives and are usually in a position to influence local policies. When resources are limited, as is often the case with community efforts, surveying influential people who have knowledge of local practices can be a good way to get information about awareness, interest, and involvement in Developmental Assets.

We will show you how to conduct a Key Leader Survey beginning on page 210 when we introduce and discuss Worksheets 8.3, 8.4, and 8.5.

D. Determine the target audience(s) for your measures

Usually, selecting your design and measures also involves deciding the target audience for your measures. If you are conducting a prevention program with 50 8th graders and have a comparison group of 50 similar 8th graders who do not receive the program, then ideally you can gather information from 100 students—everyone in each group. Also, if you plan on doing two data collection points (e.g., pre and post), remember it is always best to match the participants if you can. This means that you match each person's pre and post survey and look at changes over time. This requires a fair amount of planning to identify which survey belongs to whom. If your program is a community-wide media campaign, you may not plan to survey or collect data at two different points and you certainly can't assess everyone in the community. You will need to use a smaller *sample* of the overall population.

The larger and more representative the sample is of the overall population,

---

1. Goodman, R. M., Wandersman, A., Chinman, M., Imm, P., & Morrissey, E. (1996). An ecological assessment of community-based interventions for prevention and health promotion: Approaches to measuring community coalitions. *American Journal of Community Psychology, 24,* 1, 33–61. De la Cruz, D. S. (1997). *A quantitative evaluation to determine the effects of a community-based program on community key leaders' levels of awareness, concern, and action toward the reduction and prevention of the abuse of alcohol, tobacco, and other drugs.* Ph.D. dissertation, University of South Carolina, School of Public Health.

the more confidence you can have about stating that the results of your sample apply to the overall population. For example, a representative sample of 4th graders exposed to a community-wide antidrug media campaign might include some 4th graders from each elementary school in the community, equal numbers of boys and girls, and might reflect the ethnic/racial makeup of the community. If the community is 50% White, 35% African American, and 15% Hispanic, you should strive to sample a group with the same proportions.

E. Determine when you will collect the data

The timing of your measurements is important and will be determined by your evaluation design. If you select a pre-post design for a particular program, then you'll need to conduct one measurement *before* your participants receive the program and then again *after* they complete the program. Assessing the level of change right after the end of the program will show whether the program did what it claimed it would do.

Sometimes, if you have enough resources and you can contact the participants after the program is completed, you can measure a third time, perhaps 3, 6, or 12 months after the conclusion of the program. This is important because it's useful to determine if positive change continues or fades over time.

Typically, archival data such as health department records of large numbers of people are used to track risk factors and behaviors over long periods of time, perhaps every 6 months or every year. Although it may be unrealistic to believe that one program will affect these long-term risk factors and behaviors, more intensive community-based initiatives that exist for years can produce changes in archival data.

Tipsheet G, Protecting Evaluation Participants, on page 208, offers several important issues to consider as you prepare to conduct surveys, interviews, and other types of data collection.

Phase 2: Implement an Outcome Evaluation

F. Gather the data

Regardless of the methods you choose, the first step in actual data gathering is to determine who will be the best person(s) on your evaluation team to collect your data. Remember, your choice could affect the results. Will the participants feel comfortable with the person or people you choose? Will they provide honest information, or will they try to make themselves look good for a superior?

Tipsheet G

PROTECTING EVALUATION PARTICIPANTS

There are several important things you need to do to protect the privacy of your evaluation participants as well as to ensure the integrity of your data collection.

1. Get informed consent before you start

Potential respondents in your evaluation must be given the opportunity to give their consent to their participation. Many times this is accomplished through written consent. Participants (or their legal guardians if they are under 18) sign a consent form agreeing to take part in the evaluation. This is called obtaining "active consent." If a youth under 18 has a guardian sign for her or him, it's also customary to have the youth sign an "assent" form. Although not binding, it does signal that the youth is knowingly participating. Some funders and many states require researchers or evaluators to obtain active consent. However, in others, it's often sufficient to obtain "passive consent," in which the potential participant is given the opportunity to refuse to participate verbally, without using a consent form. In either case, your potential participants must be informed about the purpose of the evaluation, told the degree to which their answers will be kept confidential (and possibly anonymous), and told that they can decline to participate at any time with no negative consequences.

2. Keep all information you collect confidential

You should guarantee that the individual responses of your participants will not be shared with anyone except the evaluation team unless the information reveals someone with imminent intent to harm her- or himself or others (a legal statute that varies by state). Confidentiality is honored to ensure more accurate information and to protect the privacy of the participants. Common safeguards include locking the data in a secure place and limiting the access to a select group, using code numbers in computer files, and never connecting data from one person to her or his name in any written report (e.g., only report grouped data such as frequencies or averages). You should talk with an evaluator/consultant to determine what levels of confidentiality are required in your state.

3. Ensure anonymity

In many cases, if you guarantee that people's responses will be anonymous and that no one will be able to tell which responses they gave, the participants will be more honest and the data more accurate. Assuring anonymity is important to participants. However, if you plan to match subjects on a pre and post measure, you must have some identifying information upon which to match the surveys. In many cases, this may be a code, such as a combination of numbers and letters such as initials and birth date. If this is the case, it will be important to have the same code for pre and post. There are usually only one or two evaluators who will need to know which person "belongs" to which survey in case it's necessary to contact that person (to remind them to complete a survey, for example).

Can the person gathering the data be as objective as the task requires? These important issues arise in data collection regardless of the methods used.

As you implement your initiative, program, or project and begin data collection for your outcome evaluation, you may be using any of the tools we have suggested so far. We'll concentrate in this section on showing you how to use the two community change tools we previously discussed, the Tracking of Actions and the Key Leader Survey.

How to Track Community Changes

We have included two worksheets to help you track these important community changes: the Community Change Event Log Worksheet 8.1, found on page 211, and the Community Change Summary Worksheet 8.2, found on pages 212–213.[2]

When maintaining tallies from month to month of the number of community changes, only count the first instance of a new program or project in the community as a community change, since it constitutes a change in a program or practice in the community. Also, a change in policy (e.g., ordinance, law, bylaw) constitutes a community change upon its *implementation date,* as opposed to when it was passed. Not all first-time events are community changes; the event must meet all parts of the definition of a community change. For example, initiative members simply attending a seminar for the first time is not an example of an actual community change since it is not a new or modified program, policy, or practice of an organization, but an activity.

Instructions for Using the Community Change Event Log

The steps for completing Worksheet 8.1 are as follows:

- Using the criteria referenced above, record information about the community change in the Community Change Event Log. Since these changes can take a long time to realize, you will be able to track each one as it happens.
- Record the data and then answer the questions in the columns of the Event Log.

These questions are designed to guide you in deciding whether you have a genuine community change or an event that is really a step toward a community

---

2. The event log is adapted from the Community Tool Box devised by Francisco, V. T., Paine, A. L., & Fawcett, S. B. (1993). A methodology for monitoring health action coalitions. *Journal of Health Education Research: Theory and Practice, 8*(3), 403–416.

change. The Event Log helps ensure that it was your initiative or program that caused the change and that is linked to your desired outcomes. All of these criteria must be met for the event to be identified as a community change.

LEARN MORE: The Community Tool Box offers a wide variety of tools useful for community mobilization efforts. It can be found at http://ctb.ku.edu/tools/en/sub_section_tools_1364.htm.

The second worksheet, pages 212–213, is Worksheet 8.2, a Community Change Summary. It is designed to help you tally all of the community changes each month. There is room to record the number of changes as well as a brief description, which will be shorter than those you recorded in the Event Log. From this summary worksheet, you can make graphs of the changes to show stakeholders, funders, and other constituents. As an example, in the following graph, this initiative had one change in January, then another in April and in May (total of three) and so on, so that by December, there were a total of seven changes recorded since January. This graph shows that this initiative is slowly making progress.

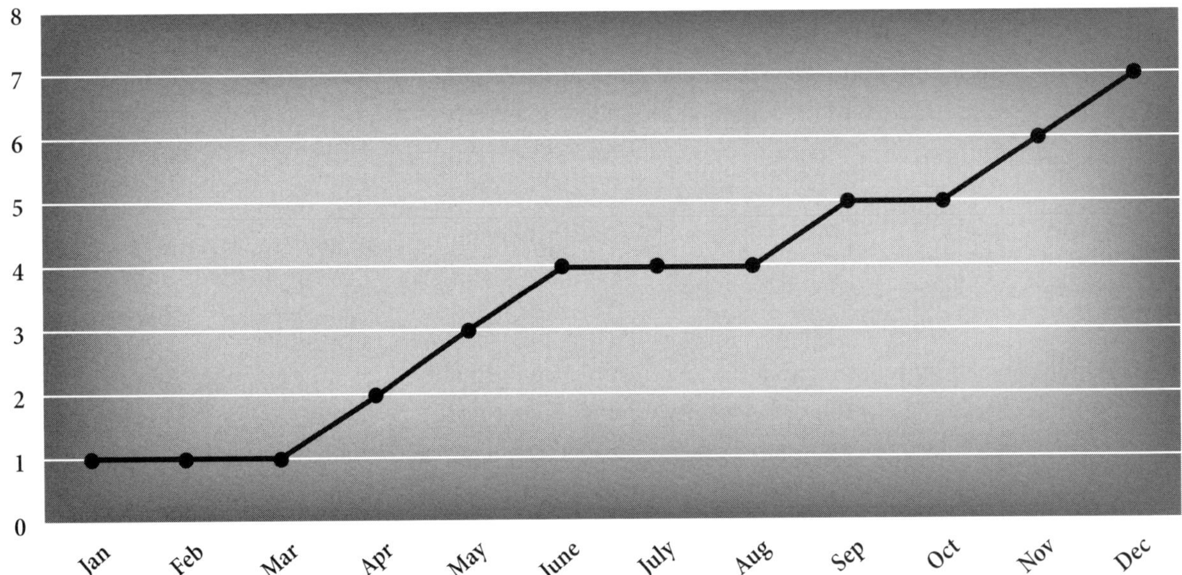

How to Conduct a Key Leader Survey

The first step in conducting a Key Leader survey is identifying the key leaders to survey. In the chart on page 214, we've identified a number of positions within a community that would qualify as key leaders. This is not an exhaustive list; you may identify other leaders who would be important depending on the type of asset-building efforts in which you are engaged.

WORKSHEET 8.1

Community Change Event Log

Initiative: ______________________ **Recorder:** ______________________

Using this form, please describe changes in *programs* (e.g., new after-school activities), *policies,* (e.g., local worksite offers flexible hours to increase parent-child time), and *practices* (e.g., new community collaboration) that are related to promoting assets.

Date (m/d/y) Was this the first time this event happened?	**Description of change** Describe the change in detail. Include: ***Why is it important?*** ***What happened as a result?*** ***Who was involved?*** ***What organizations were collaborators?***	**Linked to which outcome?** ***Does this change link to a specific desired outcome of the initiative? Which one?***	**Cause of the change?** ***How did your initiative cause the change?***

WORKSHEET 8.2

Community Change Summary

Initiative: ______________________________ **Year:** ____________

Month	**Change(s) and description**
January	# of changes = ___; Brief description of community changes
February	# of changes = ___; Brief description of community changes
March	# of changes = ___; Brief description of community changes
April	# of changes = ___; Brief description of community changes
May	# of changes = ___; Brief description of community changes
June	# of changes = ___; Brief description of community changes

Worksheet 8.2 continued on next page

Community Change Summary

Initiative: ____________________ **Year:** __________

Month	Change(s) and description
July	# of changes = ___; Brief description of community changes
August	# of changes = ___; Brief description of community changes
September	# of changes = ___; Brief description of community changes
October	# of changes = ___; Brief description of community changes
November	# of changes = ___; Brief description of community changes
December	# of changes = ___; Brief description of community changes

Sectors	Examples of key leader positions
Education	School administrators, principals, board members/chairpersons; student council president; student peer helpers; PTA president; education association president
Prevention	DARE officers, MADD chapter president; school guidance or prevention counselors, school district prevention coordinator
Community/human services	Legal services director, department of social services director, department of youth services director, housing authority director, child and family services director, Boy and Girl Scouts leaders, local chapter NAACP director, senior citizens association director, YMCA directors
Religious/spiritual	Ministers, pastors, imams, reverends, rabbis, clerics; president of a ministerial association
Government/elected officials	County council members, judges, mayors; youth members of boards and panels
Law enforcement	Crime prevention officer, parole and corrections officers, county sheriff, city police chief
Civic/business organizations	President of neighborhood councils, Chamber of Commerce, Jaycees, Rotary, Kiwanis, women's and men's clubs; American Legion post commander
Medical/health	County hospital administrator, director of substance abuse treatment center, nurse supervisor of county health department, president of medical society, leaders of mental health agencies
Public information	Editor(s) of local newspaper(s); county public information officer, Recreation Department director

The list of community sectors is long, and the list of potential key leaders is even longer. You must make a decision, based on the nature of your actions, which sectors and leaders would be important to survey. For example, if a majority of your efforts focus on schools, then it would make sense to focus your survey of key leaders on the education sector. You need to ask yourself who in the community could likely be impacted by your efforts and then survey the leaders in those areas.

The basic steps of administering the survey are:

- Identify which key leaders to survey. Aim for at least 50 key leaders.
- Send an introductory letter ahead of time to the key leaders explaining the survey and stating that it will be coming soon.

- Mail the survey to the key leaders. Include a cover letter (perhaps on brightly colored paper, to help it remain visible on a busy person's desk) and a stamped, self-addressed envelope. We suggest giving your respondents a two-week deadline in which to return the survey.
- Follow up by phone with those who don't respond. Offer to conduct the survey over the phone or send out another survey. Try to get at least 70% to respond.

CD FEATURE: We've included on the CD-ROM a sample cover letter template and Key Leader Survey Follow-up Form you can use to track returned surveys and to organize follow-up calls.

Instructions for Conducting the Key Leader Survey

The Key Leader Survey Worksheet 8.3, found on pages 217–221, has 31 items that address leaders' thoughts about the Developmental Assets model and 7 demographic items that ask the leader to describe her- or himself. The 31 items are organized into seven scales on the personal level and the organizational level.

The *personal-level questions* ask the key leader respondents to answer questions for themselves, based on their own opinions, about their community. The scales in the personal level are:

- Awareness of assets: How aware is the key leader of the Developmental Assets model being used in her or his community?
- Interest in assets: How interested is the key leader in learning about the asset model for use in her or his community?
- Involvement in assets: How involved is the key leader in asset-building work right now?
- Involvement in assets, change within the last 12 months: How has the key leader's involvement in asset-building work changed in the past 12 months?

The *organizational-level questions* ask the key leader respondents to answer for the organizations to which they belong. The scales in the organizational level are:

- Awareness of assets: How aware of the Developmental Assets model does the key leader believe people in her or his organization are?

- Involvement in assets: How interested in learning about and working with the asset model does the key leader believe people in her or his organization are?
- Collaboration in assets, change within the last 12 months: How has the collaboration around asset building changed in the past 12 months, according to the key leader?

G. Analyze the data

Now you have implemented your initiative, program, or project and gathered the data you need to complete your outcome evaluation. The next thing to do is match your data analysis to the types of information you are collecting.

- When using *quantitative data collection methods* like surveys, it's common to use quantitative data analysis methods like comparing averages and frequencies.
- When using *qualitative methods like focus groups,* it's common to use qualitative data analysis methods like content analysis.

The sidebar on page 222 shows how evaluation designs, various data collection methods, and the corresponding types of analyses are linked. This will guide you in matching your collection and analysis methods. You may also consider it worthwhile to consult an expert in data analysis procedures to ensure that the appropriate techniques are used.

CD FEATURE: You can find more information on how to calculate frequencies and interpret averages on the CD-ROM included with this book.

WORKSHEET 8.3

Key Leader Survey

This survey asks about your familiarity with the Developmental Assets model and asset-building activity in your community. The model is designed to mobilize various sectors of the community to support positive youth development. One main way this happens is through an asset-building initiative, in which people from a community collaborate to incorporate the Developmental Assets and asset building into the community's culture and practices.

1. How familiar are you with the Developmental Assets model?
(Circle the answer that best describes your personal opinion.)

Not at all familiar	A little familiar	Somewhat familiar	Very familiar
1	2	3	4

Personal Level (Circle the answer that best describes your personal opinion.)

Personal-Level Items	Not true	Slightly true	Moderately true	Very true
Personal Awareness of Assets				
2. I am aware of asset-building activity in my community.	1	2	3	4
3. I know which asset-building initiatives serve my community.	1	2	3	4
4. I can name the different types of services offered by asset-building initiatives in my community	1	2	3	4
Personal Interest in Assets				
5. I am interested in learning more about asset-building activities.	1	2	3	4
6. I am interested in learning more about the time and energy commitments that asset-building activities would require.	1	2	3	4

Survey continued on next page

Key Leader Survey *continued*

Personal-Level Items	Not true	Slightly true	Moderately true	Very true
7. I am concerned about whether my community has sufficient asset-building activities.	1	2	3	4
Personal Level of Involvement in Asset-Building Work				
8. I spend time collaborating with others in asset-building activities.	1	2	3	4
9. I am involved with the asset-building activities in my community.	1	2	3	4
10. I am interested in becoming actively involved in promoting assets in my community.	1	2	3	4
11. I know about efforts in my community to promote assets.	1	2	3	4

Personal Level of Involvement in Asset-Building Work					
	Decreased a lot	Decreased a little	Not changed	Increased a little	Increased a lot
In the past 12 months:					
12. My involvement in asset-building activities has . . .	1	2	3	4	5
13. My awareness of asset-building activities has . . .	1	2	3	4	5
14. My interest in asset-building activities has . . .	1	2	3	4	5

Survey continued on next page

Key Leader Survey *continued*

Organizational-Level Items	Not true	Slightly true	Moderately true	Very true
Organizational Level (Circle the answer that best describes your organization)				
Organizational Involvement in Assets				
15. My organization is involved in asset-building activities in our community.	1	2	3	4
16. Members of my organization are assigned to collaborate with others concerning the use of the asset model.	1	2	3	4
17. My organization has policies that incorporate the asset model.	1	2	3	4
18. As part of its mission, my organization is concerned with promoting the asset model in our community.	1	2	3	4
19. Members of my organization are currently learning what asset-building activities exist in our community.	1	2	3	4
20. My organization is interested in information about the time and energy commitments that asset-building activities would require.	1	2	3	4
Organizational Awareness of Assets				
21. In general, staff in my organization know whether asset-building activities serve our community or not.	1	2	3	4
22. In general, staff in my organization can name the different types of services offered through asset-building activities in our community.	1	2	3	4
23. In general, staff in my organization are aware of asset-building activities in our community.	1	2	3	4

Survey continued on next page

Key Leader Survey *continued*

Collaboration in Asset-Building Activities	Decreased a lot	Decreased a little	Not changed	Increased a little	Increased a lot	*Don't know enough to judge*
In the past 12 months:						
24. Our organization's involvement in asset-building activities with other organizations in our community has . . .	1	2	3	4	5	
25. Our organization's exchange of information with other organizations concerning the promotion of the assets model has . . .	1	2	3	4	5	
26. Our organization's referrals to or from other organizations concerning the promotion of the asset model have . . .	1	2	3	4	5	
27. Our organization's sharing of resources (e.g., equipment, supplies) with other organizations concerning the promotion of the asset model has . . .	1	2	3	4	5	
28. Our organization's cosponsorship of events with other organizations concerning the promotion of the asset model has . . .	1	2	3	4	5	
29. Our organization's coordination of services with other organizations concerning the promotion of the asset model has . . .	1	2	3	4	5	
30. Our organization's undertaking of joint projects with other organizations concerning the promotion of the asset model has . . .	1	2	3	4	5	
31. Our organization's participation in media coverage concerning the promotion of the asset model has . . .	1	2	3	4	5	

Survey continued on next page

Key Leader Survey *continued*

Demographic Questions

Gender—Which one describes your sex?

- ☐ Male
- ☐ Female

Race/ethnicity—Which one best describes you?

- ☐ African American or Black
- ☐ American Indian, Native American, or Indigenous
- ☐ Asian or Asian American
- ☐ Pacific Islander
- ☐ White
- ☐ Hispanic or Latino/Latina
- ☐ Other: ______________________

Occupation—Which one best describes your occupation?

- ☐ Executive, director, service manager
- ☐ Professional
- ☐ Technical
- ☐ Sales
- ☐ Administrative support
- ☐ Service
- ☐ Industrial
- ☐ Homemaker
- ☐ Unemployed
- ☐ Other: ______________________

Age, in years ____________

What is the highest level of education that you have completed?

- ☐ 8th grade or less
- ☐ Some high school
- ☐ High school graduate
- ☐ Vocational school beyond high school
- ☐ Some college
- ☐ College graduate
- ☐ Some graduate school
- ☐ Graduate degree

Which best describes your organization?

- ☐ Private business (for profit)
- ☐ Governmental agency
- ☐ Nonprofit private social service agency
- ☐ Religious organization
- ☐ School-related
- ☐ Community-based
- ☐ Other: ______________________

Length of time in current position, in years: ____________

Linking Design, Collection, and Analysis at a Glance

Design	Data collection method	Data analysis method	# of groups
Post only	Surveys/archival trend data/observation/ record review	*Compare averages.* Compare average score on your measure to archival data or a criterion from literature/previous experience—"eyeballing." *Frequencies.* Eyeball different categories of knowledge/skills/behavior at ONE point in time.	ONE (the group receiving the program or attending the event)
Pre-post	Focus groups/open-ended questions/ interviews/ participant observation/archival research	*Content analysis.* Look for themes in the experience of participants.	ONE (the group receiving the program or attending the event)
	Surveys/archival trend data/observation/ record review	*Compare averages.* Compare change over time by looking at the % change from pre to post scores or change in an average score on a measure from pre to post. *Frequencies.* Eyeball different categories of knowledge/skills/behavior at TWO points in time.	
Pre-post with comparison group OR Pre-post with control group (random assignment)	Focus groups/open-ended questions/ interviews/ participant observation/archival research	*Content analysis.* Look for change in themes over time.	TWO GROUPS (e.g., the group receiving the program, and a similar group NOT receiving the program)
	Surveys/archival trend data/observation/ record review	*Compare means.* Compare the comparison group's % change on a measure from pre to post with the program group's % change from pre to post OR compare both groups' average change scores from pre to post. *Frequencies.* Eyeball different categories of knowledge/skills/behavior of the two groups at two different times.	
Tracking of community changes	Event logs	*Assess level of achievement.* It is expected that after six months to a year, some changes should be evident.	ONE (the group conducting the asset-building projects or programs)

How to Analyze Your Key Leader Survey

After you have collected all the surveys and determined that you cannot get any more leaders to respond, it will be time to analyze the data. It can be helpful to use a spreadsheet program like Microsoft Excel to do this. Using Excel, each item on the survey will have its own column. Each key leader's responses will have their own row (see the chart below for a sample setup for your database). Once all the data are entered into the spreadsheet, then you will need to calculate averages for each of the scales according to the instructions below. When you are done, each key leader will have her or his own score for each scale. To complete the analysis, average together all of the key leaders' scores for each scale at each time point.

Sample Database Setup

	Item 1	Item 2	Item 3	Item 4, etc.
Key leader 1				
Key leader 2				
Key leader 3				
Key leader 4, etc.				

A likely situation for which you will use this information is to compare the group of key leaders at one point (i.e., at the beginning of your asset-building efforts) to a later point in time, perhaps after a year of work. The expectation is that these scores will improve (i.e., increase) because of your initiative's or program's efforts. Use Worksheet 8.4 (Guidelines for Calculating the Scale Scores for the Key Leader Survey) on pages 224–227 to help you calculate averages for each of the scales. Use the Key Leader Summary Sheet Worksheet 8.5, on page 228, to calculate percentage change across these two time points. Scores in the range 1–2 are low, 2–3 are moderate, and 3–4 are high. The desired outcomes for your key leader survey may be to reach a moderate level of awareness, interest, and involvement; or it may be to cause a significant improvement in these domains; or both. With additional outside assistance, you may be able to conduct more complex analyses, such as comparing the key leaders of one area to the leaders of another, or comparing different groups of leaders.

WORKSHEET 8.4

Guidelines for Calculating the Scale Scores for the Key Leader Survey

Personal-Level Items	Not true 1	Slightly true 2	Moderately true 3	Very true 4
Personal Awareness of Assets				
2. I am aware of asset-building activity in my community.	• ***Average the scores of the three items together to create a scale score.*** • Only calculate the scale if 2 out of the 3 items are present (nonmissing). • Higher scores mean more awareness.			
3. I know which asset-building initiatives serve my community.				
4. I can name the different types of services offered by asset-building initiatives in my community.				
Personal Interest in Assets				
5. I am interested in learning more about asset-building activities.	• ***Average the scores of the three items together to create a scale score.*** • Only calculate the scale if 2 out of the 3 items are present (nonmissing). • Higher scores mean more interest.			
6. I am interested in learning more about the time and energy commitments that asset-building activities would require.				
7. I am concerned about whether my community has sufficient asset-building activities.				
Personal Level of Involvement in Asset-Building Work				
8. I spend time collaborating with others in asset-building activities.	• ***Average the scores of the three items together to create a scale score.*** • Only calculate the scale if 2 out of the 3 items are present (nonmissing). • Higher scores mean more involvement.			
9. I am involved with the asset-building activities in my community.				
10. I am interested in becoming actively involved in promoting assets in my community.				
11. I know about efforts in my community to promote assets.				

Worksheet 8.4 continued on next page

Guidelines for Calculating the Scale Scores for the Key Leader Survey

Personal Level of Involvement in Asset-Building Work					
In the past 12 months:	Decreased a lot 1	Decreased a little 2	Not changed 3	Increased a little 4	Increased a lot 5
12. My involvement in asset-building activities has . . .	• ***Average the scores of the three items together to create a scale score.*** • Only calculate the scale if 2 out of the 3 items are present (nonmissing). • Higher scores mean more involvement.				
13. My awareness of asset-building activities has . . .					
14. My interest in asset-building activities has . . .					

Organizational Involvement in Assets				
Organizational-Level Items	**Not true 1**	**Slightly true 2**	**Moderately true 3**	**Very true 4**
15. My organization is involved in asset-building activities in our community.	• ***Average the scores of the six items together to create a scale score.*** • Only calculate the scale if 4 out of the 6 items are present (nonmissing). • Higher scores mean more involvement.			
16. Members of my organization are assigned to collaborate with others concerning the use of the asset model.				
17. My organization has policies that incorporate the asset model.				
18. As part of its mission, my organization is concerned with promoting the asset model in our community.				
19. Members of my organization are currently learning what asset-building activities exist in our community.				
20. My organization is interested in information about the time and energy commitments that asset-building activities would require.				

Worksheet 8.4 continued on next page

Guidelines for Calculating the Scale Scores for the Key Leader Survey

Organizational Awareness of Assets	
21. In general, staff in my organization know whether asset-building activities serve our community or not.	• ***Average the scores of the three items together to create a scale score.*** • Only calculate the scale if 2 out of the 3 items are present (nonmissing). • Higher scores mean more awareness.
22. In general, staff in my organization can name the different types of services offered through asset-building activities in our community.	
23. In general, staff in my organization are aware of asset-building activities in our community.	

Collaboration in Asset-Building Activities						
In the past 12 months:	Decreased a lot 1	Decreased a little 2	Not changed 3	Increased a little 4	Increased a lot 5	*Don't know*
24. Our organization's involvement in asset-building activities with other organizations in our community has . . .	• ***Average the scores of the eight items together to create a scale score.*** • Only calculate the scale if 5 out of the 8 items are present (excluding missing or the "Don't Know's"). • Higher scores mean more involvement.					
25. Our organization's exchange of information with other organizations concerning the promotion of the assets model has . . .						
26. Our organization's referrals to or from other organizations concerning the promotion of the asset model have . . .						
27. Our organization's sharing of resources (e.g., equipment, supplies) with other organizations concerning the promotion of the asset model has . . .						

Worksheet 8.4 continued on next page

Guidelines for Calculating the Scale Scores for the Key Leader Survey

In the past 12 months:	Decreased a lot 1	Decreased a little 2	Not changed 3	Increased a little 4	Increased a lot 5	*Don't know*
28. Our organization's cosponsorship of events with other organizations concerning the promotion of the asset model has . . .						
29. Our organization's coordination of services with other organizations concerning the promotion of the asset model has . . .						
30. Our organization's undertaking of joint projects with other organizations concerning the promotion of the asset model has . . .						
31. Our organization's participation in media coverage concerning the promotion of the asset model has . . .						

WORKSHEET 8.5

Key Leader Summary Sheet

Key Leader Domain Scales	Time 1 averages	Time 2 averages	Percentage change = (Time 2 – Time 1)/Time 1 × 100
Personal Level			
Awareness of assets			
Interest in assets			
Involvement in assets			
Involvement in assets—change within the past 12 months			
Organizational Level			
Involvement in assets			
Awareness of assets			
Collaboration in assets—change within the past 12 months			

Key leader surveys can be influenced by the key leaders' own biases, rather than simply reporting what they have observed in the community at large. Hence, you should use this information with caution.

H. Interpret the Data

Whatever the results, you need to review the data from both Questions #7 and #8 to help make sense and explain the results you obtained. For example, if a program or project is well implemented but does not produce positive results, you could conclude that the design or theory of the program or project was flawed and needs to be changed. (A common flaw at the community initiative level, for example, is underestimating the dosage or length of time required for change to occur.) You can conclude this only with information from both Questions #7 (process and tracking of activities) and #8 (assessing results). Invariably, whether you obtain your desired outcomes or not, people (and funders) will still ask the same questions—What did you do, and how did you get those results? The answer is usually found in the results of the process evaluation. This is why process evaluation is so important. It helps to explain the results of the outcome evaluation.

After you have all of your data from both the process and outcome evaluations, looking back to your logic model may be helpful. Your logic model shows in one place what your goals and desired outcomes are, how they are linked to certain activities, and how they would be measured. You can compare the data you collect to what you stated you were hoping for in the logic model and tell fairly quickly which activities were a success and which need to be improved.

Also, it may be useful to find patterns in the data, which can be done in many different ways. For example:

- An individual can take all the information, sort it into categories that address the different questions, then integrate it on her or his own. Discussion and modification can occur through a presentation of the initial findings to the evaluation team.
- Several people can review all the findings and then use group processes to cluster them into themes that grow out of your key evaluation questions. These themes can then be formatted into a simple report.
- Two team members can look over all the information and then do some initial sorting and summarizing of the findings individually. When they meet, they can discuss their summaries to reach consensus, create an outline of the report, and start writing, knowing that

through the collaborative act of thinking, talking, and writing, insights will begin to surface. Finally, they can present the draft of their report to the full team for review and discussion.

Phase 3: Report the Results of Your Outcome Evaluation

> *In universities, people know through* ***studies.*** *In businesses and bureaucracies, people know by* ***reports.*** *In communities, people know by . . . community* ***stories*** *[that] allow people to reach back into their common history and their individual experience for knowledge about truth and direction for the future. Professionals and institutions often threaten the stories of community by urging community people to count up things rather than communicate. Successful community associations resist efforts to impose the foreign language of studies and reports because it is a tongue that ignores their own capacities and insights.*
>
> —John McKnight

John McKnight is the cocreator (with John Kretzmann) of Asset-Based Community Development (known as ABCD). His thoughts about the different languages used by universities, bureaucracies, professionals, institutions, and communities are worth keeping in mind as you think about what findings you want to report, in what format, and to whom. This final step guides you to organize your results, interpretation, and analysis into a reporting plan that will allow you to present your findings to a variety of audiences.

Once you have gathered enough information to answer your key evaluation questions, the final step is to analyze and share what you've learned. While this approach seems simple enough in theory, too many evaluation reports never end up being used. For evaluation to be worthwhile, you need to be careful and thorough in your interpretation, and to communicate your findings in a way that maximizes the chances that they will be used in reporting, future planning, and making improvements to your efforts.

The important point here is to share your findings in such a way that those you are seeking to inform can readily understand. For example, the thick, formal, written evaluation reports required by some funders may not be at all interesting or helpful to a youth advisory council. For a youth council, you may want to creatively explore how you could share key information in ways young people would prefer and can respond to (for example, through stories or discussions that are presented or led by youth). To help you, this section briefly describes general analysis and interpretation methods, provides guidelines on what to report and what not to report, and offers a simple outline to help you organize your findings.

Telling Your Story

By following many of the steps in this and previous chapters, you already have most, if not all, of the information you need on which to base your reporting efforts. If you haven't completed summary sheets for each of your information-gathering processes, now is the time to do so.

Next, look over the data you have gathered for patterns, recurring categories of responses or themes, as well as issues, problems, and questions that still need answers. One way to guide this sort of thinking is to first name some categories of findings: for example, strengths or successes, challenges or criticisms, and suggestions or improvements. If you make a chart for each of these categories, you can jot down what you find as you go through the data, and in this manner make an initial analysis of your data. Don't forget to record who the information is from, to aid you in weighing whether you can extrapolate these findings.

Keep track separately of unexpected or puzzling patterns or findings, as well as reactions, observations, and other relevant comments from evaluation team members. These will be invaluable for determining additional avenues of investigation, writing your report(s), and planning potential next steps.

Finally, review your findings for their possible implications. Ask yourselves what the most important findings are and how they can help shape your initiative's or program's plans for improvement and future action.

Once you've gathered and analyzed your data and sorted out the findings that you want to report, you'll need to create an outline or structure for it. A number of structures could be useful and effective:

- If you are doing your evaluation mainly to meet funder requirements, that funder may have provided you with a structure to follow; if not, you can ask the funder for a sample format.
- Another option would be to organize your report by your initiative's or program's goals or by your key evaluation questions; in this case, you'll want to write an introduction and conclusion to "frame" the main sections.
- Or you can simply describe strengths, improvements, criticisms, and plans for the future—all supported by your evidence, of course.

Be aware that different stakeholders may be interested in different types and levels of information. For broad community audiences, try not to report too much data in your findings, as this can quickly become overwhelming. Instead, describe the most important and practical findings using only a few numbers and a clear explanation of what you think they mean. For a more professional audience, you might include more discussion of the statistics and types of analyses. For any audience, be careful not to overgeneralize. *Remember that unless you use a scientifically chosen, random sample, your results represent only the thinking and experience of your respondents, which may or may not be the same as that of other groups.*

The possibilities for how to creatively share your findings are broad. Perhaps you could produce a video or a Web site to share with your community. You may want to write a series of press releases for your local newspapers. Or perhaps you will invite local young people to a presentation and brainstorming session, in which you share with them what you've done so far, what you've found out, and where you're thinking of going next. You could then invite their input and participation.

At this point in your work, you may find it useful to enlist the help of a communications specialist, possibly someone within your initiative or organization who works in marketing or public relations, a writer, journalist, or editor, or perhaps someone with experience in grant writing. Then it's time to forge ahead and hammer out a first draft. Be sure to have a group of reviewers who will give the draft a quick but careful reading to look for unclear language, dubious assertions, and any spelling or grammar errors. Once you've incorporated your reviewers' comments and suggestions, print out your report, put a copy or two into your initiative's or program's archives, and distribute them.

To help you organize your thoughts and ideas about whom you'll report your findings to, we've provided a short worksheet on page 234.

Instructions for Using the How Are We Going to Report Our Findings? Worksheet

The steps for completing Worksheet 8.6 are as follows:

1. For each of your key evaluation questions, make a copy of the worksheet.
2. Identify the groups to which you need to report your findings. (Search Institute would be pleased to be included on this list, since the organization does much of its learning from practitioners in the field, like you. Send a copy to Community Liaison, Search Institute, 615 First Avenue NE, Suite 125, Minneapolis, MN 55413. Thank you!)
3. For each different group to which you need to report, identify one or two of the best methods you can think of to communicate these findings to them. While a funder or foundation may require a written report (possibly even specifying the format of the report) and a big-city newspaper may prefer a formal press release, groups such as students, parents, or initiative teams may respond positively to more creative forms of communication, such as a newsletter or

magazine articles, in-person presentations, or even a video or theatrical presentation.

4. If you are unsure of yourself in this process (especially with regard to findings that are complicated or very important to the future of your effort), identify someone more experienced in evaluation who can help you with this task.

INTEGRATE ASSETS-GTO by continuing to inform the community about your initiative or program. High-quality reporting will also continue to play an important role in improving and sustaining your work because you will be able to get feedback from your staff and constituents more easily if the results are communicated well and easy to understand. That feedback will be key in helping to improve your initiative or program. Also, since communicating your successes to current and potential funders is one of the best ways to sustain and build support for your work, reporting with quality is critical.

Looking Ahead to Sustainability

There is nothing more crucial to sustaining your work than having positive outcomes. By clearly demonstrating the effectiveness of what you've done—and how it's tied directly to your vision, goals, and community needs—you not only make a convincing case for maintaining your work, you potentially strengthen the work of your partners. By implication, you are also sustaining the efficacy of the outcomes you're measuring.

For example, when the Community Roundtable Coalition of Richland County, South Carolina, was unclear whether its funding would be renewed to continue several community-wide interventions, the coalition convened a meeting to present its outcome data to a diverse group of stakeholders. The purpose of the presentation was to discuss what outcomes were being obtained and any changes that might be needed based on the data. The stakeholders were eager to continue meeting to regularly review the results with the idea of gathering support for the interventions' outcomes if the funding were to end. A member of the coalition, a school guidance counselor, reviewed an RFP from a federal agency whose goals and desired outcomes were consistent with the goals and outcomes of the coalition's interventions. The counselor, in partnership with the coalition, wrote a successful grant proposal and received funding from a new federal agency for program continuation as well as expansion into an adjacent community. To help you build the success and sustainability of your outcomes, consider:

WORKSHEET 8.6

How Are We Going to Report Our Findings?

1. Who are the key groups to which we need to report our findings?
2. How are we going to report to each of these groups?
3. Do we need someone to check our report(s) for accuracy? If so, who could do this?

- *Providing and sharing success and information* that can help guide agency and organizational activities, government policies, and community engagement practices;
- *Providing and tracking specific outcome measures* that you and others can use to improve performance and report progress; and
- *Providing data* that can be disseminated by policy makers to further sustain the asset-building agenda.

Demonstrating strong results and sharing them with others in the community help build sustainability beyond the implementation of a single program or project. Your data support your success and help you and your stakeholders demonstrate that you are continuing to address the original priorities and goals you identified. Making adjustments as you learn also helps keep your efforts congruent and builds credibility with your partners, stakeholders, and other community members. Be honest—provide both negative and positive data to all of your audiences. Honestly look at what is working and what needs to be changed as well.

Before Going on to the Next Chapter

Celebrate! You've done a tremendous amount of work at this point. You may have plans for disseminating and reporting your results that involve community activities. You may need to find some time to take a deep breath and pause to reflect on all you've learned. You may want to have a debriefing session of some kind among the people who have worked on this effort just to tell stories to each other about what you've learned, what worked well and what you'd like to do differently next time. You may also find that you get some good feedback from youth and other community members as you present your results about what's working or could be improved. Taking some time to reflect will help you as you move into the final section of this book to address the continuous improvement and sustainability of your efforts.

PART FOUR

Improve and Sustain

You have now successfully planned, launched, monitored, and evaluated your asset-building project(s) or program(s). You have in your hands a wealth of information about how your work evolved and how your goals were met. In the next two questions, we'll help you learn from your efforts so you can continue to improve your work as you repeat your project(s) and/or program(s) or move on to new ideas. We will also help you bring together all of your ideas about how to sustain your efforts in a plan for the future.

The questions in this section include:

Question #9. What continuous quality improvement efforts do you need to improve your initiative or program over time? (CQI). This question provides a simple but systematic plan for reviewing and assessing your previous work so you can continuously improve your asset-building initiative, programs, or projects in the future. Developing a transparent process for continual review and improvement not only helps you do a better job, but also builds confidence among participants, staff, volunteers, funders, and other stakeholders. *Question #9 begins on page 239.*

Question #10. If the program or asset-building initiative is successful, how will it be sustained? (SUSTAINABILITY). This question defines sustainability and offers tips, resources, and advice from other asset-building initiatives and programs on what it takes to keep your work going. This final chapter also brings together all of the tips in the previous chapters to suggest the backbone of a sustainability plan you can customize to fit your work. *Question #10 begins on page 249.*

QUESTION #9

What continuous quality improvement efforts do you need to improve your initiative or program over time?

(CQI)

Congratulations! You have successfully planned, implemented, and evaluated your program(s) and/or project(s). You've learned a lot that was useful in the development of a specific program or project, and you now have a wealth of material and experience that will help you step back and take the big-picture view of your process. There's a great opportunity to learn from your previous efforts if processes and outcomes of programs and projects are well documented.

One of the most valuable aspects of using the steps in this Assets-GTO process is learning how to continuously improve your work. Questions #6, 7, and 8 all helped you plan and evaluate your specific program(s) and/or project(s). *Continuous quality improvement,* or CQI, involves the systematic review and assessment of *all* the previous steps you've taken in order to improve your asset-building initiatives, programs, or projects in the future. Making this CQI process a regular part of your work helps ensure that the positive changes you're implementing reverberate through your projects and programs as they should.

You likely expect to repeat many of your activities over time. You want to continue doing what's working well while also taking a deeper look at the impact you've had so your activities improve each time you repeat them. Taking some time in this step to summarize what you've learned will benefit everyone involved in your program or initiative. Your staff, volunteers, and participants will all learn together from your experience, making your asset-building initiative, projects, and programs more effective while ensuring your sustainability. A demonstrated process for continual review and improvement will also increase confidence in your work among funders and stakeholders. Finally, the use of data to improve your work builds capacity and interest among staff and volunteers to conduct evaluation.

The steps in this chapter will help you conduct a systematic review of your work from the previous eight Assets-GTO questions and come up with a plan for making changes.

Here's what you'll need to get you started:

- Completed worksheets from the previous eight chapters;
- Copies of your logic model;
- Copies of your process and outcome evaluation reports; and
- Coffee, donuts, or snacks of your choosing and comfortable chairs.

A SNAPSHOT OF THIS STEP IN ACTION

St. Louis Park High School 9th Grade Program

When staff, teachers, and administrators launched the St. Louis Park High School 9th Grade Program, they built in opportunities to continuously ask questions of everyone involved about how the program was going. Staff and teacher meetings designed to share information about how to support students also provided regular chances for people to talk about adjustments and modifications that were needed to make the entire program work better. Evaluators from the Minnesota Institute of Public Health—familiar with asset building and the larger community efforts tied into Children First—came on board early on and regularly conducted interviews, surveys, and observation sessions throughout the program's duration.

The main tools used to continuously evaluate and improve the program included:

- Staff/teacher interviews;
- Observation of specific components of the program, like "I Time";
- Interviews with participants from the Parent Advisory Group;
- Student focus groups; and
- Monitoring of local media coverage to see how news about the program was getting out into the community.

Staff, teachers, and administrators were all involved, but students and parents reportedly were also surprised to find themselves face-to-face with evaluators asking their opinions. Such a high degree of personal involvement yielded much higher quality information with which to evaluate the program's outcomes. Evaluators found during Parent Advisory Group interviews, for example, that the group was gaining in membership as a result of the 9th Grade Program's success and that staff were more actively seeking parent input on a variety of issues. Communications back and forth helped fine-tune and improve the program as it developed.

What did staff learn along the way? Despite challenges such as disruption caused by major construction at the high school, the emphasis on regular communication, coordination, and meetings among teachers, staff and administrators

How to Implement Your CQI Efforts

After completing your program(s) or project(s), the main question to ask is: How can you do things better the next time? Implementing a CQI strategy is straightforward: Use CQI Summary Worksheet 9.1 on page 244 to help you review the key results of your first eight accountability questions.

For example, you and your partners could consider whether the issues or resources identified in Question #1 have changed or whether the goals you described in Question #2 need to be refined. You may also have learned about how other asset-building initiatives or programs are addressing the same concerns, and you can consider implementing some of those learnings the next time you conduct your program or initiative projects. Obviously, you will have learned some things from your process and outcome evaluation that will also tell you what to keep doing.

A SNAPSHOT OF THIS STEP IN ACTION, *continued*

made it possible to deal with crises effectively. Program staff learned that this emphasis on communications channels was worth the extra effort it took to keep this aspect of the program strong. The perceived gains made by students in the 9th grade also began to lead to the realization of the gaps in programming for students in grades 8, 10, and 12, which the school is now working on addressing.

Along with the statistically measurable reduction in high-risk behaviors, a majority of teachers, staff, and administrators felt that making progress toward their goal of reducing academic failure was their most important outcome. When interviewed, many teachers said this not only made them feel they were doing a better job, but it helped set high expectations for the other students and improved the overall climate of the 9th grade class. These results helped motivate teachers, staff, and administrators to keep the program going and to refine it along the way to make it work better.

Teachers were specifically asked what they'd do differently if they were starting over. Some of the responses:

- Better efforts to keep the core class sizes down.
- Provide funding to continue the social worker for each class as it moves along.
- More parent involvement. Have monthly dinner meetings offered at school or places in the community.
- More systematic tracking of how our kids did.

Along with working to incorporate changes and suggestions, staff has also worked on getting more financial support from the school district and other grants to continue, as well as expand, the program. The staff is also looking for ways to improve its evaluation process to more clearly demonstrate, among other things, the relationship between asset development and the decrease in risk behavior. Staff would also eventually like to evaluate the impact of the program on teacher and staff morale and the ability of the program to show sustained impact over time.

Here are a few tips to help you prepare for your review process:

- *Let people know what's coming.* As your project or program comes to a natural ending point, start letting staff, volunteers, participants and other key stakeholders know that you're planning a systematic CQI process. If you are evaluating an ongoing initiative, you could schedule an annual CQI process at a certain time every year to gather the information you need.
- *Convene a work group.* In the same way that you might have people who really like working with data, you probably also have a group of people who would really enjoy conducting the CQI process. The CQI process will benefit from having multiple perspectives, so encourage diverse membership in this working group. Convene this group to plan and implement your work and if you wish, have them develop a summary report for your planning group and stakeholders.
- *Organize your materials before you get started.* It might be useful to review copies of all the filled-in worksheets you've produced for Questions 1–8 as you prepare to conduct your CQI process. Organizing and summarizing the key information might make it easier for your work group to fill in the questions in the CQI Summary.
- *Document what you learn in this step, too.* Just as you have been careful to document your work in the previous eight questions, you want to have a clear and concise summary of your findings in this step as well. Try to keep your answers to the questions on the CQI summary concise to help keep you focused on the most salient points, but you should feel free to record information on a separate sheet if you need more room. You may also want to include some other questions you have. Remember, you can modify the worksheet on the CD-ROM to better suit your needs.

Instructions for Using the CQI Summary Worksheet

The steps for using Worksheet 9.1 are as follows:

1. Make copies of the worksheet or modify the worksheet from the CD-ROM to fit your needs.
2. Convene your work group.
3. Make sure each member of the work group has copies of the completed worksheets from previous chapters in hand before you meet with instructions on how to review them and prepare for the CQI process.

4. Include a blank copy of the CQI Summary in your preparation packet to structure group members' thinking.
5. It might be helpful to put up large pieces of flip chart paper around your meeting room and have everyone brainstorm multiple ideas on each question. Then you can all work together to distill your learnings and ideas into the most important points for future action.
6. Designate a recorder to capture the important information on your CQI Summary.

Once you have completed your CQI review, you'll probably want to come up with a short summary of what you learned. If there are changes you plan to make as a result of your review, you might also want to develop a short plan with beginning and ending dates to help ensure the changes get incorporated into your program(s) or project(s). Be sure to report back to your participants regularly on your process.

Implementing a CQI strategy can help you **INTEGRATE ASSETS-GTO** in all the ways we first suggested in the Introduction (see Tipsheet B, page 13):

1. *Continuing to get buy-in.* By demonstrating your commitment to continuously reviewing and examining your work, you continue to build confidence and investment on all levels of the initiative, organization, or program to endorse the use of Assets-GTO.
2. *Continuing to orient new personnel and participants to Assets-GTO.* CQI helps improve orientation and training for new staff, employees, volunteers, and participants.
3. *Continuing to structure all reporting around Assets-GTO.* The CQI process helps bring all of the reports structured around the ten questions together, which further facilitates regular communication among participants and staff about operations and results. High-quality reporting will also play an important role in continually improving and sustaining your process.
4. *Continuing to provide regular access to Assets-GTO information.* As with any of the worksheets in this book, the CQI Summary can be especially effective as a communications tool for groups with a wide range of participants.
5. *Complementing strategic planning.* You can maximize your results by making the CQI process part of your larger strategic planning efforts, both at the individual program level, as well as at the agency and initiative levels. Because CQI encourages a review of the larger picture of your work, you can use it to help you assess and determine potential areas for improvement and growth.

WORKSHEET 9.1

CQI Summary

Name of person completing form:

Date:

Summary of main points to consider	Ideas from considering main points	How will you use this information to improve implementation next time?
Q #1. How have the needs and strengths of your setting changed since you previously implemented programs or projects in this setting?		
Q #2. What new goals or desired outcomes might you have? Is there a new community or group that you plan to work with to integrate your asset-building efforts?		
Q #3. What new program(s) or project(s) might you implement, given the results of the process and outcome evaluations?		
Q #4. Will these proposed new programs or projects still fit with your initiative or organization (both philosophically and logistically) and your community?		

Worksheet 9.1 continued on next page

WORKSHEET 9.1 *continued*

CQI Summary

Summary of main points to consider	Ideas from considering main points	How will you use this information to improve implementation next time?
Q #5. What additional resources might be necessary in order to repeat your successful program or project or implement new ones?		
Q #6. How well did you plan? How can you improve the planning phase the next time?		
Q #7. How well were the projects and programs implemented? What were the main conclusions from the process evaluation? How will you incorporate this information for improvement? What changes do you need to make to your process evaluation?		
Q #8. Did you achieve your goals and desired outcomes? What changes do you need to make to increase your successes? What changes do you need to make to improve the evaluation process?		

6. *Employing what you're learning to build capacity.* The CQI process can help you see new ways to more fully integrate Assets-GTO into varying levels of your work to build capacity in a variety of ways. You can apply the steps and learnings of the CQI process to a review of your operational and resources capacities, both at the initiative and program levels, to determine what you can do differently in the future.

You'll probably see changes you want to make as you review each of the steps in the Assets-GTO process using the CQI process we've outlined. If you find that your organization wants to begin to focus on more internal assets, for example, this is likely to require new goals, capacities, and evaluation methods. In contrast, if the only significant result of the CQI review is that the process evaluation showed weak implementation in some areas, that may be the only aspect that will need to be addressed the next time around.

Looking Ahead to Sustainability

The First Baptist Church of Los Angeles, California, decided to set up a recreation and arts center in its neighborhood. The congregation wanted to offer a safe place for youth along with constructive ways to spend their time. But, despite good intentions, programming, and staff supervision, the center became a gang hangout and had to close. Determined, the congregation asked the local YMCA for help in developing a more structured, controlled program that would include more values and drug education. The new program didn't reach quite as many young people, but the church was able to have an impact on the values of young people who did participate. As a result, the church made additional plans to boost recruitment.

Systematically assessing and reviewing your progress, then reconsidering and implementing changes where necessary, will keep your work vital. But also remember that while you must focus to a certain extent on the nuts and bolts of reviewing and improving a program or project, sustaining an asset-building initiative also works best when you:

- *Continue to approach community change as a dynamic, unpredictable process.* Having a template or "recipe" to work from is useful, but the way your initiative, project, or program will actually develop is like cooking gumbo—each one is different. And it's supposed to be! That's part of what makes the work fun, interesting, and truly reflective of a community's diversity.
- *Give it away.* Your role is not to provide all the answers but to unleash the processes within the community that will build the change you

collectively seek. Empower people in the community to incorporate the Developmental Assets framework in unique, creative, even informal ways. Pay attention to the community members' personal and organizational interests to help determine where to invest your initiative's (or program's) energy.

- *Trust the community.* Asset building is about developing trust and relationships with others. Participants may find that they disagree with each other on how to go about some things, but the asset framework can provide common language and common ground for people to articulate their higher purpose of caring about children and youth. The more voices at the table, the stronger your work will be.

Systematic reflection on your work will help you build sustainability. Using your vision as your touchstone and then keeping the end in mind while asking where you can do better will continually help you refresh and revitalize your work.

Before Going on to the Next Chapter

Pull together a summary of the lessons you've learned along the way, the challenges you've faced and overcome, thoughts, ideas, and experiences about what's worked and not worked, and observations from stakeholders about your process. Digest and synthesize a bit before moving on to the final stage of this process—what do you think it will take to sustain your work? Think a bit out of the box on this one. Of course, continued funding is crucial to continuing your work, but what else will it take? And if you face a situation where continued funding isn't possible, what kind of creative solutions might you, your work groups, participants, and stakeholders come up with to continue your successes?

QUESTION #10

If the program or asset-building initiative is successful, how will it be sustained?

(SUSTAINABILITY)

What does it mean to sustain your work? Many view sustainability primarily as the continuation of an initiative, program, or project after the initial funding ends. Simply making the transition from short-term funding to longer term funding can require intense focus and collaboration among partners and stakeholders. Funding and resource development are important issues, but within the context of a commitment to long-term, systemic change to better benefit children and youth, sustainability becomes a much broader issue. In addition to continued funding, sustainability in Assets-GTO also means that asset building becomes a part of how the community operates.

Along with continued funding, you want to ensure that your efforts successfully continue to exist while producing the progress and measurable outcomes you have envisioned. All the people involved need the nourishment and necessities required for a long journey of community change. Just like the healthy growth and development you wish for your young people, you want your participants, asset initiatives, and programs to thrive as well.

There certainly are challenges. Many of you have faced or will face reduced funding, shifting priorities, a loss of interest and focus, changing personnel, misunderstandings, competition, emerging crises, and fatigue. To truly sustain your work requires monitoring the fluctuating contexts in which your work takes place and constantly reassessing the fit between your goals and your community. You may be called upon to revisit the earlier stages of your plans, even reconsider your initiative's identity or your program's focus, while all the time keeping the work itself going. Developing asset-based initiatives, projects, and programs requires a high degree of agility and flexibility.

Clearly, not everything that is started should be sustained. Circumstances, personnel, and needs change over time. Perhaps a more effective or more suitable program or project becomes available; maybe the project or program you tried was not effective, or the original priority ceases to exist. Your evaluation results can help you determine whether your initiative or program is worth sustaining or not.

Along with all the uncertainty and hard work comes the reward of accomplishing your goals, actually seeing positive changes not just in your community's young people, but in your entire community as well. The improvements you've nurtured come to fruition and you begin to see asset building become a way of life, integrated into organizations and systems. There is even a kind of exhilaration in learning to live with the ebb and flow of a dynamic asset-building initiative, program, or project.

"Our initiative matured in a very vivid way," says Helen Beattie of her region's Healthy Communities • Healthy Youth (HC • HY) initiative in Hardwick, Vermont. "We had funding and leadership in the beginning to carry consciousness and mobilize people. Now the initiative is part of the fabric of the community, and many pieces live on in that fabric. The initiative is almost silent but present in the lifeblood in the way that things work. We don't have to remind the local newspapers to seek youth voice, for example. They just do it on their own. The initiative percolates at its own rate and that provides a readiness when something comes up so we don't have to always start everything from scratch."

The Foundation of Your Sustainability Plan

The plan you develop for sustaining your initiative or program will be just as unique as the community in which you live, but whether you're thinking of pursuing additional resources from local organizations, foundations, or governmental sources, consider the primary question: *Should this asset-building initiative or program be sustained?* When answering this question, consider these two points:

1. Are there data to support the success of this asset-building initiative, program, or its components?
2. Does the asset-building initiative or program continue to address the needs in your community of interest?

If the answer to either of these two questions is no, then it may be best to reconsider your efforts for sustainability. Trying to keep something going without results or relevancy can lead to increased resistance within the community. It will be difficult to get new or continued funding for initiatives or programs

A SNAPSHOT OF THIS STEP IN ACTION

Central Whidbey Youth Coalition, Coupeville, Washington

The Central Whidbey Youth Coalition (CWYC) has evolved since a group of citizens started meeting in 1988 over concerns about drug and alcohol use by young people. Located in the rural community of Coupeville, right in the middle of one of Puget Sound's most picturesque islands, CWYC is now an HC • HY initiative, and while its main focus is still drug and alcohol prevention, the coalition has become a vital source of public education and youth activities, guided by four long-term goals:

1. CWYC focuses awareness on youth issues.
2. CWYC serves as a communication, education, and coordination agency for youth issues.
3. CWYC networks and cooperates with community and governmental agencies to provide support services for youth.
4. CWYC develops and/or supports youth programs that are safe, supervised, and drug- and alcohol-free; hosted in a pleasant and supportive atmosphere; provides opportunities for youth to participate in planning; and has positive expectations for youth.

CWYC runs its own programs (After the Facts and Late Night Central are drug-free after-school and weekend drop-in programs for middle schoolers) and partners with others, such as the Coupeville School District, to support their programs (the coalition passes federal money on to the school district for an adult/peer mentoring program called Learning Partners, as well as Readiness to Learn). CWYC also supports an alcohol-free party for graduating Coupeville High School seniors and an annual three-day sailing trip for middle schoolers.

Like many coalitions and initiatives, the funding for CWYC is a patchwork of federal, state, and local dollars combined with support from a large cross section of individual and organizational participation. The issue of how to sustain the coalition is always on the table. One important way the coalition sustains itself is through an elaborate, productive network of partnerships with 27 other organizations such as the local library, hospital, and Coupeville marshall's office. These organizations donate services—such as the marshall's office, which provides safety officers at events—but more important, each organization provides a board member to CWYC.

A recent unexpected retraction of state funds forced CWYC to cut back the number of after-school drop-in sessions it offered, but the reduction also spurred the coalition to apply for more year-four Safe and Drug Free Communities money on the basis of its successful results from the first three years under this grant. The coalition is already planning to apply for year-five money, as well as go for a second five-year grant that is specifically aimed at helping initiatives develop sustainability plans. If CWYC can achieve federal funding for seven more years, it will have time to make plans to embed its programs and priorities into the community in other ways. One developing scenario—CWYC is considering transferring its after-school and weekend drop-in programs to a newly forming Boys and Girls Club that plans to launch soon out of a renovated firehouse in Coupeville.

that are not demonstrating results. And, it may be equally difficult to obtain additional resources in a particular setting such as schools if the needs and related buy-in from key stakeholders are not apparent.

If you have determined that you want to sustain your efforts, keep these key points in mind:

- ***Plan from day one.*** Your plan for sustainability starts at the beginning of your work—at the same time your program and evaluation planning begins. "Building your system *is* an act of sustainability," says Sue Allen, coordinator for the Wisconsin Positive Youth Development Initiative. "By creating a lasting collaborative system that builds expectations, including data sharing, into the way agencies, institutions, organizations, municipalities, and counties 'do business,' then we have a chance at a long-term sustainable process. Prevention *plus* building assets means we're all thriving."
- ***It's about more than money.*** Funding, lack of funding, changes in funding, and how to get and manage funding are all important issues that initiatives and programs must tackle. Diversifying your funding streams protects you from being vulnerable to budget cuts. But money alone does not create long-term sustainability, and the efforts to raise funding can actually sap the human resources and spirit that sustain effective community change efforts. Sometimes outside infusions of financial resources can diminish local ownership or dilute focus. Instead of investing tremendous amounts of time and energy in raising money, look at the broader picture of what resources are needed and develop creative ways to tap resources that already exist within the community. Connection and integration with existing organizations and institutions may become more vital than money alone when your budget is cut and you need to find a new home for your programs.

  "Our coalition philosophy is to encourage existing community resources with expertise in a specific area to take a leadership role," says Mary Schissel, director of the Mason City Youth Task Force. "We try to bring along other resources to support them." For example, the task force has identified a grouping of assets that the broader community coalition should be able to impact through youth involvement efforts. While everyone in the coalition tries to impact all the assets, certain partners take the lead on specific assets, such as the schools' focus on educational commitment. "We try to work smarter, not harder," says Schissel.

- ***Demonstrate and publicize your successes.*** Plan your communication about your work and outcomes to flow within all different levels of your community, from top to bottom and back up again, including policy makers. Decide what you want to say and who needs to hear it. And repeat yourself! Redundancy in communications is vital to getting the word out. Not only will your communications about your positive results inform the community, but they can also help with your resource development efforts as well as your efforts to influence changes in policy. In its *Evaluation Handbook,* the Kellogg Foundation advises initiatives and programs to present evaluation findings and lessons in compelling ways. "There are many far more compelling ways to present findings of an evaluation than with traditional research reports full of technical jargon and research-defined categories and criteria. Present real-life stories and real issues."
- ***Be creative, resourceful, and willing to forge new partnerships.*** The vitality of your efforts will come from the vitality and creativity of all the people who are engaged and on fire with asset building. You can cultivate shared leadership and strengthen the capacity of your initiative or program by forming partnerships with other organizations. "Partnerships are critical to the long-term success of any initiative," says Rick Phillips of Community Matters, a California training organization that specializes in community building. "Trying to develop partnerships can seem a bit daunting at first, but nothing is more powerful in addressing community issues than an effective partnership." One of Phillips's key tips—take the time it takes to nurture a strong partnership. "This allows you to bring all the players to the table, forge a shared vision, and develop a clear plan for working in concert on a common problem or issue."

If you look back at the circular diagram of the ten steps of this Assets-GTO process on page 10, you'll see that in a way, we've arrived back at the beginning. Starting with the Introduction and continuing through all ten Assets-GTO questions, we provided ideas to help you think about sustainability at every stage of the process. For those who have been able to incorporate planning for sustainability as you've worked through the steps in this book, the checklist on page 264 will provide a look back on what you've done. For those of you just getting started on your sustainability plans, the checklist can help you organize your thoughts and ideas as you begin.

Tipsheet H

WHAT DO LONG-LASTING ASSET-BUILDING INITIATIVES LOOK LIKE?

Search Institute conducted a survey of 45 initiatives it considered leaders in sustainability. Most of these initiatives were launched between 1995 and 1999 and are still operating. Nearly half are operating at the county level; the rest are predominantly city/town, multi-city or county, and school district–level initiatives. Twenty-six percent have populations under 50,000; 26 percent have populations of 150,000 or more. About 38 percent are rural; 25 percent are suburban, and 18 percent are urban. A third have budgets under \$25,000; 13 percent have budgets between \$25,000 and \$50,000, and another 11 percent have budgets between \$50,000 and \$75,000.

Here's what else Search Institute learned about these "in it for the long haul" leaders:

91%	Are currently focused on engaging youth.
86%	Have faith-based groups involved; other sectors with high involvement include business, civic organizations, city/county government, public schools, 4-H, health care, law enforcement, service clubs, and youth/family serving organizations.
86%	Have a steering or advisory committee that includes representatives from multiple sectors or organizations in the community.
84%	Say at least half of the steering/advisory committee is from their community.
84%	Are active in building receptivity and awareness.
80%	Are mobilizing and organizing for growth and change.
80%	Identify one or more organizations or places in the community using Developmental Assets in a way that goes beyond awareness building and mobilization.
76%	Are currently focused on mobilizing adults.
76%	Meet regularly.
76%	Report data from asset surveys back to the community.
73%	Have access to in-kind and cash resources from one or more sources to help support work.
67%	Currently say they have the human capacity to hold the initiative together and coordinate its work.
67%	Have a written plan to guide its work.
64%	Are addressing continuity (sustainability).
64%	Regularly evaluate or systematically reflect on their progress as an initiative.
64%	Say they are learning about making change.
62%	Are currently focused on strengthening programs.

Tipsheet H continues on next page ▶

Tipsheet H, continued

60%	Support action to promote growth and change.
53%	Are currently focused on activating sectors.
53%	Have evaluated the impact of the initiative on youth.
53%	Say they are learning about leadership.
51%	Focus work on all eight asset categories and all 40 Developmental Assets.
49%	Blend assets with other frameworks, including America's Promise, Asset-Based Community Development (ABCD), Communities That Care, and Character Counts.
47%	Say they are learning about assets.
42%	Believe they are maintaining the status quo or are stable.
38%	Say that advisory/steering committee reflects most of the community's diversity.
36%	Are currently focused on influencing civic decisions.
35%	Have produced a work plan.
29%	Have produced an annual report.
27%	Believe they are stalled.
27%	Have produced a newsletter.
27%	Have produced an evaluation report.
24%	Have evaluated the impact of the initiative on adults.
24%	Believe they are gaining momentum.
20%	Have produced a video.
16%	Say at least one third of their advisory/steering committee is young people.
7%	Believe they are losing momentum.

From the variety of activities and strategies mentioned by "long haul leaders," it is clear that initiatives do not all operate in the same way. However, we can see that a focus on engaging youth can be found across most of these initiatives, and engaging multiple sectors is also an ongoing task for those initiative leaders in it for the long haul. By looking at those items on which 75% or more agreed, you can see that most have local steering committees that understand that building receptivity and awareness and mobilizing are ongoing tasks that keep the work alive in their communities. By reading the entire list, you can see the variety of activities that initiatives can choose to pursue in their ongoing efforts to maintain visibility and deepen their own and their community's understanding of asset building.

Steps for Building Your Sustainability Plan

To begin the journey of sustainability from your initiative's or program's inception, remember to ground all of your work in these three important ways:

1. *Develop a shared vision:* Vision provides clarity, a picture that all your participants can share and use to help plan for the future. If you reach a place where it seems difficult to know what to do, you can return to your original vision as a touchstone to help clarify direction.
2. *Build strength-based relationships:* Emphasize building relationships as the basis of all your work. They will provide a platform for skill development, behavioral change, and informed decision making.
3. *Cultivate diversity:* Embracing cultural diversity changes people individually and, consequently, changes the trajectory of your program's or initiative's work in the community. Continually cultivate diverse youth and community engagement and active participation in all levels of your work.

   Remember also to emphasize building relationships among your diverse participants—focus on forming trusted relationships with members of different community groups and working with those folks first to be sure that members of each group feel safe, welcomed, and accepted in a meeting or at an event. This will help keep your work relevant, as well as strengthen and sustain your members.

To assist you in developing and customizing your own plan, following is a review of all the sustainability steps we included at the end of each chapter. You'll see that each Assets-GTO question that you applied to your initiative or program to this point can also be rephrased to pertain to your efforts at sustainability.

Question #1. Learn from Your Initial Community Assessments

Pay attention to the needs, interests, and priorities of the stakeholders (including youth) who've already joined you at the table. You want to know what's important to them and look for creative ways to develop congruence between their priorities and yours. By paying attention, you're also beginning to develop relationships, as well as a common purpose and commitment, which are all key to maintaining your work. Remember to:

- *Start to identify places in which to integrate asset building.* Your resource assessment has shown you a full range of programs and supports in the community. Identify which ones you think might be good places to start the conversation about integrating asset building into their work.

- *Offer trainings.* Community leaders and programs might be interested in what you have to offer, but don't have the resources to extend themselves. Providing trainings (even at no cost, if you can) is a way to build relationships and help create a larger, operational infrastructure.
- *Identify potential homes for your programs.* While no one likes to think about what would happen if they can't continue their program, look ahead to logical organizations or programs to take on your work if your funding ends.
- *Talk about larger policy goals now.* It never hurts to think ahead to how you might want to influence decision makers about your issues, priorities, and goals. If you are discussing now the people whom you eventually want to influence and what information you know they'll need to hear, you can build some of those ideas into your evaluation.

All of these actions will help make your work more relevant in the community. You'll have a clear understanding of how your initiative or program fits into the larger picture of what's going on in your community and you can take steps to integrate your work into community and organizational efforts.

Question #2. Develop Clear Goals and Outcomes to Provide Structure

Involving youth, diverse communities, other stakeholders, and the community in the development of your goals and outcomes builds excitement and investment in collective success. Your goals and outcomes become important features of the story you want to tell about your program or initiative and what you hope to achieve. They provide a clear road map for you and the community to follow as you implement, measure, and talk about your accomplishments. Logically linking your community's priorities with the goals and outcomes you develop makes your story easier to tell. You can more easily identify what you want to say and who you want to say it to.

To help set the stage for sustainability:

- *Develop a simple communications plan now.* Use what you're learning through your planning and evaluation efforts to continually communicate with your participants, community, and stakeholders.

- *Repeat your story.* Redundant messages about your goals, outcomes, and successes are necessary to build your identity so that your work becomes an important part of the fabric of the community.
- *Always discuss policy goals.* Continue to discuss what your policy goals are and include communications and engagement with policy makers in your plans. This will help you stay on top of relevant issues as they emerge. It will also keep policy makers aware of your work as a potential resource for them.
- *List your desired outcomes for sustainability.* For example, ask yourself: what portions of your work do you wish to sustain? What are the concrete sustainability outcomes you wish to achieve?

All of these actions will help create a viable operational infrastructure. If you develop and successfully measure realistic outcomes while making the best use of your available resources, you'll demonstrate efficacy to your stakeholders through your successful planning, decision making, and governance. This helps you build your capacity for continuing your work. Measurable outcomes not only have a positive impact on the young people you're working with, they also increase everyone's confidence so that you can garner the support and resources you'll need to repeat your successful programs or projects or broaden and deepen your initiative.

Question #3. Use What Works to Increase Your Chances of Success

By identifying and selecting appropriate, effective programs and projects early in your process, you have a better chance of implementing programs and projects that will lead to measurable outcomes. Achieving measurable outcomes increases the likelihood of your success, making it more likely that you'll be able to sustain your efforts.

Pay attention to incorporating these important elements into your work:

- *Adequate structures to support the initiative or program.* This includes aspects of the model for asset-based community capacity building, such as providing tools, training and coaching, and technical assistance.
- *Adequate expertise and buy-in among staff, volunteers and participants available to sustain the initiative or program.* Training of staff, volunteers, and participants applies here as well, especially for new people as they come on board.
- *Adoption and maintenance of the initiative or program with integrity that adequately meets stakeholder needs.* Here you are building

congruence between identified stakeholder needs and the integrity of your implementation process. This could be as simple as making sure that recommendations from young people are acted upon.

Just as incorporating evidence-based strategies into your work is good for your program or initiative practice, **proactively identifying efforts and practices you think are worth sustaining becomes an important part of your process, too.** (The list in Tipsheet H is a good place to start.)

Question #4. Ensure Fit between Your Work and the Community

Taking the time to assess the fit between your sustainability plans and your community's needs strengthens your overall efforts and makes good use of everyone's resources. Congruence and efficiency bolster sustainability. Getting to know more about the existing organizations, programs, and supports in your community also shows you where to engage multiple agencies, organizations, and community sectors that have a shared stake in what you're doing, further strengthening everyone's efforts on behalf of young people.

By taking such steps, you can:

- *Continue to secure community buy-in as you reach out to new participants;*
- *Ensure the continuation of your chosen programs and projects by having multiple stakeholders sharing in their implementation and success; and*
- *Demonstrate to other entities you engage in the future the efficacy of your plans because of the successful, collective efforts of you and your stakeholders.*

Integrating your work into existing efforts ensures sustainability. Working actively with your partners to build your collective efforts also allows you to monitor the fluctuating context of the community and readjust goals, plans, and programs when necessary.

Question #5. Develop the Organizational Capacities Needed to Strengthen Your Work

By building and maintaining the infrastructures and capacities needed to plan, do, and grow your work, you increase the likelihood that you'll be able to sustain your work. This means paying attention to the nuts and bolts of doing things like governance, decision making, documenting, managing, communicating, coordinating, and celebrating, as well as supporting the people involved by providing recognition, training, and support. Simply having regular meetings, compiling good records, and keeping communication channels open will help maintain the infrastructure.

To further support your work and build sustainability:

- *Look for ways to build formal and informal relationships among leaders, champions, and stakeholders within your initiative or program to strengthen your work;*
- *Look for ways to build formal and informal relationships across community groups, other organizations, and institutions; and*
- *Develop plans for increasing resources dedicated to your initiative, program, or projects as well as ways of securing ongoing, yet flexible, resources for your work.*

Catalyzing leadership and asset champions builds sustainability. You want to recruit adults and youth who can be part of shaping and implementing your vision while developing enough capacity within your initiative or program to withstand leaders moving on. Shared leadership promotes community ownership and helps sustain your efforts by letting people know they have important roles to play.

Question #6. Connect Vision and Outcomes through Good Planning

Both planning and doing are necessary to maintain momentum in your asset-building efforts. If you spend too much time planning, energy and enthusiasm can wane in the absence of action. If you spend too much time doing, on the other hand, you may head in a direction that doesn't lead toward your goals. We like to say that you can think of *planning* as stepping with the left foot and *doing* as stepping with the right foot. Integrating planning and doing allows you to draw on the contributions of both planners and doers in your initiative, organization, or program.

Remember to:

- *Continue recruiting effective leaders who will take appropriate actions to sustain the initiative or program.* Effective leadership will help you proactively respond to a changing environment so you can make needed adjustments while still maintaining your vision and goals.

- *Continue cultivating asset champions (youth and adult) who will guide and inspire your community change movement.* These may not be the usual community leaders or people performing in the usual formal roles, although they can be. Asset champions can help you continue to broaden the support for an initiative or program through flexible, informal, catalyzing ways.
- *Continue developing adequate policies and procedures that will help you sustain your initiative or program.* By establishing measurable goals and procedures for evaluating your progress, you will have a way of systematically reflecting on your work that helps inform your actions as you move toward your goals.

Making sure you are clear about the contributions of both planners and doers—and integrating their ideas into your work—will help you build sustainability. One of your roles is to attract many different people to the many different tasks of asset building by remaining invitational. Keep inviting and informing. Find ways to revisit your vision, but keep going.

Question #7. Implement Your Plans with Quality

Your process evaluation will yield concrete data about how well you're implementing your programs and projects, but it can also provide an opportunity for you to reflect on how well things are going. Go back to your vision and see if you are staying on course. Use this as a time to ask your stakeholders if *they* think you are on course. If you think you've strayed from your original vision, talk about ways to refocus your efforts.

Think about:

- *Actively using your goals, chosen strategies, and gathered information* to help you examine the process you're using to make sure you're staying focused but flexible;
- *Continuing to invite new people* and their fresh insights into your process; and
- *Reviewing and fine-tuning the methods you use* to assess your program or project implementation to continually ensure the integrity of your work.

Making sure you're paying attention to implementation quality and integrity that adequately meets stakeholder needs will help you build sustainability. You will not only increase your chances of success, you will also earn the trust and confidence of your partners, which will have a wider impact in other efforts. You will also have a chance to stay on top of any midcourse corrections that may be needed to keep your efforts on track.

Question #8. Find Multiple Ways to Measure and Communicate Your Outcomes

There is nothing more crucial to sustaining your work than having positive outcomes. By clearly demonstrating the effectiveness of what you've done—and how it's tied directly to your vision, goals, and community needs—you not only make a convincing case for maintaining your work, you potentially strengthen the work of your partners. By implication, you are also sustaining the efficacy of the outcomes you're measuring.

Carefully developing and following a structured plan for your projects and programs will be more effective if you have a variety of data to demonstrate your successes. You are looking to measure a variety of outcomes at various levels including individuals, community, and systems.

Build sustainability by using data to:

- *Make program adaptations monthly, quarterly, and yearly;*
- *Engage stakeholders; and*
- *Report back regularly to the community.*

Demonstrating and sharing strong results with others in the community help build sustainability beyond the implementation of a single program or project. Your data support your success. You can use what you learn to make sure you are continuing to address the original priorities and goals you identified or if you need to make adjustments to increase your congruence and credibility. Be honest—provide both negative and positive data to all of your audiences. Honestly look at what is working and what needs to be changed as well.

Question #9. Employ Continuous Improvement to Revitalize Your Work

Systematically assessing and reviewing your progress, then implementing changes where necessary will keep your work vital. But also remember that while you must focus to a certain extent on the nuts and bolts of building and sustaining a program or initiative, building Developmental Assets works best when you:

- *Continue to approach community change as a dynamic, unpredictable process.* Having a template or "recipe" to work from is useful, but the way your initiative, project, or program will actually develop is like cooking gumbo—each one is different, and it's supposed to be! That's part of what makes the work fun, interesting, and truly reflective of a community's diversity.

- *Give it away.* Your role is not to provide all the answers but to unleash the processes within the community that will build the change you collectively seek. Empower people in the community to incorporate the Developmental Assets framework in their work in unique, creative, even informal ways. Pay attention to the community members' personal and organizational interests to help determine where to invest your initiative's (or program's) energy.
- *Trust the community.* Asset building is about developing trust and relationships with others. Participants may find that they disagree with each other on how to go about some things, but the asset framework can provide common language and common ground for people to articulate their higher purpose of caring about children and youth. The more voices at the table, the stronger your work will be.

Systematic reflection on your work will help you build sustainability. Using your vision as your touchstone and then keeping the end in mind while asking where you can do better will continually help you refresh and revitalize your work.

A Final Checklist to Review Your Sustainability Plans

The steps for completing Worksheet 10.1, Sustainability Plan Checklist, are as follows:

1. Gather together your work group.
2. Make as many copies of the worksheet as you need to write on.
3. Have a brainstorming session that gives everyone a chance to reflect on each of the checklist points.
4. Decide together if you are meeting each of the sustainability goals described in the worksheet.
5. If there are areas your group thinks need improvement, make some notes about how you'll improve your sustainability plan in each area.
6. Plan to revisit, review, and revise your sustainability plans regularly.

By thinking ahead to the myriad ways you can sustain your initiative, project(s), or program(s), you'll also be prepared to deal with surprises, like funding cutbacks, funding infusions, or changes in key staff, champions, or stakeholders.

WORKSHEET 10.1

Sustainability Plan Checklist

Sustainability Goals	Yes	No	Not sure	What we can do
Vision: Our vision has been developed through the shared efforts of our coalition and community members. The vision provides clarity and allows for future-oriented planning. We have a vision team or process that provides a constant source of fresh faces and fresh ideas, keeping our initiative or program dynamic and creative.				
Relationships: We emphasize building relationships as the basis of all our work. Our relationships are based on strengths, which will provide a platform for skill development, behavioral change and informed decision making.				
Diversity: We continually cultivate diverse youth and community engagement and active participation in all levels of our work not only to keep our efforts relevant but also to strengthen and sustain our members. We also emphasize building relationships among our participants.				

Worksheet 10.1 continued on next page

WORKSHEET 10.1 *continued*

Sustainability Plan Checklist

Sustainability Goals	Yes	No	Not sure	What we can do
Q #1 **Assessment:** We have a clear understanding of how our initiative or program fits into the larger picture of what's going on in our community. We've taken steps to blend and braid our work into community and organizational efforts. We have a plan for regularly updating our formal and informal surveys of community issues and concerns as well as reassessing resources so we know when to make appropriate adjustments in our work.				
Q #2 **Goals and outcomes:** We use what we've learned through our planning and evaluation efforts to continually communicate with our participants, community, and stakeholders. We have developed a plan for what we want to say and who we want to say it to. We have also discussed, wherever relevant, what our policy goals are and included communications and engagement with policy makers in our plan.				

Worksheet 10.1 continued on next page

Sustainability Plan Checklist

Sustainability Goals	Yes	No	Not sure	What we can do
Q #3 **Effectiveness:** We're being proactive by identifying efforts we think are worth sustaining. Just as we identify and use effective strategies in our program and initiative practice, we use effective methods for sustaining our work as well.				
Q #4 **Fit:** We continue to engage multiple agencies, organizations, and community sectors that have a shared stake in what we're doing. We monitor the fluctuating context of the community and readjust when necessary. We seek to integrate our work into existing efforts to ensure sustainability. We work through roadblocks in creative, collaborative ways.				

Worksheet 10.1 continued on next page

Sustainability Plan Checklist

Sustainability Goals	Yes	No	Not sure	What we can do
Q #5 **Capacity:** We build and maintain the infrastructures and capacities needed to plan, do, and grow our work. This means paying attention to the nuts and bolts of doing our work like governance, decision making, documenting, managing, communicating, recruiting, coordinating, and celebrating as well as supporting the people involved by providing recognition, training, and support.				
Q #6 **Plan:** We integrate both planning and doing to implement our programs and projects and maintain momentum for our work. We continue to recruit effective leaders and asset champions.				

Worksheet 10.1 continued on next page

WORKSHEET 10.1 *continued*

Sustainability Plan Checklist

Sustainability Goals	Yes	No	Not sure	What we can do
Q #7 **Process:** We take time to reflect back on our vision and make sure our work remains congruent with what we set out to do. We use the goals, outcomes, and information we've developed to help us examine the process we're using to make sure we're staying focused but flexible. Our process remains open to new people and fresh insights.				
Q #8 **Outcomes:** Our data supports our success. We use what we learn to help ourselves and our stakeholders understand if we are continuing to address the original priorities and goals we identified or if we need to make adjustments to increase our congruence and credibility.				
Q #9 **Improvement:** We systematically assess and review our progress, and implement changes where necessary to keep our work vital.				
Q #10 **Sustainability:** We plan for sustainability just as we plan our goals, outcomes, projects, and programs.				

APPENDIX A

Glossary

Accountability The ability to demonstrate to key stakeholders that a program or initiative works and that it uses its resources effectively to achieve and sustain projected goals and outcomes.

Action Strategies (Search Institute) The Five Action Strategies provide a practical approach to identifying, encouraging, and linking all the people, places, activities, and programs necessary for a powerful collective effort. With an initiative, you can intensify your efforts to:

1. *Engage adults* from all walks of life to develop sustained, strength-building relationships with children and adolescents, both within families and in neighborhoods.
2. *Mobilize young people* to use their power as asset builders and change agents. This means listening to their input and including them in decision making.
3. *Activate sectors* of the community—such as schools, congregations, businesses, youth and family services, human services, and health care—to create an asset-building culture and to contribute fully to young people's positive growth and development.
4. *Invigorate programs* to become more asset rich and to be available to and accessed by all children and youth.
5. *Influence civic decisions* by connecting with decision makers and opinion leaders to leverage financial, media, and policy resources in support of this positive transformation of communities and society.

Activities	The specific actions needed to carry out each of the primary program components. For example, some of the activities needed to present a Latino Student Leadership Conference might include recruiting and training students, booking a conference location, and planning the conference's slate of workshops.
Components	The primary elements of a program. For example, a school district launches a program aimed at boosting student achievement among Latino students. The main components of that program could include (1) presenting a Latino Student Leadership Conference, (2) forming a parent advisory committee, and (3) offering Spanish lessons for teachers. The next level of detail describing the specific actions needed to implement each of those components would be the program's activities.
Developmental Assets	The 40 concrete, commonsense, positive experiences and qualities essential to raising successful young people.
Domain	Within the Communities That Care model, a term used to indicate categories of risk and protective factors such as community domain, and family domain.
Effectiveness	The ability of a program or initiative to achieve its stated goals and produce measurable outcomes.
Evidence-Based (or Research-Based)	A classification for programs/initiatives that have been shown through scientific study to produce consistently positive results.
Fidelity	The extent to which the program or initiative is implemented in the exact way that the developer intended. This is often balanced with adaptation, which is the degree to which programs or initiatives are adapted or customized to fit local needs and conditions.
Getting To Outcomes (GTO)	A system of accountability that includes ten elements of effective planning, implementation, and evaluation. GTO is a process of addressing ten questions to increase the likelihood that programs/initiatives are able to achieve their desired results and demonstrate accountability.
Goals	Statements that indicate overall direction and reflect projected future long-term impact.
Initiative	An organized, community-wide mobilization effort.

Logic Model	A flow chart or table that describes what an initiative or program expects to achieve and how it's all expected to work, based on a chain of events. The model shows the logical relationships among goals, desired outcomes, components, and activities.
Outcomes	The specific changes in knowledge, attitudes, skills, and behaviors expected to occur as the result of actions. In Assets-GTO, outcome statements are developed by addressing: what will change (outcome), for whom (population), by how much (increase or decrease), by when (specified date), as measured by (data source). Outcomes can be short, intermediate, or long term.
Outcomes Evaluation	Systematic process of collecting, analyzing, and interpreting data to assess and evaluate what outcomes a program or initiative has achieved.
Process Evaluation	Assessing what activities were implemented, the quality of the implementation, and the strengths and weaknesses of the implementation. Process evaluation is used to produce useful feedback for ongoing improvement, to determine which activities were more successful than others, and to document successful processes for future replication.
Program or Project	A structured, intentional set of activities conducted by initiatives and/or organizations.
Qualitative Data	Information about a program/initiative gathered in narrative form by talking to or observing people. Often presented as text, qualitative data serve to illuminate evaluation findings derived from quantitative methods.
Quantitative Data	Information about a program/initiative gathered in numeric form. Quantitative methods deal most often with numbers that are analyzed with statistics to test hypotheses and track the strength and direction of effects.
Stakeholders	People who have a vested interest in the development, implementation, progress, and success of any community, initiative, or program plans.
Strategies	See "Action Strategies."

APPENDIX B

Research on and Evidence for the Developmental Assets Model

MARC MANNES, PH.D.

This appendix provides the research background and general application of the Developmental Assets model and also describes the current evidence base for it, showing that assessing the cumulative benefits of Developmental Assets for individual youth can help to:

- Explain the prevention of and protection from high-risk behaviors;
- Explain the expression of thriving behaviors; and
- Explain academic achievement and commitment to learning.

You will find it helpful as background for asset-building efforts, as well as for sharing with program and initiative leaders and funders. In addition, you will find useful information here, as you develop your targeted program(s) and project(s), to support your focus on asset building and your use of measures of Developmental Assets in your evaluation.

The Developmental Assets Model

Search Institute's Developmental Assets (or asset) model is based on a set of theoretical hypotheses and empirical evidence that helping youth experience healthy developmental resources and opportunities, and helping them to successfully achieve developmental tasks is one of the best ways to prevent negative behaviors and outcomes and to promote positive behaviors and outcomes. The asset model is based on a synthesis of multiple lines of inquiry aimed at identifying the "building blocks" of development that contribute to three types of healthy outcomes:

- The prevention of high-risk behaviors (e.g., substance use, violence, early sexual intercourse, school failure);
- The enhancement of thriving behaviors (e.g., school success, affirmation of diversity, the proactive approach to nutrition and exercise); and
- Resilience, or the capacity to function adequately in the face of adversity.

The asset model identifies factors (40 Developmental Assets) that are empirically predictive of these healthy outcomes consistently across sex, race/ethnicity, and family income (Benson, Scales, Leffert, & Roehlkepartain, 1999; Leffert et al., 1998). All 40 Developmental Assets comprising the asset model are supported by empirical literature (Scales & Leffert, 2004).

The asset model also weaves together core themes from developmental systems and developmental dynamic systems theories that point to the developmental significance of positive relationships between young people and adults, among young people and their peers, and between young people and the various community and social settings that touch their lives. It draws support from research and evaluation studies that show that programmatic approaches that are narrowly focused on reducing or preventing risks are less effective than more comprehensive approaches that focus on meeting young people's broad developmental needs (e.g., Roth, Brooks-Gunn, Murray, & Foster, 1998; Seligman & Csikszentmihalyi, 2000; Schorr, 1993).

The Asset Model's Theoretical and Research Roots

The asset model is conceptually aligned with a number of recent syntheses of research on adolescent development, including the National Research Council and Institute of Medicine (Eccles & Gootman, 2002); the working group on positive youth development within the Society for Research in Adolescence (Roth et al., 1998), and the American Academy of Political and Social Science (Damon, 2004). It represents an integrative and applied framework of strength-based theories and research that constitute the field of "positive youth development" (Benson, Scales, Hamilton, & Sesma, 2004). It is also consistent with one of the core dynamics of positive youth development that involves the active interplay of ecological and individual factors in moving youth toward health-promoting actions and behaviors. The asset model reflects an exceptional balance of ecological influences (the external assets) and individual-level engagement (internal assets).

The asset model also has an important lifespan relevance by virtue of offering a theoretical basis for understanding positive development across multiple age groups. Empirically based Developmental Assets frameworks have been crafted for middle childhood or upper elementary school years (Scales, Sesma, & Bolstrom, 2004) and early childhood or preschool years (see www.search-institute.org).

In addition to incorporating the application of knowledge associated with strength-based development, the asset model is also based on the theory and research that show a number of discrete qualities and features minimize the influence of risk factors and enhance the likelihood of successful development.

For example, attributes related to resilience and competence are central to developmental strengths. Resilience refers to "the emergence of good adaptation in the context of high-risk exposure or significant threats to development" (Masten & Curtis, 2000, p. 530). Garmezy (1985), for example, noted that resilient children seem to have three broad categories of factors operating to protect them: (1) individual dispositions, such as an easygoing temperament and high intelligence, (2) cohesive families, including a close relationship with a parent, and (3) the ability to attract and use sources of social support, including relationships with nonparental adults and positive school experiences. Masten and Curtis (2000) defined "competence" as "adaptational success in the developmental tasks expected of individuals of a given age in a particular cultural and historical context" (p. 533). Research has suggested that competence exhibits a coherent structure in children and adolescents, being comprised of academic, conduct, and social success throughout childhood and adolescence (Masten et al., 1995).

Numerous elements, defined as protective factors, have also been identified as playing an important role in protecting children from risk and encouraging successful adaptation. Protective factors include a high commitment to school, high self-efficacy, and an external support system that encourages coping and positive values (Hawkins, Catalano, & Miller, 1992). For Benard (2004), resilience for young people is defined as the presence of caring relationships, high expectations, and opportunities to participate in and contribute to in family, school, and community life.

In Jessor, Turbin, and Costa's (1998) longitudinal study of urban high school students, risk and protective factors each accounted for relatively similar proportions of variance in school success and delinquency prevention, both concurrently and across time. The most important predictors among the risk factors were low expectations for success, low self-esteem, hopelessness, and having friends as models for problem behavior. In contrast, the key protective factors were attitudinal intolerance of deviance, positive orientation to health, and having friends as models for conventional behavior. The findings also suggested that risk was moderated by protection, such that young people with higher levels of risk factors were more likely to have successful outcomes if they also had higher levels of protection.

The concept of "connectedness" to others, derived from positive relationships, is also central to strength-based development. By "connectedness" we mean the quality and stability of the emotional bonds of support and caring that exist between children and caregivers, children and peers, and among the adults in young people's worlds. Scores of studies have reported that positive connections to parents and other adults contribute to better well-being across a variety of behavioral and psychological outcomes at specific moments in time, as well as across time (reviewed in Scales & Leffert, 1999). Especially for children and adolescents of color, relationships with adults in the extended family may be particularly important supplemental or compensatory sources of connectedness (Scales & Gibbons, 1996).

Pettit, Bates, and Dodge's (1997) longitudinal study of more than 500 Tennessee and Indiana families with kindergartners showed that the quality of supportive parenting children received as kindergartners (e.g., parental warmth and involvement, proactive teaching, calm discussion) contributed a small (1–3%) but unique variance to the prediction of their functioning in both kindergarten and grade 6, including whether they exhibited problem behaviors, were socially skillful, and performed well in school. This study was notable for showing that the presence of positive parenting, not only the absence of harsh parenting, plays an important role in contributing to child well-being in both the short and longer term.

Relationships with adults in school and community settings also provide valuable sources of connection. In the National Longitudinal Study on Adolescent Health, Resnick and colleagues (1997) reported that young people who experienced closer connections to their families and schools were significantly less likely than other adolescents to engage in a variety of risk-taking behaviors. Each of the contexts (family and school) by itself explained relatively modest portions (5%–18%) of the variance across outcomes such as emotional distress, violence, and substance use. However, analyses showed that the emotional connectedness variables (such as feeling loved and wanted at home, feeling close to people at school, and feeling that teachers treated them fairly) were more important contributors than other variables such as simple parent presence, the activities parents and adolescents did together, feelings about student prejudice at school, or the school's attendance or dropout rates. Even for age at first sexual intercourse, an outcome where other variables did make a contribution, emotional connectedness still played a critical role. Young people with high levels of parent/family connectedness were 15% less likely than those with low levels ever to have had sexual intercourse. Those with high levels of school connectedness were even more positively affected: They were 23% less likely ever to have had sexual intercourse.

Community Application of the Asset Model

In addition to being well grounded in scientific theory and research, the asset model has demonstrated widespread practical application. This is in part a natural outgrowth of the asset model's deliberateness in calling attention to the many and varied community sources of developmental strengths and a consequence of the availability of Search Institute resources and products describing strategies and practices those sources can employ to support the positive development of young people. The asset model not only considers the more obvious venue of youth programs, some of which are designed to fill the "gap periods" when youth are not engaged in more formal socializing systems (Benson & Pittman, 2001), but uniquely emphasizes the connections between and transactions across other community settings and contexts that are too often overlooked or underappreciated (Bronfenbrenner, 1979; Scales & Leffert, 1999). The asset model serves as a point of departure from, and a counterpoint to, most research as well as policy, program, and practice efforts that tend to focus only on a single source, or "delivery system," for developmental well-being, such as families, schools, neighborhoods, youth organizations, or religious communities.

The asset model stimulates mobilization, planning, and implementation processes in hundreds and hundreds of communities throughout North America that are striving to become "developmentally attentive" places for young people. Communities that focus on asset building use the Developmental Assets to establish a language of the common good, secure a working consensus on core values that undergird healthy development, and then take concrete steps to raise good kids. The common language the asset model introduces to community conversations enhances the prospects of reaching a consensus that can help shape incentives for adult engagement with children and youth. The consensus also serves to stimulate and influence the formation of developmentally supportive social norms, and leads to the provision of opportunities and resources that can bring developmental well-being to fruition.

A developmentally attentive community acts to see that youth experience multiple developmentally rich life settings, and that all youth, not just those deemed to be at-risk and/or served by standard prevention or risk-reduction programs, are beneficiaries. The developmentally attentive community works to activate the strength-building capacity of its residents of all ages, promote collective action that seeks to recreate community infrastructure more conducive to positive development, and delineate pathways for a more equitable access to all facets of its revitalized infrastructure.

The asset model also appears to hold global applicability. Asset-building implementation is occurring in Canada, Brazil, Singapore, and Australia, as interested parties see the relevance and utility of the model in serving the youth of these nations.

Many communities make use of the Search Institute survey entitled *Profiles of Student Life: Attitudes and Behaviors* (A&B) to initiate their asset-building endeavors. Search Institute began using the A&B in 1989, and since that time has been conducting studies of 6th- to 12th-grade students in public and private schools throughout the United States that complete the instrument. The A&B was revised in 1996 to measure each of the 40 Developmental Assets, gather data on a set of items defined as developmental deficits, and measure a collection of high-risk behaviors drawn from federally funded research studies. Finally, the survey tries to identify the degree to which young people manifest what are referred to as thriving indicators, representing optimal expressions of healthy and responsible behavior. The A&B is administered anonymously in a classroom setting with standardized instructions.

The completed surveys are mailed back to Search Institute, where the data are processed and an aggregate report is produced and sent back to the community. The aggregate report provides a developmental profile of community youth, and also paints a portrait of the human development community system for young people. Through 2004, more than 3,000 communities have had their youth complete the A&B one or more times, and about 2 million adolescents have completed the instrument at least once.

Analyses of aggregate national samples of adolescents completing the survey during a particular school year have been conducted for 1989–1990, 1996–1997, and 1999–2000, and for the year 2003. Aggregate national reports have been created in 1990, 1999, and 2005. The data collected from administering the A&B are the foundation for analysis and establishment of the evidence base documenting the benefits of using the asset model.

Evidence Supporting the Developmental Benefits of Using the Asset Model

There is a consistent and growing body of evidence based on correlational and regression statistical analyses that points to the cumulative influence, importance, and power of the Developmental Assets in relation to significant dimensions of young people's lives. Analysis of various data collected by Search Institute, along with the evaluation of various initiatives conducted by third-party evaluators, makes the case that assessing the cumulative benefits of Developmental Assets for individual youth can help to:

- Increase an understanding of what constitutes risk;
- Explain the prevention of high-risk behaviors;
- Explain protection from high-risk behaviors;
- Explain the expression of thriving behaviors;
- Better understand relationships between asset categories and risk and thriving developmental outcomes; and,
- Explain academic achievement and commitment to learning.

In addition, Search Institute research and third-party evaluations are helping to make the case that there are cumulative benefits of a programmatic, community-based, and statewide application of the asset model, including:

- Positive developmental impacts on youth in areas such as grade point average; stronger sense of belonging, self-confidence, and self-efficacy; possessing a more positive view of the future, a stronger degree of empathy for others, and a higher valuing of community service; a greater number of interactions with a wider circle of adults; and having strengthened relationships with significant adults in their lives;
- Decreases in alcohol, tobacco, and other drug use by youth;
- Decreases in academic failure;
- Increased commitment to school as demonstrated by improved attendance of students;
- Expressions of adult leadership for asset building;
- Successful community mobilization around asset building;
- Positive results for youth from redundancy and reinforcement of asset building across community settings;
- Changes in the behaviors of agencies serving youth;
- Youth and adults having more positive interactions with one another; and
- An increase in asset levels for youth over time.

The Cumulative Benefits of Assets for Individual Youth

Various studies generate a greater understanding regarding the developmental robustness of assets for individual young people. The evidence suggests that the more Developmental Assets young people experience and possess in their lives, the less likely they are to succumb to risks, the healthier, more caring, and more responsible they are likely to be, the more inclined they are to manifest markers of optimal development, and the more likely they are to be successful in school.

Helping to Deepen an Understanding of What Constitutes Risk

Low levels of Developmental Assets appear to be a better predictor of engaging in risk behaviors than many of the more widely used sociodemographic risk factors, such as living in poverty, being from a single-parent family, and dropping out of school. An analysis of data from students in a Minnesota community was conducted to ascertain the relationship between high-risk behaviors and a more traditional risk measure: poverty (which, in this case, is measured by eligibility for free or reduced-price lunches).

The study indicated that experiencing fewer than ten assets is two to five times as powerful in predicting risk as poverty. For example, young people (regardless of their levels of assets) who live in low-income families are twice as likely as other youth to engage in antisocial behavior. In contrast, low-asset girls (regardless of their family economic status) are nine times as likely as other girls to engage in antisocial behavior as other girls, and low-asset boys are four times as likely as other boys to engage in antisocial behavior. These findings suggest that using asset levels as a primary means of identifying youth at risk may be better than relying on more standard demographic measures.

A comparison was also made between young people who reported low levels of assets (0–10) with those who reported 11 or more assets, and their relative risk for various negative behaviors. Results showed youth with few assets as many times more at risk of engaging in all of the negative behaviors than those with more assets. This relationship holds true for both females and males. For example, females reporting few assets are six times as likely as other females to report school problems (including lower grades and skipping school). Males with few assets are five times as likely as other males to be at risk for using drugs.

Helping to Explain the Prevention of High-Risk Behaviors

In their study of nearly 100,000 6th–12th graders, Benson and colleagues (1999) noted that the higher the number of assets students reported they have, the less likely they were to report engaging in a variety of high-risk behavior patterns. For example, 53% of young people who are viewed as asset poor and report 0–10 assets have used alcohol three or more times in the past month or have gotten drunk at least once in the last two weeks, but only 3% of students viewed as asset rich, with 31–40 assets, report such problem alcohol use. The 30% of students with average levels of assets (11–20) are ten times more likely to have problems with alcohol use than asset-rich students.

Similar correlational patterns are evident with other common risky behaviors for youth, including tobacco use, drug use, sexual intercourse, depression and/or attempted suicide, antisocial behavior, violence, school problems, driving and alcohol, and gambling. Asset-rich students are many times less likely to engage in these behaviors than even asset-average youth, much less asset-poor youth.

Using regression techniques on the same sample, Leffert and colleagues (1998) reported that certain clusters of Developmental Assets explained a considerable proportion of the variance associated with those high-risk behavior patterns. All of the 40 assets were introduced into stepwise regressions as predictor variables, after first entering gender, grade, racial/ethnic background, family composition, and maternal education (as a proxy for socioeconomic status). A predictor variable was considered meaningful if it added at least 1% to the variance of the risk behavior patterns. Although slightly different clusters of assets were meaningful in explaining different outcomes, the total model (with demographic variables) accounted for 21–41% of the variance, and the assets themselves contributed 16–35%. Developmental Assets were most meaningful in predicting depression and/or suicide attempts, school problems, violence, and alcohol use, and had somewhat less explanatory power for tobacco use, sexual intercourse, and gambling.

An overall risk index of 24 different high-risk behaviors also was created. The total regression models (assets plus demographics) explained 66% of the variance of the risk index, and assets alone explained 57%. Across the risk index and various risk-behavior patterns, the Developmental Assets that most often were retained as meaningful predictors were positive peer influence, the value of restraint, peaceful conflict resolution, school engagement, resistance skills, and time at home. Achievement motivation was a unique predictor of school problems, and a sense of purpose and self-esteem uniquely explained depression and/or suicide attempts.

Moreover, consistent with the studies of other researchers (e.g., Jessor & Jessor, 1977; Ketterlinus, Lamb, Nitz, & Elster, 1992), Benson and colleagues (1999) show that risk behaviors tend to co-occur. That is, young people who engage in one high-risk behavior pattern are several times more likely to engage in other patterns of risky behavior. For example, 71% of the young people who regularly use tobacco also have problems with alcohol use, whereas among those who don't use tobacco only 17% have a problem with alcohol use. Similarly, 69% of those who engage in antisocial behavior also engage in violence, versus only 22% who engage in violence but not antisocial behavior. The risk behaviors Search Institute has found to be the most likely to co-occur with other patterns of risk are problem alcohol use, tobacco use, and other illicit drug use, as well as antisocial behavior. Students who engage in any of those risk patterns are more than four times as likely as other students to engage in at least three additional risk behavior patterns.

In addition, for both middle and high school students, there are certain patterns of risk that, when students engage in them, mark those students as developmentally out of step with the majority of their peers. For example, middle school students who engage in problem alcohol use or who have had sexual intercourse three or more times are not so different from high school students in those risk patterns, but are distinctly different from most other middle school students, their peers. Similarly, high school students who engage in violence are less like their high school–age peers, and more like middle school students, who actually report more violent behavior than older adolescents. At each grade level, young people who engage in risk patterns that are developmentally out of sync with those engaged in by their peers appear to be at an especially heightened risk of engaging in other risk patterns. As Benson and colleagues (1999) wrote, the existence of these differences "isolates them from the majority of their peers, places them in contact with more negative influences, and increases the probability that their behavior will become more and more dangerous and destructive" (p. 68).

Helping to Explain Protection from High-Risk Behaviors

In addition to providing a preventive function, the Developmental Assets demonstrate their viability as protective factors in the sense that they work against youth engagement in risk behaviors. The protective value of the Developmental Assets is best illustrated by findings that show how the number of risky behavioral patterns co-occur as a function of asset levels. The average number of 10 high-risk behavior patterns reported by young people drops sharply, by half or more, with each successive increase in the level of assets they report. Asset-poor young people with 0–10 assets report 4.4 high-risk behavior patterns. Youth with 11–20 assets report 2.4 risk patterns, while those with 21–30 assets report just 1 high risk behavior pattern. Asset-rich youth, with 31–40 assets, report just .3 risk patterns.

It is important to note that these findings are also consistent among youth of color. The same pattern of asset-rich multiracial, African American, Latino/Latina, Asian American, and American Indian youth being less likely to engage in these high-risk behaviors than their asset-poor counterparts is evident from an analysis of the data. Asset-average youth of color (those experiencing on average 23 or 24 Developmental Assets) tend to engage in no high-risk behaviors, whereas asset-poor youth of color (experiencing only 6–9 assets) engage in 9 or 10 high-risk behaviors.

Developmental Assets and Risk Behavior Patterns by Asset Levels*

High-risk behavior pattern		Percentage reporting behavior pattern			
Category	Definition	Assets			
		0–11	11–20	21–30	31–40
Alcohol	Has used alcohol three or more times in the past month or got drunk once in the past two weeks.	45	26	11	3
Tobacco	Smokes one or more cigarettes every day or uses chewing tobacco frequently.	22	9	3	0
Illicit drugs	Used illicit drugs three or more times in the past year.	38	18	6	1
Sexual activity	Has had sexual intercourse three or more times in lifetime	34	23	11	3
Depression/suicide	Is frequently depressed and/or has attempted suicide.	44	29	15	5
Antisocial behavior	Has been involved in three or more incidents of shoplifting, trouble with police, or vandalism in the past year.	47	22	7	1
Violence	Has engaged in three or more acts of fighting, hitting, injuring a person, carrying or using a weapon, or threatening physical harm in the past year.	62	38	18	6
School problems	Has skipped school two or more days in the past month and/or has below a C average.	44	23	10	4
Driving and alcohol	Has driven after drinking or ridden with a drinking drive three or more times in the past year.	33	19	8	2
Gambling	Has gambled three or more times in the past year.	27	18	10	3

*Based on studies of 6th- to 12-grade public school students during 2003. Sample includes 148,189 students in 202 communities.

Helping to Explain the Expression of Thriving Behaviors

The concept of thriving encompasses something very different from the relative absence of pathology. Instead, it seeks to articulate the conceptual elements of thriving along with more explicit indicators of highly successful and even

Developmental Assets and Thriving Indicators, by Asset Level*

Thriving indicators		Percentage reporting behavior			
Category	Definition	Assets			
		0–11	11–20	21–30	31–40
School success	Students grades are A- or higher.	9	19	34	54
Prosocial behavior	Student provides help to others 1 hour or more per week.	62	79	89	96
Affirmation of diversity	Student places high value on interacting with people of other racial and ethnic backgrounds.	39	60	76	89
Leadership	Student reports being a leader in a group or organization in the last 12 months.	48	66	78	87
Danger avoidance	Student reports avoiding behaviors that are dangerous.	9	19	31	44
Health promotion	Student reports an active interest in nutrition and exercise.	27	48	69	88
Delay of gratification	Student "saves money for something special rather than spending it all right away."	27	41	56	72
Resilience	Student reports he/she "does not give up when things get difficult."	56	67	78	86

*Based on studies of 6th- to 12-grade public school students during 2003. Sample includes 148,189 students in 202 communities.

optimal development. Search Institute's set of thriving indicators are school success, helping others, valuing diversity, maintaining physical health, exhibiting leadership, resisting danger, delaying gratification, and overcoming adversity.

There is some conceptual similarity between the notion of Developmental Assets and that of thriving indicators, in that both concepts focus on the presence of strengths in young people's lives. However, assets are conceptualized as the building blocks of developmental success, whereas thriving indicators are seen as signs or markers of highly successful development. In other words, Developmental Assets are seen as predictors of the outcomes represented by thriving indicators. Experiencing and possessing assets define conditions under which the attainment of those thriving outcomes is made more likely.

Benson and colleagues (1999) reported that Developmental Assets show similar patterns of relations with thriving indicators as they do with high-risk behavior patterns. The promotional function of the Developmental Assets that fosters highly successful development is best illustrated by findings that show how thriving patterns co-occur as a function of asset levels. The proportion of young people who enjoy the co-occurrence of at least six of the eight thriving behaviors studied by Benson and colleagues (1999) is dramatically greater among asset-rich youth than among youth with just average levels of assets or those youth that are asset-poor. For all eight thriving indicators studied, the proportion of students saying they experience them increases with each rise in asset level. For example, only 7% of asset-poor students with 0–10 assets say they get mostly A's at school, whereas 53% of asset-rich young people with 31–40 assets report such thriving. Although the patterns typically are not as dramatic as the relation of assets to risk behaviors, the trends are the same.

The difference is especially striking as a function of how vulnerable young people are. For example, among young people who experience none of five developmental deficits (alone at home, TV overexposure, physical abuse, victim of violence, attending drinking parties) and who experience 31–40 assets, 79% report at least six of the eight thriving indicators. But, among those who report 11–20 assets, yet also experience none of the deficits, just 14% have six of the eight thriving indicators. In other words, asset-rich youth are six times more likely to experience these indicators of thriving.

Among the most vulnerable youth, those with all five deficits, the level of assets makes a profound difference: Nearly 60% of those highly vulnerable youth with high assets have six of the eight thriving indicators, but just 11% of highly vulnerable youth with only average levels of assets indicate they manifest the indicators of thriving.

Similar patterns are also evident among youth of color. Youth from all racial/ethnic groups are more likely to exhibit multiple thriving behaviors if they experience more Developmental Assets. Youth of color exhibiting all eight thriving behaviors have, on average, 29–32 of the 40 assets, whereas youth exhibiting none of the thriving behaviors have, on average, 7 or 8 Developmental Assets. Findings from a study conducted among economically poor Latino/Latina and African American urban high school students showed that the average number of thriving behaviors increased by 24% among students experiencing 21–30 assets versus students with 11–20 assets. Also, among these students the ones experiencing 11–20 assets had a 52% increase in thriving behaviors over their counterparts with only 0–10 assets (Scales et al., 2005).

In order to better understand the role Developmental Assets may play in explaining thriving indicators among youth of color, Scales, Benson, Leffert, and Blyth (2000) drew from the Benson and colleagues (1999) sample of nearly 100,000 6th–12th graders a subsample of 1,000 students in each of six racial/ethnic groups (African American, Asian American, Hispanic/Latino, Native

American, Multiracial, and White youth). As in Leffert and colleagues (1998), the 40 assets were entered into stepwise regressions after the demographic variables had first been entered as a block, and those that were retained as meaningful predictors explained at least 1% of the variance in a thriving indicator.

Scales and colleagues (2000) reported that clusters of the assets explained 47–54% of a thriving index (comprised of all the indicators) across racial/ethnic groups, and 10–43% of seven specific thriving outcomes across racial/ethnic groups, over and above demographic variables. With demographic variables included, the total models explained 48–57% of the variance of the thriving index, and 11–48% of the individual thriving indicators. The asset clusters best explained valuing diversity, school success, physical health, helping others, leadership, and delay of gratification, and, likely due to measurement issues, were less strong as an explanation for overcoming adversity.

In both the Leffert and colleagues (1998) and Scales and colleagues (2000) analyses of assets and risk behaviors, and assets and thriving indicators, respectively, the amounts of variance explained by Developmental Assets was much greater than that explained by demographic variables and comparable to that found in other studies using different predictor variables.

These findings suggest that the explanatory power of the asset model is at least as compelling as, even somewhat greater than, that of traditional demographic variables such as gender, race, and socioeconomic status.

More important, clusters of Developmental Assets explained a proportion of variance comparable to that reported in other studies of similar phenomena. For example, Resnick and colleagues (1997) used numerous demographic, individual, family, and school variables to explain 7–30% of most of the risk behavior outcomes among middle and high school students in the National Longitudinal Study on Adolescent Health (violence was the exception, with about 50% being explained). Similarly, Roeser and Eccles (1998) were able to explain about 11–30% of middle school effects on various academic motivation and achievement outcomes.

Garmezy (1991) observed that risk factors may have a more direct influence on youth than protective factors, since the latter, like assets, may interact with and modify risk factors. If this were true, the unique contribution of strength-based variables would be more difficult to establish. Moreover, assets may interact not only with risk factors but also with each other. In both Leffert and colleagues (1998) and Scales and colleagues (2000), numerous assets other than the ones cited, including many that theoretically could have been meaningful contributors to specific outcomes, contributed small amounts to variance, but did not reach the 1% cutoff.

The evidence suggests that a "considerable amount of unexplained indirect influence connects many of the developmental assets" and various outcomes (Scales et al., 2000, p. 44). Given that possibility, the proportion of variance that the Developmental Assets can explain must be considered consequential, and underscores the utility of strength-based approaches for understanding the developmental trajectories of young people.

Helping to Better Understand Relationships between Asset Categories and Risk and Thriving Developmental Outcomes

Analyses of the relationships between each of the eight categories of assets and a range of positive and negative outcomes were based on 700 high school students in one community who completed the A&B in 2001. Findings show that three categories of assets—Boundaries and Expectations, Constructive Use of Time, and Commitment to Learning—are most strongly associated with reductions in several high-risk behaviors that include alcohol, drugs, and tobacco use; drinking and driving; and school problems. Similar analyses were also conducted to examine relationships between asset categories and indicators of thriving behavior. The external categories of Support and Boundaries and Expectations, along with the internal categories of Social Competencies and Positive Identity, are most associated with the maintaining health outcome, whereas Social Competencies and Positive Identity are most associated with valuing diversity.

Helping to Explain Academic Achievement and Commitment to Learning

Research reviewed in Scales and Leffert (2004), and Starkman, Scales, and Roberts (1999) shows that Developmental Assets are related to, and may well contribute to, students' academic success through their collective effects on:

- Promoting supportive and caring relationships among students, teachers, and others;
- Increasing student motivation and engagement;
- Increasing the value that students attach to education;
- Increasing the effectiveness of students' study habits;
- Strengthening social norms and expectations that promote achievement; and
- Increasing parent involvement and student attendance.

In an analysis of nearly 100,000 6th- to 12th-grade students, Benson and colleagues (1999) found that asset-rich students who report experiencing 31–40 of the assets that encompass the above factors are 2.8 times more likely (53% vs. 19%) to report getting mostly A's in school than students who indicate they only have an average level (11–20) of the assets.

From an analysis of 6,000 6th–12th graders, equally divided across six major racial/ethnic groups (African American, Asian American, Hispanic/Latino, Native American, White, and Multiracial students), Scales and colleagues (2000) reported that several Developmental Assets (including school engagement, achievement motivation, time in youth programs, time at home, and personal power) together predicted or explained from moderate to substantial proportions of the variance (19–31%, depending on student race/ethnicity) in student-reported grades (over and above demographic variables). The clusters of Developmental Assets were especially good predictors for White, Asian American, and Multiracial youth.

The analyses cited above used student self-reported grades as the primary dependent variable. Although student self-reports of grades have been shown to have a high correlation with actual grades (Crockett, Schulenberg, & Petersen, 1987), they still are subject to errors of recall or intentional bias. In a study of more than 1,000 middle and high school students, Search Institute researchers used actual grades and class rank as indicators, in addition to self-reported student grades. They found that students experiencing higher levels of Developmental Assets generally had higher actual grades in English, science, social studies, and mathematics, as well as higher cumulative GPAs. Those students also had higher class ranks.

In cross-sectional studies of students living in St. Louis Park, Minnesota, asset levels were strongly associated with their actual grade point average, class rank, risk behaviors, and thriving at the same time. In terms of GPA, the total number of assets is correlated with GPA at a level of .35 for females and .45 for males, indicating that between one-third and one-half of differences in GPAs among students can be accounted for by the level of assets they report. Similarly with regard to class rank, the correlations are .33 for females and .40 for males.

In addition, possessing high levels of assets seemed to be related to narrowing of traditional equity gaps in achievement. Boys with higher levels of assets had higher GPAs, closer to those of girls, than did boys with lower levels of assets. Girls with higher levels of assets had higher grades in math, closer to those of boys, than did girls with lower levels of assets (Leffert, Scales, Vraa, Libbey, & Benson, 2001).

In terms of assessing the relationship between academic achievement and Developmental Assets, the amount of variance the assets explain is greater than that of demographics, and comparable to that found in other studies using different predictor variables. In Leffert and colleagues' (2001) study of assets and academic achievement, demographics explained about 10–12% and asset clusters 12–24% of the variance in outcomes such as actual grades, GPA, and class rank.

The Academic and Prevention Inseparable Study (API) conducted by the Orange County Department of Education in California sought to identify specific factors and promising practices that simultaneously enhance youth development and increase student achievement. The intent of the study was to understand how prevention and youth development activities correlate with academic achievement. The asset model was used as the youth development tool for implementing academic and prevention activities. The program focused on the Commitment to Learning category of the asset model. That category is composed of five assets: achievement motivation, school engagement, homework, bonding to school, and reading for pleasure. The study was conducted in four schools in Orange County between May 2000 and May 2002.

An experimental group (one elementary and one middle school) and a control group (one elementary and one middle school) were formed. The schools in both groups had similar characteristics in terms of basic demographics, geographic area, test scores, number of English as second language learners, and socioeconomic background. Data was collected from students and adults in both the experimental and control groups using a pre- and post-test instrument. Analysis of the data revealed the following findings significant at the .05 level:

- Elementary and middle school students not exposed to consistent prevention and youth development activities showed a significant decrease in their commitment to learning;
- Elementary and middle school students exposed to consistent prevention and youth development activities showed a significant increase in their test scores and commitment to learning;
- Elementary and middle school students exposed to consistent prevention and youth development activities reported they were more connected to teachers, school, and community;
- Elementary and middle school students exposed to consistent prevention and youth development activities reported feeling safer in school; and
- Teachers' attitudes toward their work environment and level of involvement with youth showed improvement when promoting a "positive school culture" and empowering students at their school.

The Cumulative Benefits of a Community and Statewide Focus on Assets for Youth

The ecological orientation and community emphasis of the asset model argues that the greater the degree of positive developmental redundancy in family life and across community settings that shape and influence the lives of young people, the greater the contributions to their health, success, and developmental well-being. Here the focus is on the simultaneous reinforcing experiences of assets across the different contexts of a young person's total ecology, such as family, peers, school, neighborhood, and community, that allows young people to perceive and feel safe, supported, and capable. Young people who experience such cumulative redundancy ought to be even more likely to enjoy protection from risk and to thrive than young people who do not. Data analysis supports these assumptions.

In an early Search Institute study of more than 47,000 6th–12th graders, Benson (1990) reported that to be the case. Adolescents engaged in four developmentally rich settings (family, school, structured youth activity, and faith community) evidenced six times fewer risk behaviors than adolescents without similar contextual redundancy. Research conducted by others provides additional supporting evidence. In a longitudinal study of nearly 1,000 New Zealand 16-year-olds who had been studied since birth, Ferguson and Lynskey (1996) reported that adolescents who were resilient in the face of family adversity experienced strengths in several domains. Logistic regression showed the resilient adolescents had stronger personal characteristics such as a higher IQ. They also had fewer friendships with delinquent peers (analogous to the Search Institute asset of positive peer influence) and lower rates of novelty seeking (analogous to the asset of resistance skills and the thriving indicator of resisting danger).

Sanders's (1998) study of more than 800 urban African American students in grade 8 lends further support to the hypothesis that strengths piling up within families and across certain community settings magnify the protective and thriving effects of positive experiences in single contexts. In Sanders's study, parent and teacher support significantly predicted school conduct and achievement ideology; parent support and church involvement significantly predicted academic self-concept; and teacher support and church involvement significantly predicted student GPA, over and above the influence of demographic variables. When school conduct, academic self-concept, and achievement ideology were added to the prediction of GPA, the contribution of support across the three contexts of family, school, and community (church) diminished. This finding suggests that support affected academic achievement through its impact on promoting positive conduct behavior at school and positive self-perceptions of academic ability. This study also suggests that the interactions among constructs variously labeled strengths, protective factors, or assets can be complex. Therefore, caution is advised when trying to conclude that any single asset, or small number of assets, reflects the "most important" influence for a given outcome.

Additionally, Sanders reported that when all three support contexts—family, school, and church—were combined, the effect on academic self-concept (which most strongly predicted actual achievement) and achievement ideology were stronger than the unique effects of any of the individual contexts. (The combined effect on school conduct was comparable to the individual effect from teacher support.) This finding suggested that "when students receive support from the family, church, and school simultaneously, the effects on their attitudes about self and the importance of schooling are magnified" (p. 402).

In the National Longitudinal Study of Adolescent Health (Resnick et al., 1997), evidence of the cumulative community effects on risky behaviors also can be observed. For example, family context variables alone explained just 8.5% of middle school students' alcohol use, and 6% of high school students' use. But when demographics, the school context, and individual characteristics such as self-esteem, religious connectedness, and GPA were entered, the final regression model could explain about 13% of alcohol use variance for middle and high school youth. Although the total variance explained does not appear to be impressive, the increase in explanatory power achieved by considering strengths across various contexts was more than 50% for middle school students and more than double for high school students.

Clarifying the Benefits of an Asset-Building Community Initiative

The Children First initiative in St. Louis Park, Minnesota, was the first Healthy Communities • Healthy Youth initiative and is the longest running community-wide asset-building initiative in the country. Cross-sectional research findings in St. Louis Park have been consistent with data discussed earlier. Hence, the asset model performs a prevention function in the sense that the more assets young people have and/or experience, the less likely they are to engage in a wide range of high-risk behaviors. The asset model also assumes a promotion function in terms of the more assets young people have and/or experience, the more likely they are to engage in a wide range of thriving behaviors. Finally, the asset model fosters resilience for young people because the more assets youth tell us they have in their lives, the more likely they are to manifest resilience and overcome challenges or obstacles in life.

An Increase in Asset Levels over Time

When the overall findings from an administration of the A&B to a 2001 St. Louis Park cohort are compared with the results from the first time the survey was administered to a 1997 cohort, two historical changes in assets are evident. First, for all grades 6 through 12, students report significantly higher average levels of assets in 2001 compared to 1997. Thus, on the whole, youth in St. Louis Park reported having about two more assets in 2001 than the youth reported in 1997. Second, in 2001, it appears that young people were experiencing, on average, less of a decline in assets in early adolescence, were bottoming out earlier, and were showing a more substantial rebound in assets by grade 12. All of these changes are factors indicative of a more successful adolescence and transition to adulthood. While these changes cannot be directly attributed solely to asset-building efforts in St. Louis Park, the data are encouraging, and it is reasonable to assume that St. Louis Park's children and youth have benefited a great deal from the community's innovative asset-building efforts.

A Decrease in High-Risk Behaviors over Time

Similar trends are evident when examining changes in high-risk behavior patterns between the 1999 and 2001 cohorts. Youth in St. Louis Park reported less involvement in risk-behavior patterns on average in 2001 when compared to 1997.

The Influence of Assets over Time

A recent longitudinal study (Sharma & Griffin, 2003) based on the St. Louis Park initiative and completed in 2003 adds important new insights regarding the relationships between Developmental Assets and youth outcomes. Analyses show that assets are significantly related to youth outcomes three years later. That is, the level of assets young people report in grade 8 gives an indication of how they will be doing three years later. The specific correlations between number of assets identified in 1998 and their relationship to grade point average, high-risk behaviors, and thriving three years later in 2001 for both boys and girls are all significant ($p < .01$). Moreover, the average magnitude of more than .30 for the correlations indicates moderate predictive power over three years.

Clarifying the Benefits of an Asset-Building Statewide Initiative

Between 1997 and 2002, The Colorado Trust funded a statewide initiative dedicated to promoting the use of the asset model. The trust contracted OMNI Research and Training, Inc. (a social science research firm based in Denver), to assess the initiative's impact as a catalyst for:

1. Adult asset champions intent on fostering the spread and reach of the Developmental Assets;
2. Mobilizing communities statewide for asset-building efforts;
3. Transforming the work of youth-serving organizations; and
4. Youth themselves.

Employing multiple methods, including key informant interviews, focus groups, site visits, and other participant observation techniques, document reviews, and surveys, OMNI uncovered a range of impacts.

Expression of Adult Leadership

Asset champions took active steps to encourage, inspire, and coach others around the value of asset building, kept the assets in the forefront of people's thought and action, and sought to move the asset model agenda forward within their respective organizations and among colleagues through professional networks. In terms of asset champion diffusion of the asset model, OMNI determined that personal stories and experiential learning activities were key communication mechanisms that helped convey the asset message to new audiences. A closely related, and apparently successful, strategy entailed ensuring that youth themselves learned about the Developmental Assets and had opportunities to think about and actually employ them in their daily lives. Finally, it was important to expand the number of asset champions by stoking the involvement and commitment of increasing numbers of adults.

Community Mobilization

The OMNI evaluation study determined that mobilization of communities throughout Colorado was spearheaded by a statewide organization (Assets for Colorado Youth) whose mission was to build organizational competencies in areas such as resource development, interorganizational networking, and acquisition of specialized knowledge of specific sectors and Spanish-language communities. Several of the lessons that emerged from the OMNI assessment of mobilization included supporting the transition from individual awareness and interest to community and organizationally based action; being highly strategic about how to disseminate the asset model; and regularly convening asset builders and celebrating successes and accomplishments. OMNI found that by promoting new collaborations among diverse community sectors, more than 600 entities reported using, or supporting the use of, the asset model within the first five years of the statewide initiative.

Changing Agencies That Serve Youth

The transformation of youth-serving organizations encompassed infusing the Developmental Assets into organizational culture and operations, along with fostering meaningful youth engagement. According to the OMNI evaluation report, staff working in organizations striving to become asset builders experienced changes in terms of staff development, youth involvement, community outreach, stakeholder involvement, and partnerships with other organizations in the community on shared goals. OMNI also noted evidence of these asset-building organizations enhancing the effectiveness of the service infrastructure in their communities across the state. Finally, organizations appeared to make more progress when they applied the nine core elements of youth engagement.

Results for Youth

OMNI study findings also demonstrated how a statewide and community-wide initiative can make positive impacts in the lives of young people. Youth reported gains in their sense of belonging, self-confidence, and self-efficacy, possessing a more positive view of the future, a stronger degree of empathy for others, and a higher valuing of community service (Leahy et al., 2003). Youth also reported having a greater number of interactions with a wider circle of adults and having strengthened relationships with significant adults in their lives. Both youth and adults found their interactions with one another were more positive.

Clarifying the Benefits of an Asset-Building Program

The 9th Grade Program at St. Louis Park High School was not integrally linked to the longitudinal study of St. Louis Park youth discussed earlier, but the findings from the evaluation of this program begin to document how a programmatic asset-building effort can make a difference. The 9th Grade Program was conceived when a high school counselor sought to address a wide range of ongoing concerns in the 9th grade. In the fall of 1999, the school district received a Center for Substance Abuse Prevention (CSAP) State Incentive Grant from the Minnesota Department of Children, Families, and Learning to implement the full new program through spring 2003. The 9th Grade Program was based on asset-building research, principles, and practices. All program elements were selected based on their connection to specific Developmental Assets that had been previously shown to be associated with reductions in the specific problems that were raising concerns regarding 9th-grade students. An independent evaluation of the 9th Grade Program by the Minnesota Institute of Public Health (MIPH) concluded that "this multi-faceted program has promise to reduce the likelihood that illegal substance abuse and other risk behaviors interfere with students' ability to be successful in school. . . . Initial findings are promising, and it appears that the 9th grade program has successfully met program developers' expectations to decrease illegal alcohol, tobacco and other drug use, decrease academic failure, and increase commitment to school as demonstrated by improved attendance of 9th-grade students."

The evaluation found that academic failure rates have noticeably declined over the course of this project. The percentage of students receiving either one or two (or more) Fs decreased to half by fall 2002. Truancy rates show a less dramatic but nonetheless downward trend as well. Student rates of alcohol, tobacco, and marijuana usage declined from 1998 to 2001. Use rates are lower compared to overall Minnesota rates, and rates for males are lower than for males in a neighboring district.

Conclusion

In summary, analysis of various data collected by Search Institute, along with the evaluation of various initiatives conducted by third-party evaluators, makes the case that assessing the cumulative benefits of Developmental Assets for individual youth can help to:

- Explain the prevention of and protection from high-risk behaviors;
- Explain the expression of thriving behaviors; and
- Explain academic achievement and commitment to learning.

Search Institute plans on continuing to conduct research and evaluation to build the evidence base for the asset model and encourages external parties to conduct inquiries that will further explain and deepen an understanding of the positive consequences of utilizing Developmental Assets to improve the lives of youth and the community environments that touch those lives.

References

Benard, B. (2004). *Resiliency: What we have learned.* San Francisco: WestEd.

Benson, P. L. (1990). *The troubled journey: A portrait of 6th–12th grade youth.* Minneapolis, MN: Search Institute.

Benson, P. L., Leffert, N., Scales, P. C., & Blyth, D. A. (1998). Beyond the 'village' rhetoric: creating healthy communities for children and adolescents. *Applied Developmental Science, 2*(3), 138–159.

Benson, P. L., & Pittman, K. (2001). *Trends in youth development: Visions, realities, and challenges.* Norwell, MA: Kluwer Academic Publishers.

Benson, P. L., Scales, P. C., Hamilton, S. F., & Sesma, A., Jr. (2004). Positive youth development: Theory, research, and application. In W. W. Damon & R. M. Lerner (Eds.), *Handbook of child psychology: Vol. 1. Theoretical models of human development.* New York: John Wiley.

Benson, P. L., Scales, P., Leffert, N., & Roehlkepartain, E. (1999). *The fragile foundation: The state of developmental assets among American youth.* Minneapolis, MN: Search Institute.

Bronfenbrenner, U. (1979). *The ecology of human development.* Cambridge, MA: Harvard University Press.

Crockett, L. J., Schulenberg, J. E., & Petersen, A. C. (1987). Congruence between objective and self-report data in a sample of young adolescents. *Journal of Adolescent Research, 2*(4), 383–392.

Damon, W. (2004). What is positive youth development? *The Annals of the American Academy of Political and Social Science, 591*(1), 13–24.

Eccles, J. S., & Gootman, J. A. (2002). *Community programs to promote youth development.* Washington, DC: National Academy Press.

Ferguson, D. M., & Lynskey, M. T. (1996). Adolescent resiliency to family adversity. *Journal of Child Psychology and Psychiatry and Allied Disciplines, 37*(3), 281–292.

Garmezy, N. (1985). Stress-resistant children: The search for protective factors. In J. E. Stevenson (Ed.), *Recent research in developmental psychopathology* (pp. 213–233). New York: Elsevier Science.

Garmezy, N. (1991). Resilience and vulnerability to adverse developmental outcomes associated with poverty. *American Behavioral Scientist, 34*(4), 416–430.

Hawkins, J. D., Catalano, R. F., & Miller, J. Y. (1992). Risk and protective factors for alcohol and other drug problems in adolescence and early adulthood: Implications for substance abuse prevention. *Psychological Bulletin, 112,* 64–105.

Jessor, R., & Jessor, S. L. (1977). *Problem behaviour and psychosocial development: A longitudinal study of youth.* New York: Academic Press.

Jessor, R., Turbin, M. S., & Costa, F. M. (1998). Risk and protection in successful outcomes among disadvantaged adolescents. *Applied Developmental Science, 2*(4), 194–208.

Ketterlinus, R. D., Lamb, M. E., Nitz, K., & Elster, A. B. (1992). Adolescent nonsexual and sex-related problem behaviors. *Journal of Adolescent Research, 7,* 431–456.

Leahy, S. K., Nearing, K. J., Acosta, D. W., Erickson, G. W., & Lechuga, C. (2003). *Creating social change: The growth of a statewide movement.* Denver: The Colorado Trust.

Leffert, N., Scales, P. C., Vraa, R., Libbey, H., & Benson, P. L. (2001). *The impact of developmental assets on adolescents' academic achievement.* Minneapolis, MN: Search Institute.

Leffert, N., Benson, P. L., Scales, P. C., Sharma, A. R., Drake, D. R., & Blyth, D. A. (1998). Developmental assets: Measurement and prediction of risk behaviors among adolescents. *Applied Developmental Science, 2*(4), 209–230.

Masten, A. S., Coatsworth, J. D., Neemann, J., Gest, S. D., A. Tellegen, A., & Garmezy, N. (1995). The structure and coherence of competence from childhood through adolescence. *Child Development, 66,* 1635–1659.

Masten, A. S. & Curtis, W. J. (2000). Integrating competence and psychopathology: Pathways toward a comprehensive science of adaptation in development. *Development & Psychopathology, 12,* 529–550.

Pettit, G. S., Bates, J. E., & Dodge, K. A. (1997). Supportive parenting, ecological context, and children's adjustment. *Child Development, 68,* 908–923.

Resnick, M. D., Bearman, P. S., Blum, R. W., Bauman, K. E., Harris, K. M., & Jones, J. (1997). Protecting adolescents from harm: Findings from the National Longitudinal Study on Adolescent Health. *Journal of the American Medical Association, 278*(10), 823–832 .

Roeser, R. W., & Eccles, J. S. (1998). Adolescents' perceptions of middle school: Relation to longitudinal changes in academic and psychological adjustment. *Journal of Research on Adolescence. 8*(1), 123–158.

Roth, J., Brooks-Gunn, J., Murray, L., & Foster, W. (1998). Promoting healthy adolescents: Synthesis of youth development program evaluations. *Journal of Research on Adolescence, 8*(4), 423–459.

Sanders, M. G. (1998). The effects of school, family, and community support on the academic achievement of African-American adolescents. *Urban Education, 33*(3), 395–409.

Scales, P. C., Benson, P. L., Leffert, N., & Blyth, D. A. (2000). Contribution of developmental assets to the prediction of thriving among adolescents. *Applied Developmental Science, 4*(1), 27–46.

Scales, P. C., Foster, K., Mannes, M., Horst, M., Pinto, K. C., & Rutherford, A. (2005). School-business partnerships, developmental assets, and positive outcomes among urban high school students: A mixed-methods study. *Urban Education, 40*(2), 144–189.

Scales, P. C., & Gibbons, J. L. (1996). Extended family members and unrelated adults in the lives of young adolescents: A research agenda. *Journal of Early Adolescence, 16* (4), 365–389.

Scales, P. C., & Leffert, N. (2004). *Developmental assets: A synthesis of the scientific research on adolescent development,* 2nd ed. Minneapolis, MN: Search Institute.

Scales, P. C., & Leffert, N. (1999). *Developmental assets: A synthesis of the scientific research on adolescent development.* Minneapolis, MN: Search Institute.

Scales, P. C., Sesma, A., & Bolstrom, B. (2004). *Coming into their own: How developmental assets promote positive growth in middle childhood.* Minneapolis, MN: Search Institute.

Schorr, L. (1993). Applying what we already know about successful social policy. *The American Prospect, 4*(13), 43–54.

Seligman, M. E. P., & Csikszentmihalyi, M. (2000). Positive psychology: An introduction. *American Psychologist, 55*(1), 5–14.

Sharma, A., & Griffin, T. (2003). *Saint Louis Park 9th grade program summative evaluation report.* Retrieved May 25, 2004, from http://education.umn.edu/CAREI/Programs/SIG/Eval_plans/default.html.

Starkman, N., Scales, P.C., & Roberts, C. (1999*). Great places to learn: How asset-building schools help students succeed.* Minneapolis: Search Institute.

Getting To Outcomes: Research and Evidence

MATTHEW CHINMAN, PH.D.
PAM IMM, PH.D.
ABRAHAM WANDERSMAN, PH.D.

Introduction

Research has demonstrated that both behavioral health problems and positive development in youth are amenable to intervention. However, this is only the case when the appropriate policy or strategy is adopted, implemented with quality, monitored for effectiveness, and sustained over long periods of time. While researchers have developed many successful programs and policies, local schools and communities often face significant challenges in achieving the same positive outcomes, including the significant amount of knowledge and skills required, the amount of resources needed, and the policies that need to be in place. Drs. Chinman, Imm, and Wandersman specifically developed the Getting To Outcomes (GTO) model to address this apparent gap between prevention science and practice by providing practitioners with methods and tools to develop a comprehensive and systematic approach to accountability. As shown in Figure 1, the GTO system is based on ten accountability questions that are logically linked and must be addressed to promote true program accountability. The process consists of six planning (1–6) and two (7–8) evaluation steps (process and outcomes), and the use of data to improve and sustain programs (9–10). These steps are presented in greater detail in Table 1.

Theory of GTO

GTO weaves together several overlapping theoretical strands of evaluation and "accountability," which is defined here as the systematic inclusion of all the critical elements of program planning, implementation, and evaluation in order

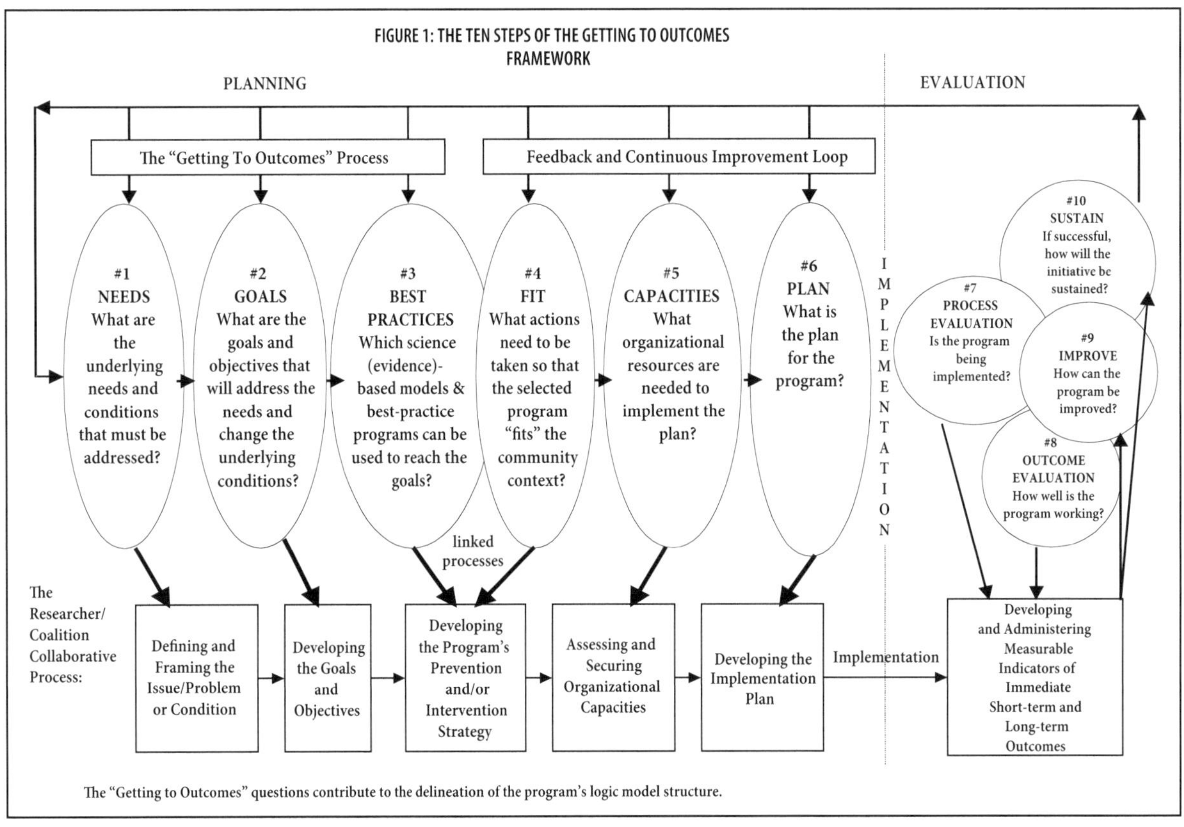

to achieve results (Wandersman, Imm, Chinman, & Kaftarian, 2000). Alone, each theory is incomplete in providing the type of guidance needed for prevention practitioners to achieve positive results. First, the GTO approach is based on traditional program evaluation, conducted by external (neutral and objective) evaluators to assess the effects of programs created and implemented by practitioners (Rossi, Lipsey, & Freeman, 2004). While traditional evaluation is the foundation, in recent years additional approaches to evaluation have been proposed that support more collaborative relationships between evaluators and practitioners, such as participatory evaluation (e.g., Choudhary & Tandon, 1988; Papineau & Kiely, 1994; Shapiro, 1988).

Empowerment evaluation is the second theoretical strand of GTO. While still retaining the basic tenets of evaluation, it calls for evaluators to provide program implementers with both the tools and the opportunities to plan, implement with quality, evaluate outcomes, and develop a continuous quality improvement system for themselves, thereby increasing the probability of achieving results (Fetterman & Wandersman, 2005).

The third theoretical strand of GTO is results based accountability (RBA). Based in part on Osborne and Graebler (1992) and on the Government Performance and Results Act of 1993, RBA moves practitioners away from collecting only process or output information, such as counting the number served, toward answering bottom-line questions about program effectiveness.

The fourth strand is continuous quality improvement, a technique in Total Quality Management (TQM). Developed for industry, TQM suggests using an ongoing process to improve quality, reduce errors and costs, and increase customer satisfaction (e.g., Deming, 1986; Juran, 1989) and has been successful in health care settings (Morrissey & Wandersman, 1995).

Getting To Outcomes 2004: Methods and Tools for Planning, Evaluation, and Accountability

The Getting To Outcomes model was developed to address the gap between prevention science and practice. The original ten-step model is fully explained in the RAND manual, *Getting To Outcomes 2004: Promoting Accountability Through Methods and Tools for Planning, Implementation, and Evaluation* (Chinman, Imm, & Wandersman, 2004). The first version was developed by Wandersman (2000) for the Center for Substance Abuse Prevention, and included a comprehensive synthesis of the literature on planning and evaluation (e.g., Bond, Boyd, Raphael, & Sizemore, 1997; Hatry, Houten, Plantz, & Taylor, 1996; Loud, 1992; Sloboda & David, 1997). That version was awarded Best Self-Help Manual by the American Evaluation Association in 2001. The current manual was significantly revised and published by RAND in 2004 (available for download at www.rand.org/publications/TR/TR101).

While the total GTO model consists of two additional components (face-to-face training and ongoing on-site technical assistance), the RAND-published GTO manual is the centerpiece, as it has all of the text explaining the model and tools to assist with program planning, implementation, evaluation, and sustaining activities. These tools, mostly Word documents, are contained on a CD-ROM (or can be downloaded from the above Web site) that accompanies each manual so that they can be tailored for each user. RAND publications must pass a quality review by RAND and outside experts. Phyllis Ellickson, Ph.D. (developer of the model program Project ALERT), and Karol Kumpfer, Ph.D. (former director of the Center for Substance Abuse Prevention and developer of the model program Strengthening Families), reviewed the manual and certified that it met RAND's quality standards. In addition to the revisions to the manual, beginning in 2002, RAND staff began testing a revised training and technical assistance intervention to support GTO implementation (see below). Information about each chapter is presented in Table 1.

Evidence for the Impact of the Getting To Outcomes Model

The GTO model has been demonstrating its impact for several years. For example, an earlier version of the GTO manual was used with an elementary school in rural South Carolina to build character, increase social and academic competence, and

TABLE 1

Ten Accountability Questions, Chapter Summaries, and Literatures of GTO

Accountability Questions	Chapter Summary (This chapter of GTO . . .)	Literature for answering question
1. What are the underlying needs and conditions to address?	provides information about conducting a needs and resource assessment and links to additional resources.	Needs assessment, resource assessment
2. What are the goals, priority populations, and objectives (i.e., desired outcomes)?	provides worksheets for clarifying priority populations and to create realistic and measurable goals and desired outcomes.	Goal setting
3. Which science-(evidence-) based models and best-practice programs can be useful in reaching the goals?	overviews evidence-based programming and what works in prevention across various domains (e.g., individual, family, peer, school, and community) and provides links to the body of science- or evidence-based program literature.	Science and best practices
4. What actions need to be taken so the selected program fits the community context?	prompts readers to review the characteristics of existing programs and priority populations to reduce duplication and facilitate collaboration with other area programs.	Collaboration, cultural competence
5. What organizational readers are needed to implement the program?	readers are prompted to assess several aspects of organizational capacity or the resources the organization possesses to direct and sustain a program.	Capacity building
6. What is the plan for this program?	presents worksheets for key planning elements such as an implementation timeline, assignments of responsibility, needed and available resources, and locations for activities.	Planning
7. How will the quality of program and/or initiative implementation be assessed?	provides several tools to assist practitioners in assessing which activities were implemented, the quality of the implementation, and the strengths and weaknesses of the implementation.	Process evaluation
8. How well did the program work?	presents outcome evaluation and a basic framework for measurement; four evaluation designs (post only, pre-post, pre-post with comparison, pre-post with control); brief overviews of quantitative and qualitative methods; and topics including sample size, timing of assessments, informed consent, confidentiality and anonymity, data storage, and establishing benchmarks.	Outcome and impact evaluation
9. How will CQI strategies be incorporated?	prompts practitioners to reassess Accountability Questions 1–8 after completing the program to systematically assess and feed back evaluation information about planning, implementation, and outcomes to improve the program.	Total Quality Management, continuous quality improvement
10. If the program is successful, how will it be sustained?	presents several factors that practitioners should consider when attempting to sustain an effective program: (a) "buy-in", (b) effectiveness, (c) diversity of funding, (d) staff training, (e) presence of a program champion, and (f) political capital of the program.	Sustainability and institutionalization

NOTE: GTO = Getting To Outcomes; CQI = continuous quality improvement.

improve classroom behavior (Dalton, Elias, Wandersman, 2001; Everhart & Wandersman, 2000). In that effort, Wandersman and colleagues collaborated with members of a community-based prevention coalition—using GTO—to plan, implement, and evaluate their programs implemented in the local elementary school. Compared to a school without the program or GTO, children in the experimental school exhibited significantly lower levels of acting-out behavior, higher levels of on-task behavior, improved spelling and reading grades, and increased levels of self-esteem. Later, in 2001, the GTO manual won an award for the best self-help manual from the American Evaluation Association.

Beyond its use at the local level, the ten questions of the GTO model have been used to organize the prevention systems of entire states (Chinman et al., 2001). An example of such a system is the South Carolina State Incentive Grant program. In the fall of 2001, the South Carolina Department of Alcohol and Other Drug Abuse Services (SCDAODAS) received a SIG (state improvement grant) from CSAP through the South Carolina governor's office designed to be a catalyst for significant improvements in substance abuse prevention services at both state and local levels. As part of the SIG, the state developed a comprehensive statewide plan for implementing effective prevention strategies. At the local level, community residents and organizations formed 19 community coalitions that applied for and received minigrants to implement evidence-based prevention programs.

To promote good program development, implementation, evaluation, and accountability, and to increase the likelihood of positive results, the state agency that oversees drug treatment and prevention decided to use the ten GTO questions as the framework for the administration of these minigrants. The first step in creating a GTO system for the SIG was to require that all applicants consider elements of successful programming by designing the minigrant application around the ten questions. To further systematize GTO, SIG staff, funders, and administrators monitor program implementation using common GTO forms, write feedback reports using a common GTO format based on elements discussed in the GTO model, and regularly deliver technical assistance and training on the GTO approach to the 19 community coalitions. The benefit of using a common GTO structure has been that it has provided local programs with effectiveness data they can use to improve their programs, has promoted accountability at the local and state levels, and has contributed to the refinement of evidence-based prevention programming. In terms of impact, the 19 individual coalitions each collected the same pre and post survey data on their programs' recipients, youth ages 12–17. Averaging across the recipients from all 19 coalitions, they found significant improvement in the perceived risk of drug use, favorable attitudes toward drug use, and perceptions of peer norms about youth drug use. There were also nonsignificant reductions in cigarette use and marijuana use.

Starting in 2002, we received funding from the Centers for Disease Control and Prevention for the study "Participatory Research of an Empowerment Evaluation System" (CCR921459-02, Chinman, PI). This study assessed how and to what extent four programs across two community-based coalitions (in Santa Barbara, CA, and Columbia, SC) utilized the GTO model and its corresponding impact on their capacity to implement high-quality prevention programming (Chinman, Early, et al., 2004, 2005). The four programs were:

- *Program 1:* A media campaign across a whole school district to educate youth about how, in reality, most youth do not use drugs and alcohol (i.e., a social norms campaign).
- *Program 2:* A parenting skills education program.
- *Program 3:* School resource personnel that conduct universal and selective prevention programs as well as some one-on-one counseling in high schools.
- *Program 4:* A teen court that diverts first-time youth offenders from the criminal justice system and uses a jury of their peers to impose sentences that include peer groups, alcohol and drug education, or community service.

The GTO intervention was composed of three components: (1) a GTO manual of text and tools, (2) face-to-face training, and (3) on-site technical assistance. We distributed GTO manuals and delivered a yearly full-day training in the GTO approach to participating program staff and coalition members. The study has been using several assessment strategies. To track GTO implementation, we had our technical assistance staff document the time they spent on each GTO step throughout the project, and we conducted focus groups with the coalition staff after a year of GTO implementation. To assess the impact of GTO on prevention capacity at the individual level, we conducted a coalition-wide survey at baseline and after one year of GTO implementation with both coalitions. To assess the impact of GTO on prevention capacity at the program level, we conducted interviews with program staff using the "GTO-IC Map" at baseline and after one year of GTO implementation with both the GTO and comparison programs (i.e., programs in the coalitions not receiving the GTO package). Finally, we analyzed the data that each of the four programs collected to assess how effective the programs facilitated by GTO were in reaching positive outcomes.

Tracking GTO implementation. A year into the project, we conducted two focus groups with the participating staff from each of the two coalitions. We asked staff about what was and was not helpful about GTO, what were the challenges to using the model. Staff from both coalitions were similar in their responses that, overall, GTO provided them with "a new language" about how to make their programs more accountable. Also, it helped them be more "proactive," "focused," and "orderly" so that key details about the programs were not accidentally neglected. In particular, staff noted that GTO helped them with various aspects of planning such as communicating with grant writers, understanding the limits of their own capacity, structuring priorities, developing realistic goals and objectives, and assessing whether new potential programs were evidence based. Staff also stated that they received a great deal of assistance with evaluation, including collecting better data with new and improved outcomes measures. Staff stated that there were challenges to using GTO, including a lack of time (sometimes it was difficult to fit GTO into their day-to-day routine), a lack of resources, and having to overcome an organizational culture that did not value evaluation. Some found GTO challenging to understand given its length and their lack of familiarity with the concepts GTO contains. These reactions came after a year, and we are in the process of conducting in-depth interviews with participating staff to assess these issues following two years of GTO implementation.

A key component to the GTO intervention was the delivery of GTO-based technical assistance. This took the form of weekly meetings between GTO and program staff for about an hour and a half to two hours. This assistance involved GTO staff providing additional information about the GTO model and help with using each step to guide their respective program or initiative, including:

- Developing realistic goals and objectives (GTO Step 2);
- Ensuring program fit by tailoring programs or initiatives as needed (GTO Step 4);
- Securing the needed resources to ensure high-quality implementation (GTO Step 5);
- Planning the delivery to ensure that all aspects of the program or initiative are included (GTO Step 6);
- Conducting process and outcome evaluations (GTO Steps 7 & 8);
- Using the process and outcome data to improve current and future administrations (GTO Step 9); and
- Working to sustain effective programs or initiatives (GTO Step 10)

Based on the technical assistance (TA) literature (Mitchell et al., 2004; O'Donnell et al., 2000; Stevenson et al., 2002) and our previous experience, we use a TA process that has structured steps but was flexible enough to allow the program staff to dictate the focus. These steps included a technical assistance needs assessment, to assess the needs of each program, and a technical assistance planning process to guide the TA and facilitate the tracking of progress.

Given that each program was free to use the technical assistance as it saw fit, the breakdown of TA effort expended across the ten GTO steps showed interesting patterns (see Table 2 below). While each of the four GTO programs was very different from the others in terms of content, histories, and funding sources and amounts, they showed a similar pattern of technical assistance use. The programs tended to want the most assistance with planning and process and outcome evaluation. This result also reflects that these programs were established and running for years. Therefore, they gave less emphasis to tasks like needs assessment, goals, and best practices.

GTO's impact on prevention capacity. To assess prevention capacity of the individual coalition members, we used a paper-and-pencil survey. The survey defined capacity at the individual level as the members' frequency of engaging in the actual practices of the various prevention tasks in the GTO model (goals and objectives, evaluation, etc). Currently, we have administered the survey to the participating coalitions twice, once at baseline and again after a year of GTO implementation. Not all of the coalition members are participating in GTO, setting up a natural comparison to those who are. We analyzed the data in two ways. First, after adjusting for demographic characteristics (gender, age, coalition site, and position in the coalition), we compared those program staff *assigned* to the GTO condition to those in the coalitions who did not receive the GTO intervention. We found that those in the GTO condition showed greater improvement in the areas of Fit, Capacities, Planning, Outcome Evaluation, Continuous Quality Improvement, and Sustainability compared to those who did not receive the GTO intervention. Then we assessed the impact of GTO based not on assignment but upon how much of a "dose" of GTO a person received. Based on whether they had participated in GTO training, read the GTO manual, planned to use GTO, talked with colleagues about GTO, or tried to get resources for GTO, each person received a GTO use score from 0 to 5.

Using this data, we analyzed the relationship between GTO use and the amount of improvement in how often the coalition members performed the various prevention practices. We found that those with greater GTO use scores showed more improvement over the course of the year than those with

TABLE 2

Percentage of Time Spent on GTO Technical Assistance by GTO Step

	The four GTO programs			
GTO Step	**1**	**2**	**3**	**4**
1. Needs	2%	2%	1%	1%
2. Goals	1%	3%	2%	2%
3. Best prac.	2%	0%	3%	1%
4. Fit	1%	1%	2%	0%
5. Capacities	3%	8%	17%	6%
6. Plan	13%	17%	34%	6%
7. Proc. eval.	27%	29%	27%	32%
8. Out. eval.	32%	33%	8%	37%
9. CQI	9%	4%	5%	9%
10. Sustain	9%	2%	1%	5%
TOTAL Hrs.	280.55	125.83	250.00	321.50

lower scores for the areas of Best Practices Fit, Capacities, Planning, Process Evaluation, Outcome Evaluation, Continuous Quality Improvement, and Sustainability. Thus, in general, those who were either assigned to the GTO condition or received greater GTO exposure showed more improvement in how often they engaged in various prevention practices (as indicated with an "X" in Table 3 below) compared to those in the no-GTO group or who received less GTO exposure.

To assess prevention capacity at the individual level, we used a tool called the Innovation Configuration (IC) Map (Hall & Hord, 1987; Hall & Hord, 2001). Based on the idea that innovations are often implemented differently than intended, it is a framework that can be tailored to evaluate the *quality* of any innovation, in this case the steps of prevention prescribed by GTO. We developed, with direct participation from the developer of the original IC Map Dr. Gene Hall, a *GTO*-IC Map, which has 14 items (called "components") tied to each

TABLE 3

GTO's Impact on Prevention Practices

Prevention practices related to GTO's ten steps **How often in the last 12 months did you:**	**GTO group vs. no-GTO group**	**More GTO use vs. less GTO use**
GTO Step 1: . . . examine the current level of alcohol and drug use and the factors that cause them		
GTO Step 2: . . . develop goals to address needs (e.g., to reduce substance abuse)		
GTO Step 3: . . . locate and evaluate strategies that have been shown through research to be effective		X
GTO Step 4: . . . examine whether strategies duplicate existing efforts	X	X
GTO Step 5: . . . assess capacities (funds, expertise, equipment) needed to implement its strategies	X	X
GTO Step 6: . . . develop a detailed implementation plan (e.g., staff roles, timelines, target population locations) for strategies	X	X
GTO Step 7: . . . evaluate whether strategies are implemented according to plan		X
GTO Step 8: . . . evaluate how well strategies produced the desired improvements in the participants	X	X
GTO Step 9: . . . use evaluation feedback to improve strategies	X	X
GTO Step 10: . . . take actions to keep strategies running	X	X

X = GTO group/Greater GTO use improves more than non-GTO/less GTO use group step of GTO (Process evaluation, Outcome Evaluation, and Continuous Quality Improvement had two components each). Each component has seven response choices, described with specific observable behaviors that range from "highly faithful to (=7)" to "highly divergent from (=1)" GTO. Thus, this measure defined prevention capacity at the program level as the *quality* with which the program as a whole engages in the prevention tasks outlined by GTO's ten steps. Through interviews with program staff, supplemented with observations and document reviews, we made GTO-IC Map ratings on four GTO programs and four comparison programs at two points in time (baseline and after two years of GTO implementation). Using two raters, the average inter-rater reliability was .78. Averaging across all areas of prevention, the GTO groups improved almost three times as much as the comparison programs (42% vs. 15%). In particular, the areas that showed the largest significant differential improvement versus the comparison programs (in % change) were Goals (40% vs. 14%), Capacity (36% vs. –9%), Planning (29% vs. 0%), Process Evaluation (50% vs. 9%), Outcome Evaluation (80% vs. 41%), and Continuous Quality Improvement (49% vs. 3%).

We also correlated the average amount of change among the four GTO programs' GTO-IC Map ratings with the number of hours spent on each GTO step, which yielded a very high correlation of .55 (shown in the chart below). This result reinforces how important the GTO-based technical assistance was in improving the programs' prevention capacity.

Individual program evaluations. While all these evaluations are ongoing, the four programs have collected sufficient amounts of data to make some conclusions about their progress. Programs 2–4 (parenting, school resource personnel,

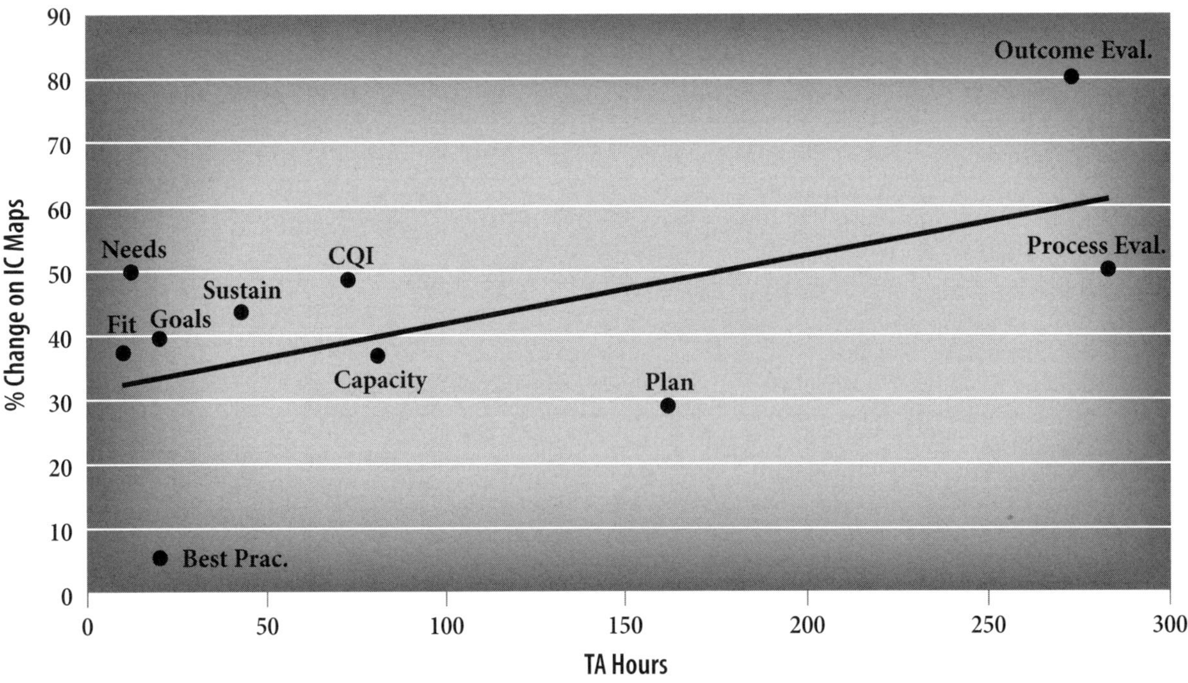

and teen court programs) used attendance and completion data to track implementation and pre-post survey designs to track outcomes. Program 1 (social norms campaign) used annual school surveys.

The school resource personnel outcome evaluation involved 91 participants completing pre-post surveys and found significant improvement in 30-day marijuana and alcohol use, drug use control, and overall school performance and no improvement in self-reported grades and attendance, school bonding, and mood. The teen court evaluation involved 50 participants—referred for both drug and nondrug offenses—completing pre and post surveys. Paired comparisons showed significant improvement in marijuana use, drug knowledge, decision-making skills, and perceived school importance. There was no improvement in perceptions of harm from drugs, drug resistance skills, perceptions of parental expectations about teen drug use, or antisocial attitudes and behaviors. The parenting program outcome evaluation involved 24 participants completing pre-post surveys and found significant improvement in the intentions to use a variety of positive parenting practices such as family meetings, setting clear rules, and coaching children on resistance skills.The social norm campaign evaluation involved yearly school surveys of about 3,500 middle and 3,700 high school students in 2003 and 2004. Compared to 2003, both groups of middle and high school students in 2004 reported having more negative attitudes toward alcohol, tobacco, and drug use and less use over the past 30 days.

In all programs, implementation data showed significant variation in participant exposure. Tracking of the outcome evaluations showed that the surveying was not always uniform, resulting in the loss of some data. However, the teen court evaluation represented a significant advance, as there were no evaluation activities in place before the use of the GTO model. Regarding the other programs, the previously existing evaluations were significantly improved by the use of the GTO model. In addition, the issues of program participation and evaluation quality are now being addressed through GTO's continuous quality improvement process, and already outcome evaluation surveying has improved in all of the programs.

Conclusions

Although encouraging, one must interpret these data with some caution. To date, these efforts represent quasi-experimental and observational designs, which make it difficult to causally link with certainty GTO implementation with the resulting improvement in prevention capacity and youth outcomes. For example, the GTO-IC Map measure has only been administered to a small number of programs, preventing the use of reliable statistical methods. However, the data collected from these three efforts suggest that GTO builds the capacity of local practitioners, facilitating the implementation of prevention with improved quality.

We continue to engage in research on how to increase organizational and community capacity for tailoring, implementing, and sustaining effective interventions with GTO. Research about bridging this gap in dissemination practice is critical to improving the ability to disseminate the most effective prevention strategies. The GTO model is specifically designed to enhance local capacity for prevention; further researching its effect on both capacity and youth outcomes will have important implications for how practitioners deliver prevention programs that improve community health and welfare.

References

Bond, S. L., Boyd, S. E., Raphael, J. B., & Sizemore, B. A. (1997). *Taking stock: A practical guide to evaluating your own programs.* Chapel Hill, NC: Horizon Research, Inc.

Chinman, M., Principal Investigator. Centers for Disease Control and Prevention: *Participatory research of an empowerment evaluation system (CCR921459-02),* 2002–2005.

Chinman, M., Early, D., Ebener, P., Hunter, S., Imm, P., Jenkins, P., Sheldon, J., & Wandersman, A. (2004). Getting To Outcomes: A community-based participatory approach to preventive interventions. *Journal of Interprofessional Care, 18,* 441–443.

Chinman, M., Hannah, G., Wandersman, A., Ebener, P., Hunter, S., Imm, P., & Sheldon, J. (2005). Developing a community science research agenda for building community capacity for effective preventive interventions. *American Journal of Community Psychology,* 3/4, 143–157.

Chinman, M., Imm, P., & Wandersman, A. (2004). *Getting To Outcomes 2004: Promoting Accountability through Methods and Tools for Planning, Implementation, and Evaluation.* Santa Monica, CA: RAND Corporation, TR-TR101. Available at http://www.rand.org/publications/TR/TR101/

Chinman, M., Imm, P., Wandersman, A., Kaftarian, S., Neal, J., Pendleton, K. T., & Ringwalt, C. (2001). Using the Getting To Outcomes (GTO) model in a statewide prevention initiative. *Health Promotion Practice, 2,* 302–309.

Choudhary, A., & Tandon, R. (1988). *Participatory evaluation.* New Delhi, India: Society for Participatory Research in Asia.

Dalton, J., Elias, M., & Wandersman, A. (2001). *Community psychology: Linking individuals and communities.* Stamford, CT: Wadsworth.

Deming, W. E. (1986). *Out of the crisis.* Cambridge, MA: MIT Press.

Everhart, K., & Wandersman, A. (2000). Applying comprehensive quality programming and empowerment evaluation to reduce implementation barriers. *Journal of Educational and Psychological Consultation, 11*(2), 177–191.

Fetterman, D., & Wandersman, A. (2005). *Empowerment evaluation principles in practice.* New York: Guilford Press.

Hall, G. E., & Hord, S. M. (1987). *Change in schools facilitating the process.* Albany: State University of New York Press.

Hall, G. E., & Hord, S. M. (2001). *Implementing change.* Boston: Allyn and Bacon.

Hatry, H., Houten, T. V., Plantz, M. C., & Taylor, M. (1996). *Measuring program outcomes: A practical approach.* Alexandria, VA: United Way of America.

Juran, J. M. (1989). *Juran on leadership for quality.* New York: Free Press.

Loud, M. L. (1992). *Guidelines for health programme & project evaluation planning.* Zurich, Switzerland: Swiss Federal Office of Public Health.

Mitchell, R., Stone-Wiggins, B., Stevenson, J. F., & Florin, P. (2004). Cultivating capacity: Outcomes of a statewide support system for prevention coalitions. *Journal of Prevention and Intervention in the Community, 27,* 67–87.

Morrissey, E., & Wandersman, A. (1995). Total quality management in health care settings: A preliminary framework for successful implementation. In L. Ginsberg and P. Keys (Eds.), *New management in human services* (pp. 171–194). Washington DC: National Association of Social Workers.

O'Donnell, L. O., Scattergood, P., Adler, M., San Doval, A., Barker, M., Kelly, J. A., et al. (2000). The role of technical assistance in the replication of effective HIV interventions. *AIDS Education and Prevention, 12*(Suppl. A), 99–111.

Osborne, D., & Gaebler, T. (1992). *Reinventing government: How the entrepreneurial spirit is transforming the public sector.* Reading, MA: Addison-Wesley.

Papineau, D., & Kiely, M.C. (1994). Participatory evaluation: Empowering stakeholders in a community economic development organization. *Community Psychologist, 27*(2), 56–57.

Rossi, P., Lipsey, M., & Freeman, H. (2004). *Evaluation: A systematic approach.* 7th ed. Thousand Oaks, CA: Sage.

Shapiro, J. P. (1988). Participatory evaluation: Toward a transformation of assessment for women's studies programs and projects. *Educational Evaluation and Policy Analysis, 10*(3), 191–199.

Sloboda, Z., & David, S. L. (1997). *Preventing drug use among children and adolescents* (NIH Publication No. 97-4212). Washington, DC: U.S. Department of Health and Human Services.

Stevenson, J. F., Florin, P., Mills, D. S., & Andrade, M. (2002). Building evaluation capacity in human service organizations: A case study. *Evaluation and Program Planning, 25*(3), 233–243.

Wandersman, A., Imm, P., Chinman, M., & Kaftarian, S. (2000). Getting To Outcomes: A results-based approach to accountability. *Evaluation and Program Planning, 23,* 389–395.

Acknowledgments

It has taken more than a year and numerous drafts to take this book from the original inception to completion. I could not have done it alone, nor would I have wanted to. It's been far more interesting and enjoyable a process sharing the book's development with a wide circle of intelligent, creative, committed colleagues.

I must first thank Peter Benson and Abe Wandersman for their original vision, seeing the potential to blend and braid both of their "big ideas" into the model presented in this book.

I would also like to thank Peter and others at Search Institute who demonstrated their confidence by allowing me to shape the content of this book. For their continued support during the writing of this book, either by their direct participation, assistance to me, or allowing the use of their work, I especially thank Marc Mannes, Gene Roehlkepartain, Peter Scales, Pat Seppanen, Nancy Tellet-Royce, Kristin Johnstad, Anitra Budd, Shenita Lewis, Lynette Ward, Tim Duffey, Debbie Grillo, Faith Dietz, Tania Gutsche, Art Sesma, William Mesaros, Yvonne Pearson, James Conway, Jennifer Griffin-Wiesner, and Linda Davich.

I continue to benefit both professionally and personally from the experiences, thoughtfulness, and generosity of a wonderful community of people who are out there every day doing the work of building developmentally attentive communities on behalf of all our young people. For their particular contributions to this book, I would like to thank Susan Allen, Nancy Ashley, Thomas Berkas, Shane Butterfield, Mike Diamanti, Angela Jerabek, Becky Judd, Renie Kehres, Suzanne Holm, Sarah Hunter, María Guajardo Lucero, Jaci Miller, Loretta Novince, Lee Rush, Susan Savell, and Mary Schissel.

Once again, I must especially acknowledge the work of my editor, Kay Hong, a fabulous partner in the creation of this book. She has a knack for giving free rein to my creativity while reining me in at the appropriate times. She is a consummate professional (and just a heck of a lot of fun to work with).

Finally, I happily and heartily thank my fellow authors, Abe, Pam, and Matt, for all of their efforts in bringing this book to fruition. In the world of authorship, it is extremely rare to find one person, let alone three people, who would so graciously work with a complete stranger to rewrite their material. I have not often met such dedicated people, and their commitment to making communities better places to live infuses not only their written word, but their way of working in the world. It has been a genuine pleasure to work as part of a team with them.

Deborah Fisher

We would like to acknowledge those who have shaped our thinking and who have offered suggestions for making the manuscript better. We were inspired by the commitment and enthusiasm of Search Institute staff and by community members who use the Developmental Assets model; their commitment motivated us to collaborate on the integration of assets and GTO for the purpose of enhancing communities.

First, we would like to thank our colleague and coauthor, Deborah Fisher, for taking the lead in figuring out what an integration of assets and GTO would actually look like—helping us move from vision to reality, and with a lively writing style. We would also like to thank Mary Lynn Batson and Nicole Modeen, who provided new ideas, edited text, and offered their experiences. Thanks also to those who reviewed the manuscript and provided specific feedback: Marc Mannes, Angela Jerabek, Jennifer Rauhouse, Renie Kehres, David Osher, Mary Ackerman, Mike Diamanti, and Nancy Tellett-Royce; Paul Flaspohler and Marc Mclaughlin of Miami University of Ohio; and Vincent Francisco from UNC-Greensboro.

We would also like to acknowledge Renie Kehres, Kate Thomsen, Kathy Miller, the ADAPEP Counselors at BOCES in New York, Larry Pasti, and Denise Dyer not only for educating us about youth development but also for showing it to us in action through their vision, attitudes, and commitment to youth. Last, but far from least, we would like to thank Kay Hong, who is the exemplar of a hands-on editor. She added much quality to this work.

Pam Imm, Matthew Chinman, and Abe Wandersman

About the Authors

Deborah Fisher is a writer with more than thirty years' experience in print and online magazine work, project management, and nonfiction books. She is a former Minnesota Public Radio legal affairs reporter and NPR contributor. She specializes in writing, working with communities, and conducting workshops on positive youth development and family issues, including Developmental Assets for Search Institute. Her most recent books include *Just When I Needed You: True Stories of Adults Who Made a Difference in the Lives of Young People* and *Getting To Outcomes with Developmental Assets: Ten Steps to Measuring Success in Youth Programs and Communities.* Her Web site is www.deborahfisher.org.

Pamela S. Imm, Ph.D., received her doctorate in clinical and community psychology from the University of South Carolina in 1996. She has extensive experience in the areas of program development, program evaluation, and applied research. She has presented at national conferences and has served as an evaluation consultant for the Center for Substance Abuse Prevention, the Department of Education, and the Community Anti-Drug Coalitions of America. Dr. Imm is a coauthor of the empowerment evaluation manual *Getting To Outcomes (GTO): Methods and Tools for Planning, Self-Assessment, and Accountability.* Dr. Imm most enjoys working with local community-based coalitions to help them integrate evaluation and research-based concepts into their work. She has published in the areas of alcohol and drug abuse prevention, evaluation research, and models of effective programming.

Dr. Matthew Chinman is a licensed clinical psychologist and a behavioral scientist at the RAND Corporation and Health Science Specialist at the West Los

Angeles VA Healthcare Center. His recent focus has been to develop and assess strategies to enhance the capacity of community-based prevention practitioners. He is co-developer of the Getting To Outcomes (GTO) system and the lead author of the RAND Corporation technical report, *Getting To Outcomes 2004: Promoting Accountability through Methods and Tools for Planning, Implementation, and Evaluation.* GTO was awarded "best practice process" status by the Center for Substance Abuse Prevention and won an award for the best self-help manual from the American Evaluation Association. He is currently the PI of a grant from the Centers for Disease Control and Prevention to examine how the Getting To Outcomes system helps improve community capacity in substance abuse prevention practitioners. Dr. Chinman has published on such topics as program evaluation methodology, empowerment evaluation, adolescent empowerment, coalition functioning, and peer support.

Abraham Wandersman, Ph.D., is a professor of psychology at the University of South Carolina-Columbia. He received his Ph.D. from Cornell University in the following areas of specialization: social psychology, environmental psychology, and social organization and change. He was interim co-director of the Institute for Families in Society at the University of South Carolina. Dr. Wandersman performs research and program evaluation on citizen participation in community organizations and coalitions and on interagency collaboration. He is a coauthor of *Prevention Plus III* and a coeditor *of Empowerment Evaluation: Knowledge and Tools for Self Assessment and Accountability* and of many other books and articles. In 1998, he received the Myrdal Award for Evaluation Practice from the American Evaluation Association. In 2000, he was elected president of Division 27 of the American Psychological Association (Community Psychology), the Society for Community Research and Action. In 2001, he was first author on a paper on PIE (planning, implementation, evaluation), which won a presidential prize from the American Evaluation Association for Mainstreaming Evaluation. In 2004, he coauthored the RAND publication *Getting To Outcomes 2004: Promoting Accountability through Methods and Tools for Planning, Implementation, and Evaluation.* In 2005, Dr. Wandersman was awarded the Distinguished Theory and Research Contributions Award by the Society for Community Research and action. He is working on the development of empowerment evaluation systems using GTO in the areas of intimate partner violence prevention and sexual violence prevention for the Division of Violence Prevention of CDC.